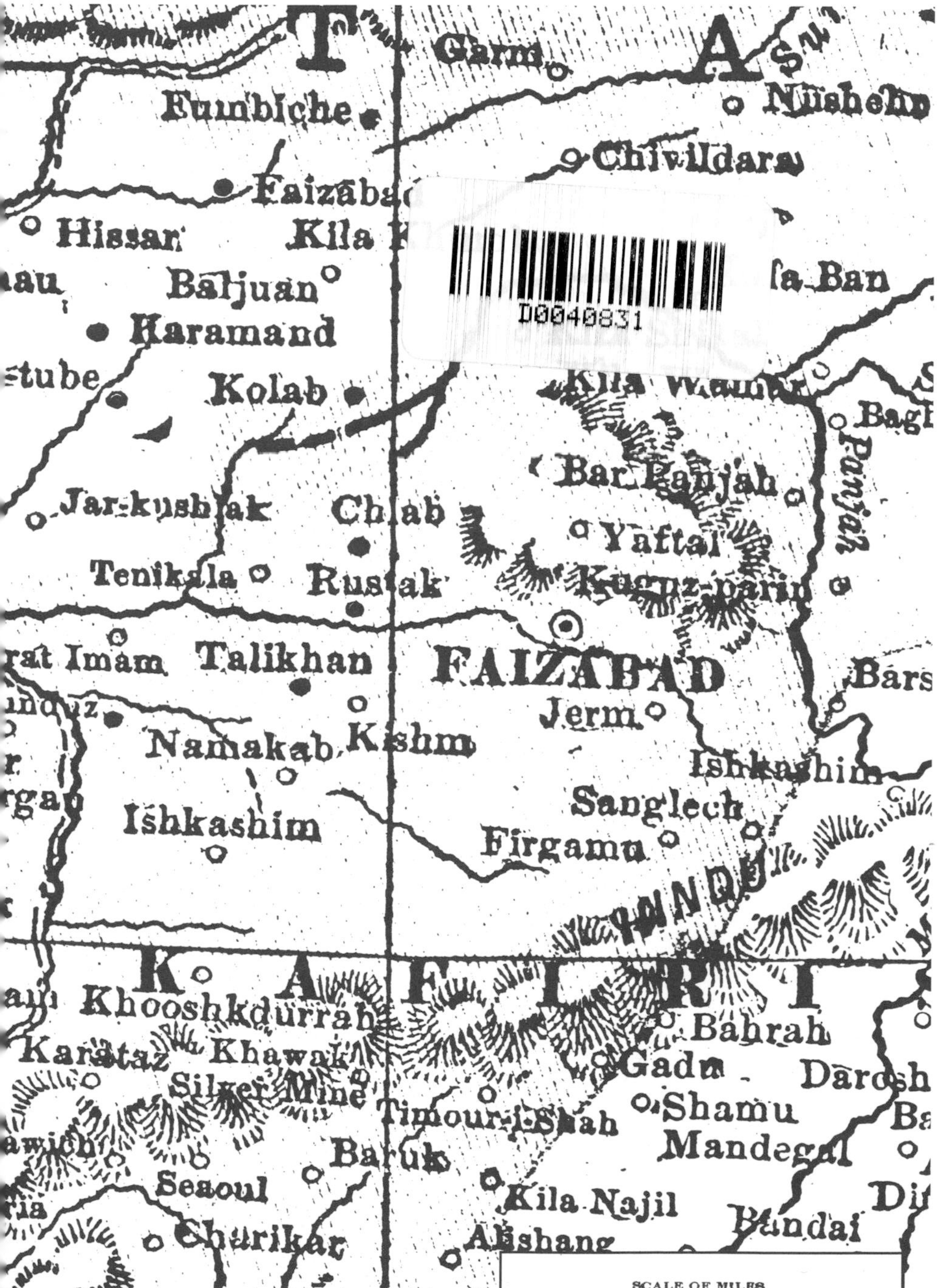

T Garm A

Fumbiche

Nushehr

Chivildara

Faizabad

Hissar Kila F

fa Ban

au Baljuan

Haramand

Kila Wamu

Bagl

stube Kolab

Panjah

Bar Panjah

Jar-kushlak Chab

Yaftal

Teniksla Rustak

Kucuz-parin

Bars

rat Imam Talikhan FAIZABAD

Jerm

Namakab Kishm

Ishkashim

ga

Sanglech

Ishkashim

Firgamu

INDU

K A F I R I

Khooshkdurrah

Bahrah

Karataz Khawak

Gadu Darosh

Silver Mine Timour-i-Shah

Shamu Ba

Baruk

Mandegal

Seaoul

Kila Najil

Bandai Di

ria Churikar

Alishang

k-serai Tigadf

KAR

Kunar

SCALE OF MILES

0   40   80   120   160

TO AFGHANISTAN AND BACK

ISBN 1-56163-325-9
© 2002 Ted Rall
Photos: © 2002 Judy Chang unless otherwise credited.
Printed in Hong Kong

5   4   3   2   1

Library of Congress Cataloging-in-Publication Data
Rall, Ted.
  To Afghanistan and back / by Ted Rall.
    p. cm.
  ISBN 1-56163-325-9 (cloth)
    1. Afghanistan--Description and travel. 2. Afghanistan--History--2001-3. War on
Terrorism, 2001- I. Title.

DS352 .R25 2002
958.104'6--dc21

                                                              2002016537

TO AFGHANISTAN AND BACK

A Graphic Travelogue by

TED RALL

NANTIER · BEALL · MINOUSTCHINE
Publishing inc.
new york

Also Available by Ted Rall from NBM:
2024, $16.95 hc, $9.95 pb.
My War With Brian, $8.95
Real Americans Admit: The Worst Thing I've Ever Done!, $8.95

Edited by Ted Rall from NBM:
Attitude: The New Subversive Political Cartoonists, $15.95

Other Books by Ted Rall:
Waking Up In America (St. Martin's Press), 1992
All The Rules Have Changed (Rip Off Press), 1995
Revenge of the Latchkey Kids (Workman Publishing), 1998
Search and Destroy (Andrews & McMeel), 2001

Ted Rall Online: www.RALL.com

We have over 150 titles, write
for our color catalog:
NBM
555 8th Ave., Suite 1202
New York, NY 10018
www.nbmpublishing.com

Back Cover: The Kunduz front line near Khanabad. Photo: Judy Chang.

"Death and Boredom on the Front Line," "Taliban Family Values" and
"How We Lost the Afghan War" originally appeared in *The Village Voice*.

First, thanks are owed to David G. Hall at KFI Radio in Los Angeles and
Doug Simmons at *The Village Voice* for funding the trip chronicled in these pages. Terry Nantier at NBM
published this book; Martin Satryb art directed, and J.P. Trostle did design and layout. David Stanford and
Sue Roush at Universal Press Syndicate edited the text. Sadoullo Khasanov of Mountain Travel Company
Central in Dushanbe got me into Afghanistan and, more importantly, got me out.

Contents

This is for
the people
who died.

Introduction

by Bill Maher

Shortly after the outbreak of hostilities in Afghanistan last October, award-winning cartoonist Ted Rall and his bride were deep in the heart of Pashtun country dodging 15,000-pound bunker-busters and haggling with locals over the price of drinking water so filthy a duck wouldn't shit in it. And you thought your second honeymoon was uninspired.

Taking pen in hand, Ted proceeded to skewer the insanity of the situation, not just with drawings but also with his prose, a series of dispatches as compelling and artfully rendered as anything I've read since...well, since *Dispatches*, Michael Herr's acclaimed book on his Vietnam War experiences. And while I don't always agree with Ted on the current conflict, the fact is he was there. Actually, Ted had traveled extensively throughout all the 'stan countries long before September 11th became a registered trademark. And since 9-11 he's seen, firsthand, what happens when a 5,000-pound precision-guided missile hits precisely the wrong target. Whereas the closest I've ever been to a genuine Afghan conflict was arguing prices with Akmed the rug salesman at this darling little boutique on Melrose.

Despite our occasional disagreements, Ted serves as a great guest on *Politically Incorrect*. Whatever our ideological differences, I know that when I pick up a book by Ted Rall my hackles will soon rise, my thoughts will be provoked, and my funny bone will be tickled. So good luck with the book, Ted, you revolting little America-hating pinko. And I mean that in the best possible way.

Bill Maher is host of the television show Politically Incorrect.

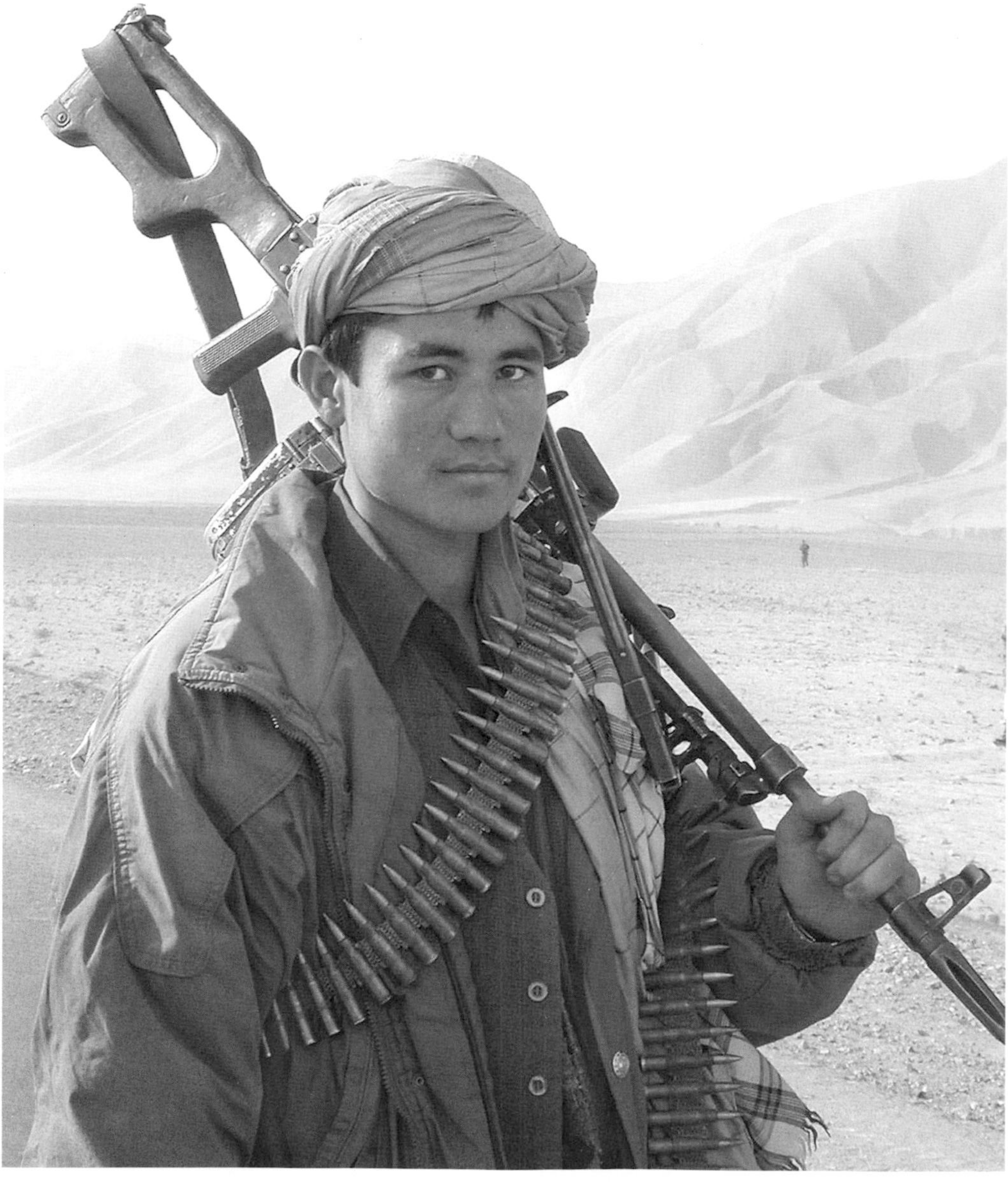

Northern Alliance soldier, age 14.

Foreword

by Ted Rall

In 1933, the author Sherwood Anderson traveled throughout the United States. To get a sense of the national mood, he talked to everyone from factory owners to hobos about the Depression. He titled his resulting essay collection *Puzzled America.*

Though the circumstances are very different, America is puzzled again. Until now, terrorism has always been something that happened in other countries or that could be quickly forgotten. How could the richest, most powerful state ever created be caught so flat-footed? Why, after all the foreign aid we've sent to poorer nations, would anyone hate us so much? And who are 'they', anyway?

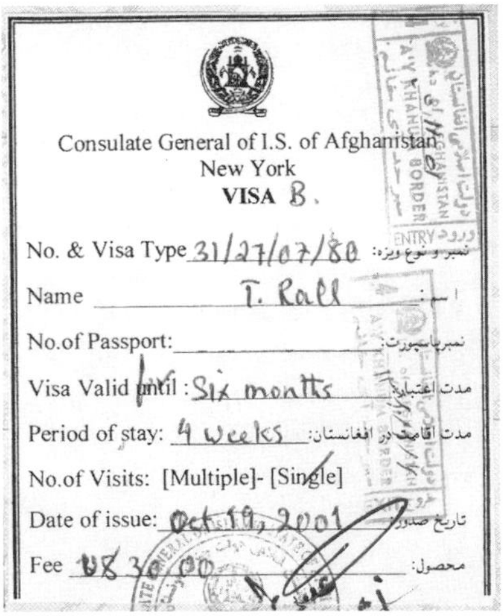

Consulate General of I.S. of Afghanistan
New York
VISA B.

No. & Visa Type 31/27/07/80
Name T. Rall
No.of Passport:
Visa Valid until : Six months
Period of stay: 4 weeks
No.of Visits: [Multiple]- [Single]
Date of issue: Oct 19, 2001
Fee US 30.00

Visa issued by Northern Alliance.

Weeks after the 2001 suicide bombings of the World Trade Center and Pentagon, the people of the wealthiest nation on earth launched an intensive, high-technology bombing campaign against the poorest. U.S. policymakers were so unfamiliar with the region that the Central Intelligence Agency was forced to issue a public appeal for Americans fluent in Pashto and Tajik, yet these same people considered themselves qualified to radically restructure Afghanistan's fundamental culture and politics.

My agent Maryanne Patey, my wife Judy and I went to discover the results of our war upon ordinary Afghans. We never expected to find The Truth, because that's impossible. We did, however, attempt to separate propaganda from reality; in other words, to eliminate some of our puzzlement. This book is part of that effort.

Ted Rall, war correspondent. The Kunduz front is on the other side of the wall.

This book is told from my perspective (rather than jointly) for several reasons. First, Afghanistan's prevailing gender apartheid often caused me to have interactions that my female companions could not, and vice versa. Second, I was still so stunned by the intensity of my experience at the time of writing that I was lucky to be able to articulate my own thoughts, much less synthesize our communal experiences into a coherent group narrative format. Finally, as a reader I've always found single-person point-of-view easier to follow, particularly vis-à-vis the graphic-novel portion of this text.

All of us have friends and relatives who demanded to know why we risked traveling to a famously dangerous place, while carrying passports issued by a country then dropping bombs on the locals. My reply was always the same: "It's just a few weeks. Millions of people live there their entire lives."

Please think of them when you read this.

Ted Rall
New York City

1. Giving War
A Chance

So we're going to war against Afghanistan. Big deal. We've been at war with Afghanistan for years.

This New War is merely an escalation of genocide by trade sanction, this time with a few old-fashioned bombs and covert commando raids thrown in for popular effect. And while the explosions will look cool on cable TV news and the vague rumors of American death squads trekking through the mountains will sound dashing in a Rudyard Kipling-cum-Rambo kind of way, it will accomplish exactly nothing.

On the other hand, this brand of ham-fisted foreign policy ensures that America will never run out of enemies.

On September 24th, Secretary of State Colin Powell promised that the Bush Administration would finally cough up definitive proof of Saudi dissident Osama bin Laden's involvement in the suicide plane bombings of the Pentagon and World Trade Center: "I think in the near future, we will be able to put out a paper, a document, that will describe quite clearly the evidence that we have linking him to this attack."

For the sake of argument, let's assume that Powell is telling the truth: that bin Laden, and by extension his Taliban hosts in Afghanistan, financed, ordered or otherwise directly participated in the murder of 3,000 Americans.

Clearly, then, bin Laden ought to be hunted down and captured "dead or alive," in the John Wayne-informed lexicon of our appointed acting president. The Taliban should likewise suffer political capital punishment—being deposed by an overwhelming invasion force. Under military occupation, bin Laden's Al Qaeda network would be rounded up and shut down. Ditto for the training camps that educate terrorist wannabes for *jihad* against Western democracies. Within a year, cybercafes catering to backpacking college kids would spring up across Kabul.

Unfortunately, it won't make any difference. Most of the training camps for such radical guerrilla outfits as the Islamic Movement of Uzbekistan, which made a name for itself a few years back with its annual raids on southern Kyrgyzstan, are in Pakistan, Tajikistan and southern Kyrgyzstan. The Tajik and Kyrgyz governments are far too impoverished, politically weak and poorly armed to eject these insurgents, but both value their ten-year-old independence from the Soviet Union too much to allow foreign troops into their territory to do the job. *Madrassas* (religious schools) in the Baluchistan and Northwest Frontier Provinces of Pakistan continue to serve up Jihad 101, but the fragile military government of General Pervez Musharraf, ethnically aligned and beholden to the Taliban for battling the Indians in disputed Kashmir province, will never risk the wrath of Muslim extremists in their own country by shutting them down. Bottom line: bombing, destroying and militarily-occupying Afghanistan only shuts down a small fraction of the terrorist training facilities.

Now, let's escalate from the madness of an Afghan invasion (remember how well the same idea worked out for Britain and the USSR?) to full-fledged mayhem on a monumental scale. Assuming that we get the approval—and still better, military backing—of Russia's Vladimir Putin, U.S. troops could fan out across Central Asia. Tajikistan would come easy. Kyrgyzstan wouldn't require much effort. Pakistan is a nuclear state nowadays; perhaps we could pay them to close the *madrassas*.

It still wouldn't make much difference.

Tens of thousands of Arab fundamentalist militants have already graduated from those Taliban-affiliated training facilities. They're in Egypt, Saudi Arabia, Libya, the United Arab Emirates, Qatar, Syria...and Florida. They belong to dozens of distinct organizations, each enjoying individual sources of financing and adhering to separate

EVEN IF AFGHANISTAN, OSAMA BIN LADEN AND THE OTHER 16,000,000 PEOPLE LIVING THERE WERE NUKED, IT WOULDN'T MATTER—MOST OF THE JIHAD CAMPS AREN'T THERE ANYWAY.
CHIN
IRAN
PAKISTAN
INDIA
EVEN IF WE OBLITERATED ALL OF THEIR TRAINING CENTERS IN PAKISTAN, TAJIKISTAN AND KYRGYZSTAN, IT WOULDN'T MATTER—THEIR FORMER STUDENTS ARE NOW ALL OVER THE WORLD.
TAMPA TRIBUNE
TAJIKISTAN BOMBED
JIHAD U.
EVEN IF WE TRACKED DOWN EVERY SINGLE MUSLIM MILITANT ON THE PLANET AND KILLED THEM, IT WOULDN'T MATTER—THEIR FRIENDS AND RELATIVES WOULD TAKE THEIR PLACES.
EVEN IF IT MATTERED, IT WOULDN'T HELP.

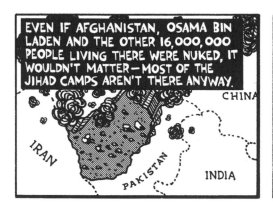

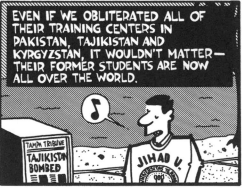

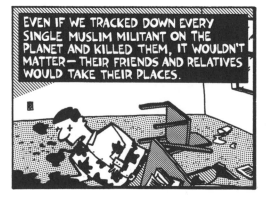

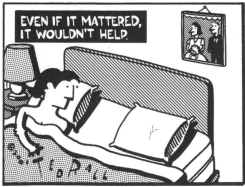

American F-16 preparing to bomb Bangi, Afghanistan.

goals and ideologies. Putting their alma maters out of business won't prevent them from carrying out future attacks on the U.S.

Nonetheless, it's always possible to carry a hypothetical war on terrorism to its logical extreme: somehow, perhaps using satellite surveillance and pixie dust, the U.S. and its allies successfully hunt down every single member of every militant Islamic organization in the world and either jail or kill them. Who knows how? Anyway—

It *still* wouldn't matter. Those dead and jailed militants have mothers, fathers, sisters and brothers. They have friends. And countless ordinary Muslim people would watch, driven to vengeance by the extraordinary ruthlessness of such a massive assault by America on individuals whose only proven sins are their beliefs. A new army of jihadists would rise from the ashes of Bush's 21st century crusade.

Nonetheless, America must have its vengeance. We're not the kind of people to sit around and mourn a few thousand dead office workers when there's some serious ass to kick. So we'll bomb or invade or something. It won't matter, but that doesn't matter. It's what we do.

Taliban POWs at the Taloqan town jail. The man at left claimed to be Uzbek—note the Uzbek hat—but guards said he was Pakistani. (Photo: Maryanne Patey.)

2. The New Great Game

Nursultan Nazarbayev has a terrible problem. He's the president and former Communist Party boss of Kazakhstan, the second-largest republic of the former Soviet Union. A few years ago, the giant country struck oil in the eastern portion of the Caspian Sea. Geologists estimate that sitting beneath the wind-blown steppes of Kazakhstan are 50 billion barrels of oil—by far the biggest untapped reserves in the world. (Saudi Arabia, currently the world's largest oil producer, is believed to have about 30 billion barrels remaining. Kazakhstan, meanwhile, may have unconfirmed reserves of up to 260 billion barrels.)

Kazakhstan's Soviet-subsidized economy collapsed immediately after independence in 1991. When I visited the then-capital of Almaty in 1997, I was struck by its utter absence of elderly people. One after another, Kazakhs confided that their parents had died of malnutrition during the brutal winters of 1993 and 1994. Middle-class residents of a superpower had been reduced to abject poverty virtually overnight; thirtysomething women who appeared sixtysomething hocked their wedding silver in underpasses next to reps for the Kazakh state art museum trying to move enough socialist realist paintings for a dollar each to keep the lights on. The average Kazakh earned $20 a month; those unwilling or unable to steal died of gangrene adjacent to long-winded tales of woe written on cardboard.

Autocrats tend to die badly during periods of downward mobility. Nazarbayev, therefore, has spent most of the last decade trying to get his land-locked oil out to sea. Once the oil starts flowing, it won't take long before Kazakhstan replaces Kuwait as the land of Benzes and ugly gold jewelry. But the longer the pipeline, the more expensive and vulnerable to sabotage it is. The shortest route runs through Iran but Kazakhstan is too closely aligned with the U.S. to offend it by cutting a deal with Teheran. Russia has helpfully offered to build a line connecting Kazakh oil rigs to the Black Sea, but neighboring Turkmenistan has experienced trouble with the Russians—they tend to divert the oil for their own uses without bothering to pay for it. There's even a plan to run crude out to the Pacific through China, but the proposed 5,300-mile line would be far too long to prove profitable.

The logical alternative, then, is Unocal's plan, which is to extend Turkmenistan's

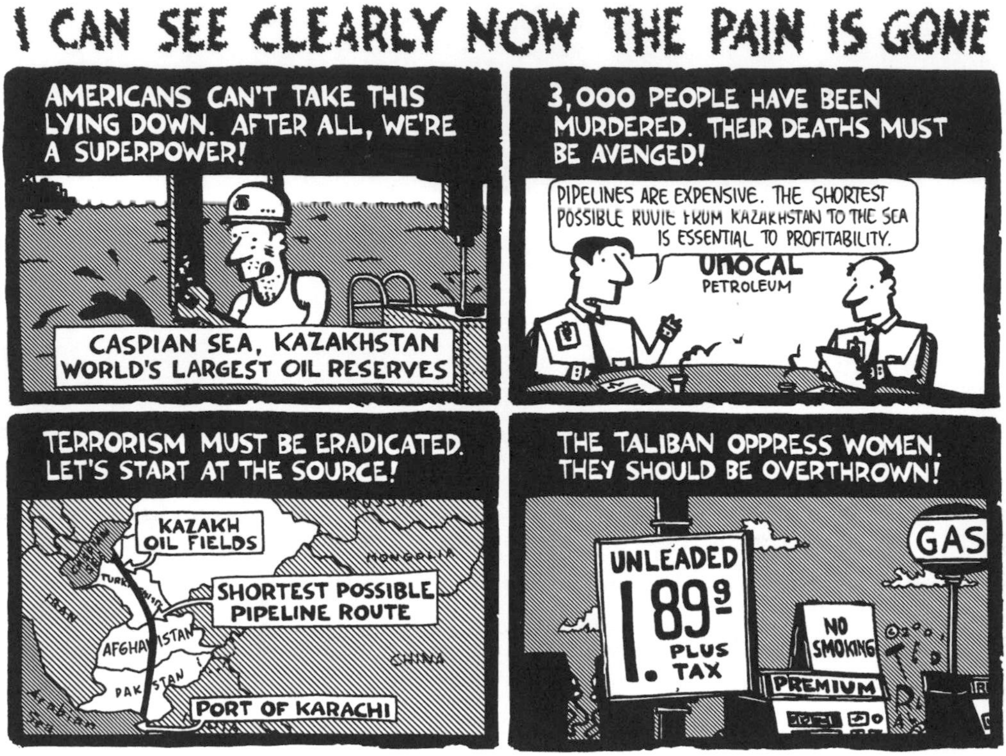
I CAN SEE CLEARLY NOW THE PAIN IS GONE
AMERICANS CAN'T TAKE THIS LYING DOWN. AFTER ALL, WE'RE A SUPERPOWER!
CASPIAN SEA, KAZAKHSTAN
WORLD'S LARGEST OIL RESERVES
3,000 PEOPLE HAVE BEEN MURDERED. THEIR DEATHS MUST BE AVENGED!
PIPELINES ARE EXPENSIVE. THE SHORTEST POSSIBLE ROUTE FROM KAZAKHSTAN TO THE SEA IS ESSENTIAL TO PROFITABILITY.
UNOCAL
PETROLEUM
TERRORISM MUST BE ERADICATED. LET'S START AT THE SOURCE!
KAZAKH OIL FIELDS
SHORTEST POSSIBLE PIPELINE ROUTE
MONGOLIA
IRAN
CHINA
PORT OF KARACHI
Arabian Sea
THE TALIBAN OPPRESS WOMEN. THEY SHOULD BE OVERTHROWN!
UNLEADED
1.89 9/10
PLUS TAX
NO SMOKING
PREMIUM
GAS

existing system west to the Kazakh field on the Caspian and southeast to the Pakistani port of Karachi on the Arabian Sea. That project runs through Afghanistan.

As Central Asian expert Ahmed Rashid describes in his 2000 book "Taliban: Militant Islam, Oil and Fundamentalism in Central Asia," the U.S. and Pakistan decided to install a stable regime into place in Afghanistan around 1994—a regime that would end the country's civil war and thus ensure the safety of the Unocal pipeline project. Impressed by the ruthlessness and willingness of the then-emerging Taliban to cut a pipeline deal, the U.S. State Department and Pakistan's Interservices Intelligence (I.S.I.) agency agreed to funnel arms and funding to the Taliban in their war against the ethnically Tajik Northern Alliance. As recently as 1999, U.S. taxpayers paid the entire annual salary of every single Taliban government official, all in the hopes of returning to the days of dollar-a-gallon gas. Pakistan, naturally, would pick up revenues from a Karachi oil port facility. Harkening to 19th century power politics between Russia and British India, Rashid dubbed the struggle for control of post-Soviet Central Asia "the new Great Game."

Predictably, the Taliban Frankenstein got out of control. The regime's unholy alliance with Osama bin Laden's terror network, their penchant for invading their neighbors and their production of 50 percent of the world's opium made them unlikely partners for the desired oil deal. Then-President Bill Clinton's 1998 cruise missile attack on Afghanistan briefly brought the Taliban back into line—they even eradicated opium poppy cultivation in less than a year—but they nonetheless continued supporting countless militant Islamic groups. When a group whose members had trained in Afghanistan hijacked four airplanes and used them to kill more than 3,000 Americans on September 11th, Washington's patience with its former client finally expired.

Finally, the Bushies had the perfect excuse to do what the U.S. had wanted all along—invade and/or install an old-school puppet regime in Kabul. Realpolitik no more cares about the 3,000 dead than it concerns itself with oppressed women in Afghanistan; this ersatz war by a phony president is solely about getting an oil pipeline deal done without interference from annoying local middlemen.

Central Asian politics, however, is a house of cards: every time you remove one element, the whole thing comes crashing down. Muslim extremists in both Pakistan and Afghanistan, for instance, will support additional terror attacks on the U.S. to avenge the elimination of the Taliban. A U.S.-installed Northern Alliance can't hold Kabul without an army of occupation because Afghan legitimacy hinges on capturing the capital on your own. And even if we do this the right way by funding and training the Northern Alliance so that they can seize power themselves, Pakistan's ethnic Pashtun government won't long stand the replacement of their Pashtun brothers in the Taliban by Northern Alliance Tajiks. Without Pakistani cooperation, there's no getting the oil out and there's no chance for long-term stability in Afghanistan.

As Bush would say, make no mistake: this is about oil. It's always about oil. And to twist a late '90s cliché, it's only boring because it's true.

WORLDS of SEPARATION

IF YOU HAVEN'T HEARD FROM SOMEONE, IS IT REASONABLE TO ASSUME THAT THEY'RE DEAD?

WHAT IF YOU THINK SOMEONE YOU CARE ABOUT IS DEAD? HOW MUCH SHOULD YOU GRIEVE?

IF SOMEONE YOU KNOW BUT AREN'T PARTICULARLY CLOSE TO IS DEAD, HOW MUCH SHOULD YOU HURT?

IF IT'S SOMEONE YOU ACTIVELY DISLIKED BUT YOU WOULD NEVER HAVE WISHED DEAD, ARE YOU ALLOWED TO FEEL UPSET?

P5 REMEMBER YOUR LEVEL

IF YOU DIDN'T KNOW ANY OF THE VICTIMS, HOW MUCH SHOULD YOU CARE?

YOU *ARE* A VICTIM.

3. Nineteen Guys Who Shook The World

NEW YORK, September 18

"Power is an illusion," columnist Jimmy Breslin wrote during Watergate. At no time in our lives has that truism been more evident.

The demise of the Soviet Union, we know as surely as we can know anything nowadays, left us Americans in charge of the planet. What we never considered was how little it took to bring down our rival superpower: the C.I.A. dumping dollars on the floors of Moscow lavatories to destabilize the ruble. A nuclear meltdown at Chernobyl.

Afghanistan.

It happened to them. Now it's happening to us.

Integral to the shaking fists and flag-waving hysteria and the funerals—thousands and thousands and thousands more of those to come, by the way—is a rage born of impotence. Conservatives applaud and liberals deplore our expensive governmental monitoring systems—what would we have argued about had we known that neither the C.I.A. nor the N.S.A. knew what was going to go down September 11th? For what does it profit a country to starve its schools if its fattened Pentagon can't even protect *its own headquarters* from a terrorist attack?

The United States has finally been unmasked as the greatest Potemkin ever conceived—"great magnificent shapes, castles and kingdoms," in Breslin's words. Or to paraphrase Edward G. Robinson's classic dis of Fred MacMurray in "Double Indemnity": We thought we were smart, but we were wrong. We're just a little bigger.

Air-traffic controllers realized fairly quickly that those four jets had been hijacked. American Flight 11, out of Boston, took 46 minutes to hit Tower One of the World Trade Center. United Flight 175 struck Tower Two 65 minutes after leaving Boston. Most damning, American Flight 77 was aloft a total of 88 minutes—*nearly an hour and a half*—making it from Washington/Dulles to southern Ohio en route to Los Angeles before turning around. Math: the flight did a 180-degree turn at least 44 minutes away from the Pentagon. Why weren't our F-16s on top of that plane within 10 minutes? Why wasn't it shot down during the next 34 minutes after that? The answer, sheepishly admitted and buried deeply amid assorted tales of horror, was that there is no policy for forcing down a civilian airliner.

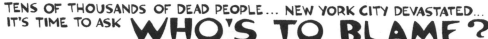

TENS OF THOUSANDS OF DEAD PEOPLE... NEW YORK CITY DEVASTATED...
IT'S TIME TO ASK WHO'S TO BLAME?
ANNOYING LIBERAL DEMOCRATS COULD HAVE PROPOSED A SWEEPING BAN OF BOX-CUTTERS, PENKNIVES AND SHARP AND/OR POINTY OBJECTS—BUT THEY DIDN'T. COULD THEY BE PART OF THE CONSPIRACY?
THE JIHAD THANKS YOU FOR YOUR HELP!
HEY—SWISS ARMY KNIVES DON'T KILL PEOPLE!
THE WRIGHT BROTHERS CREATED THEIR HEINOUS FLYING MISSILES WITHOUT EVER CONSIDERING THE CONSEQUENCES OF THEIR INVENTION. THEY'RE SCUM!
WE CLONED YOU AND WILBUR SO WE COULD EXECUTE YOU.
BUT I INVENTED AVIATION!
GOD COULD HAVE CRUDDED UP THE WEATHER, PREVENTING AIR TRAVEL. SO COULD THOSE CLOUD SEEDER GUYS. THEIR NEGLIGENCE IS UNFORGIVABLE!
WE REALLY OUGHT TO DO SOME WORK.
SCREW THAT—I WORK IN MYSTERIOUS WAYS! HA HA!
Chet's CLOUD SEEDING
THE HIJACKERS GREW UP IN THE THIRD WORLD. THE THIRD WORLD MUST PAY FOR THE SINS OF THEIR PROGENY!
IT'S NOT MY FAULT I'M A TERRORIST—I NEVER GOT A $300 TAX CUT!

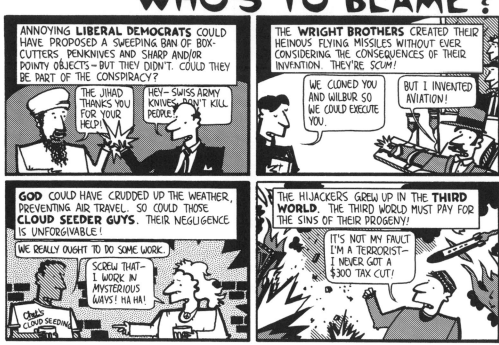

Unless, of course, there was. The Air Force denies shooting down United Flight 93, which crashed and burned in Shanksville, Pennsylvania, the government's silence certifying celled-in media stories of heroic passengers rebelling against their captors. Those accounts, however, are cast into doubt by the government's refusal to release the plane's voice cockpit recorder tapes to the public. It's a safe bet, after all, that a bold struggle for control would at least make it out in transcript form. So it's possible that Bush or other officials made a terrible, yet courageous, decision to act; if so, the need to keep it secret provides ample testimony to the aftermath of last year's election-that-never-was—if Bush is the perfect president for this time, he's the empty-headed embodiment of our national cluelessness.

America's embarrassment of embarrassments continues apace. C.I.A. superspooks admit that their posse of white Mormons from Utah never learned Pashto or Tajik, Afghanistan's two principal languages. The loss of four planes and a few days of airport closures decimates the biggest airline industry in the world, resonating through the economy in the form of the biggest stock-market crash ever. Half a dozen buildings accounting for less than one percent of New York City's office space vanish; the national economy plunges decidedly into recession and beyond.

What would we do if we really *were* at war? How can the richest superpower in the history of mankind have been brought so low by 19 guys?

The United States, it turns out, entered the 21st century atop a crumbling house of cards. When the Soviet Union went away, we lost the ideological and economic competition that had kept us sharp after World War II. We became complacent, smug and arrogant. History, Francis Fukuyama told us in 1993, had ended. Global free-market capitalism, epitomized and led by United States corporations, represented the pinnacle of achievement of historical evolution. A power vacuum opened in Central Asia. Afghanistan disintegrated into civil war, anarchy and religious madness. Surrounding republics—Uzbekistan, Kyrgyzstan, Tajikistan, Pakistan—were sucked into a vortex of instability and anti-Western sentiment fueled by clumsy U.S. attempts to suck all the oil out of the region without paying off any of the locals. This, and America's blank check to Israel, inspired tens of thousands of militant Muslims to their facile conclusion: Sometimes the bull in the china shop won't leave voluntarily. That's when you kill it.

Osama and his jihad boys sized us up fairly well. Behind the high-tech metal detectors in our airports were underpaid incompetents. Manning our tactical defenses were dimwitted dolts devoid of imagination. Bolstering our outsized economy was a mountain of debt and an easily-spooked securities market. And behind the boast that the World Trade Center could withstand a collision with a jet was the horrible, awful truth: no amount of bluster can annul the laws of physics. As the cliché goes, we believed our own hype and now we're paying the price.

Our close-to-the-bone brand of capitalism turned out to be our economic Achilles' heel. Corporations that fill metal tubes with highly-combustible fuel and upper-middle-

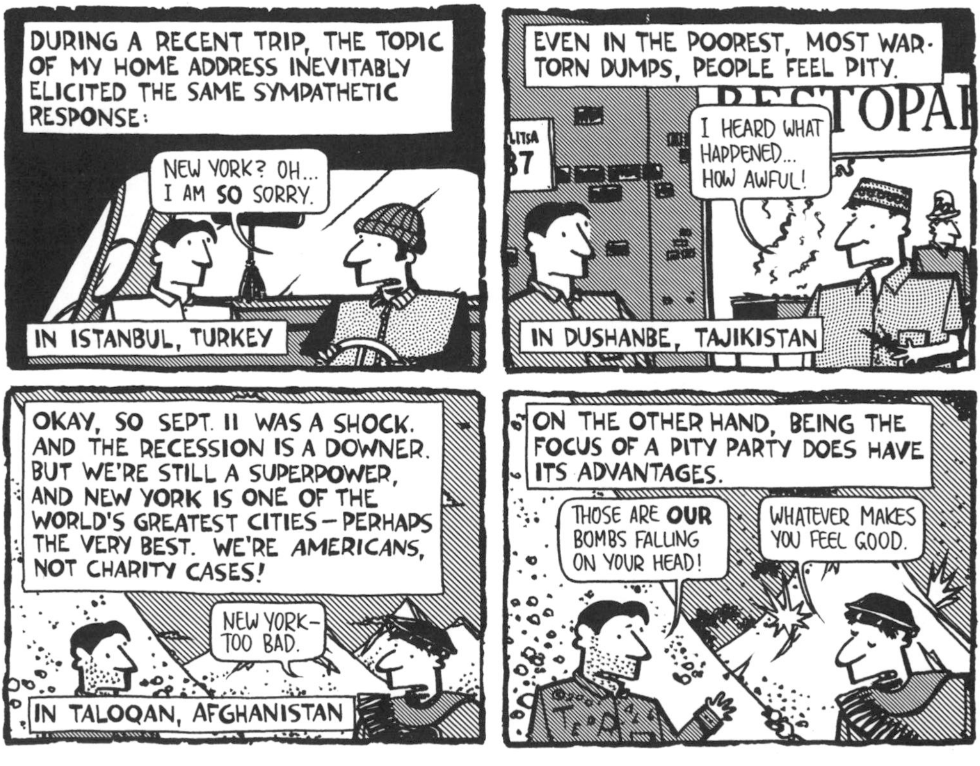
DURING A RECENT TRIP, THE TOPIC OF MY HOME ADDRESS INEVITABLY ELICITED THE SAME SYMPATHETIC RESPONSE:
NEW YORK? OH... I AM SO SORRY.
IN ISTANBUL, TURKEY
EVEN IN THE POOREST, MOST WAR-TORN DUMPS, PEOPLE FEEL PITY.
I HEARD WHAT HAPPENED... HOW AWFUL!
IN DUSHANBE, TAJIKISTAN
OKAY, SO SEPT. 11 WAS A SHOCK. AND THE RECESSION IS A DOWNER. BUT WE'RE STILL A SUPERPOWER, AND NEW YORK IS ONE OF THE WORLD'S GREATEST CITIES—PERHAPS THE VERY BEST. WE'RE AMERICANS, NOT CHARITY CASES!
NEW YORK—TOO BAD.
IN TALOQAN, AFGHANISTAN
ON THE OTHER HAND, BEING THE FOCUS OF A PITY PARTY DOES HAVE ITS ADVANTAGES.
THOSE ARE OUR BOMBS FALLING ON YOUR HEAD!
WHATEVER MAKES YOU FEEL GOOD.

class citizens and propel them eight miles over the surface of the earth at high speeds ought to be prepared for an occasional mishap, but they're not—and neither are insurers who are, after all, in the business of risk appraisal. A week of reduced productivity has ruined crops (no crop dusters during the flight ban) and trashed the economies of states dependent on tourism. This, since George W. Bush and his tax-cutting maniacs have forgotten, is why governments and companies both need savings and surpluses. "It's my money," Republicans like to say, "and I can use it better than the government can." Worst of all, decades of increasing disparity of wealth has made it impossible for ordinary people to help out the only way they really could, by spending discretionary income. Now that we've let them steal all of our money, where are all the jobs rich people are supposed to create? This is the way empires end, with a bang and a whine.

4. Capitalism Comes to Central Asia

DUSHANBE, TAJIKISTAN, November 22

My fixer—no self-respecting Westerner does Central Asia without one, without a local to smooth his way—tried to take me to the Hotel Dushanbe. But I'm no sucker. I didn't let the big rooms or working boilers seduce me.

"Take me to the Hotel Tajikistan!" I insisted to Sadoullo. An anguished look crossed Sadoullo's face: "But it's...cheaper."

In Tajikistan, as back home in Manhattan, cheap means bad. But here in the waning days of the Afghan war rush, the Hotel Tajikistan is *the* place to be. Dushanbe, the worn-out capital of the most-failed of former Soviet Republics, sight of a not-unlike-Afghanistan civil war during the '90s, is the jumping-off point for anyone who wants to get into Afghanistan, a country with no international airport. And the Hotel Tajikistan has become a Scene: There are more "journos" in the lobby than in the entire *New York Times* building.

When you catch Christiane Amanpour and the rest of the talking heads broadcasting from the roof of the Islamabad Marriott in Pakistan, know this: People who don't know jack about this part of the world go to Pakistan to get into Afghanistan. You would, too, if you looked at a map; the Khyber Pass offers the best geographical connector between Afghanistan and the outside world. But the Pakistani-Afghan border has been closed since U.S. bombs started falling; the closest thing to actual action is interviews with Afghan refugees at camps in Peshawar and Quetta.

Tajikistan has received remarkably little coverage in America's New War, as cable TV news calls it. When the Taliban still ruled, the Tajik-dominated Northern Alliance used the country as a supply

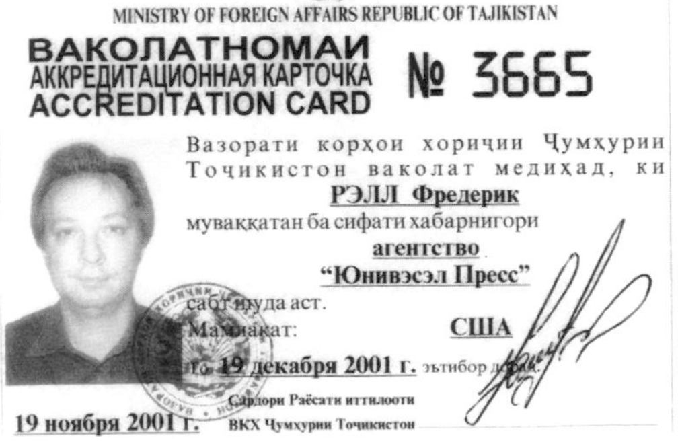

ВАЗОРАТИ КОРҲОИ ХОРИҶИИ ҶУМҲУРИИ ТОҶИКИСТОН

МИНИСТЕРСТВО ИНОСТРАННЫХ ДЕЛ РЕСПУБЛИКИ ТАДЖИКИСТАН

MINISTRY OF FOREIGN AFFAIRS REPUBLIC OF TAJIKISTAN

ВАКОЛАТНОМАИ
АККРЕДИТАЦИОННАЯ КАРТОЧКА
ACCREDITATION CARD

№ 3665

Вазорати корҳои хориҷии Ҷумҳурии Тоҷикистон ваколат медиҳад, ки

РЭЛЛ Фредерик

муваққатан ба сифати хабарнигори

агентство

"Юнивэсэл Пресс"

сабт шуда аст.

Мамлакат: США

то 19 декабря 2001 г. эътибор дорад.

Сардори Раёсати иттилооти ВКХ Ҷумҳурии Тоҷикистон

19 ноября 2001 г.

Tajik press card, required to enter the restricted zone near Afghanistan.

line—opium paste and emeralds out, guns in. Even when the Islamic State of Afghanistan controlled just five percent of the country, the Alliance ran a regular helicopter shuttle between Dushanbe and Faizabad, Afghanistan. Now, that chopper and government-sponsored journalist convoys have become the only reliable routes in and out of the land of the mujaheddin.

"Are you with a relief agency?" a thinned-lipped 50ish lady from Seattle asks me in the elevator, obviously sizing up my suitability for a middle-of-nowhere one-nighter.

"Journalism," I reply, "talk radio and *The Village Voice*."

"Ohhhh," she says.

We both know what that "oh" means.

The aid agency workers, mainly Christians and retro-granola types, consider the journalists vultures of the lowest order, gleefully snapping pictures of gore and cruel acts. The laptop and video-feed set look at the aid workers with a mix of pity and contempt, for they believe their efforts are both pointless (feeding a few thousand while millions starve) and self-interested (converting Muslims to Christianity).

Both are right. The real winners here are the Afghans and Tajiks sufficiently educated in English and the ways of the marketplace to exploit the army of expense-account-funded scribblers and proselytizers in their midst.

Refugee passing a bombed-out Afghan village, Kunduz Province. (Photo: Maryanne Patey.)

LIVE FROM THE SUBCONTINENT IT'S REFUGEE REVUE!
WE'D BEEN STARVING FOR YEARS DUE TO THE DROUGHT. AFTER MY WIFE DIED, I TOOK HER BROTHER AND OUR DAUGHTER AND LEFT OUR FARM.
SOME SOLDIERS ACCUSED MY BROTHER OF DESERTION; THEY SHOT HIM ON THE SPOT. MY DAUGHTER DIED IN THE MOUNTAINS; IT WAS JUST TOO COLD. I'VE MADE IT TO FREEDOM, BUT NOW FREEDOM IS ALL I HAVE.
WOW. WHAT A STORY.
I'LL GIVE YOU 4 MINUTES DURING EAST COAST PRIME-TIME.
WHAT ABOUT THAT GREAT KICKER? 7 MINUTES LIVE PLUS 3 REBROAD-CASTS OR I TAKE THIS TO MSNBC.

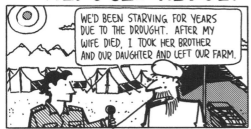

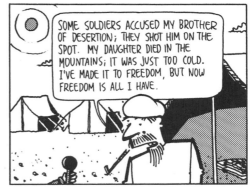

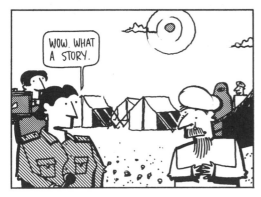

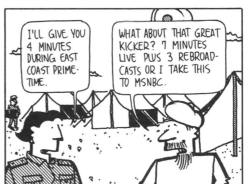

The Northern Alliance charges $550 for a one-way helicopter ride that takes 20 minutes; to increase revenue they sell twice as many tickets as there are seats and let Darwinistic fisticuffs work out the difference. The same experience, minus the double booking, cost just $130 a year ago. English/Dari/Pashto translators go for more than $100 a day in a nation with an average monthly income of $1.40. Even a 20-mile taxi ride, at most a buck a year ago, will set back the accounting department at CNN $40 or more.

According to the Afghan embassy, a few hundred journalists are running around inflating the Afghan economy; every week, roughly 40 to 80 more enter the country. The war hasn't been completely gentrified, however; the car convoy, which travels some of the worst mountain roads anywhere on the planet "for eight or nine hours, or maybe three days," according to my fixer, costs a mere $400 per car. Before the war you could've done the same thing for $80.

"I just hope the Taliban hold out at Kunduz," I overheard a guy from German Channel 4 say in the elevator here at the hotel. Many residents of Dushanbe feel the same way.

Taking a break at the front.

5. Death and Boredom on the Front Line

TALOQAN, AFGHANISTAN, November 25

Afghans are different from you and me. We live in a world in which more people are alive than have ever lived and died. Theirs is the diametric opposite. Afghanistan is defined by things that used to be: people, ideas, Buddha statues, cities. Journalistic hyperbole has no place here; even the most abused adjectives fall short in a country where Soviet tank treads serve as speed bumps. The poor are poorer than words can describe, the anarchy of armed-to-the-teeth 11-year-old soldiers more prevalent than anyone would care to admit, the destruction so complete that, as upon viewing the Grand Canyon for the first time, the brain can't process the quantity or perfect genius of the horror.

Like "Three Kings" come to life, this third Afghan war is characterized by surreal boredom, for locals and foreigners alike, with a dash of genuine death tossed in just to keep things interesting.

Nowhere is this truer than in the provincial capital of Taloqan. Dozens of Western journalists, a few from the country that started this whole thing, scurry about this town, captured by the Northern Alliance just days ago, wallowing in inanity as they place bets on their own chances of coming home alive.

"So," my new neighbor, who rode a Northern Alliance tank into Taloqan for *The Washington Post*, asks me seconds after my arrival, "What are you doing for power?"

Laptops and satellite phones and short-wave radios have us paying taxi drivers $20 a shot to drain their car batteries, running foul-smelling generators over the four-day road trip over the Tajik border, and endlessly clicking the annual rechargers from REI. Lost in the lust for direct current is the oft-told yet incomprehensible statistic of the average salary—$1.40 per month—and even paying the $20 to recharge the phone isn't pushing that buck-forty very far.

"Who's your translator?" is the second question any Euro will ask you, because a bad translator can cost you both your story and your life. A good one, on the other hand, doesn't have to speak English. He fixes things with the Foreign Ministry so that you can go to the front, scores you a cheap rental car—ideally with a cigarette lighter so you can recharge your sat phone—and finds you food during the diurnal Ramadan witching hours.

At night, the bombs come.

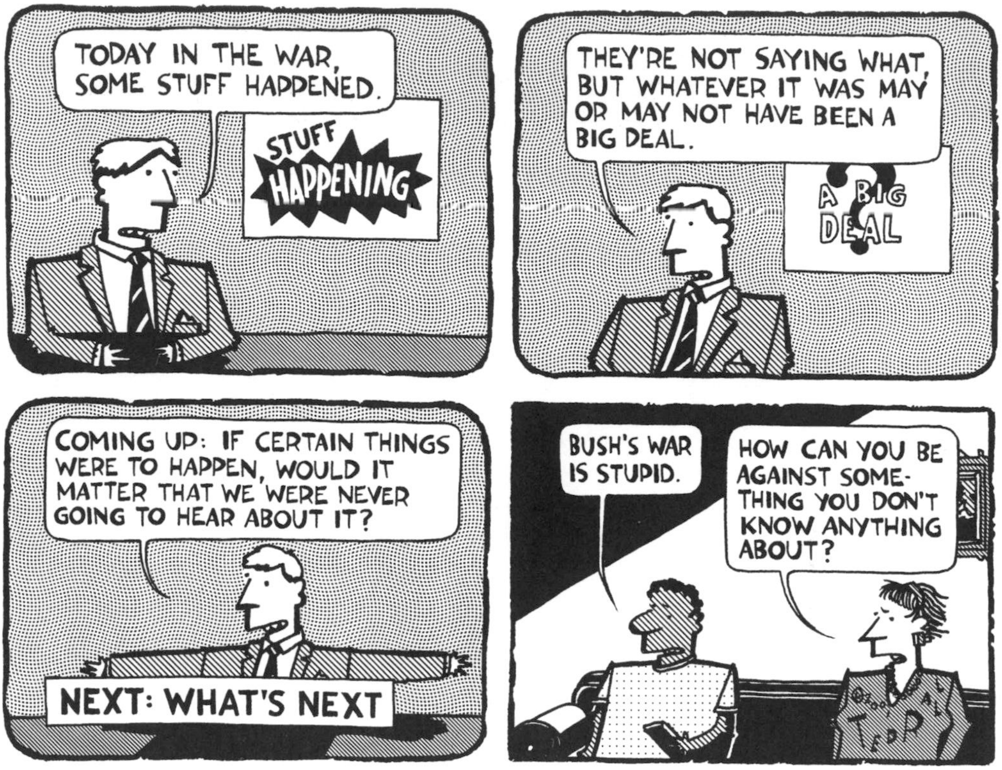
TODAY IN THE WAR, SOME STUFF HAPPENED.
STUFF HAPPENING
THEY'RE NOT SAYING WHAT, BUT WHATEVER IT WAS MAY OR MAY NOT HAVE BEEN A BIG DEAL.
A BIG DEAL
COMING UP: IF CERTAIN THINGS WERE TO HAPPEN, WOULD IT MATTER THAT WE WERE NEVER GOING TO HEAR ABOUT IT?
NEXT: WHAT'S NEXT
BUSH'S WAR IS STUPID.
HOW CAN YOU BE AGAINST SOMETHING YOU DON'T KNOW ANYTHING ABOUT?

The siege of Kunduz, which is important because the place sits at the intersection of two of the five paved highways in the country, rages 20 miles to the west. Mostly the bombs, big 5,000-pounders according to Saloqhan, a jovial Northern Alliance commander who briefs me each morning, fall on the Taliban sector of Kunduz. One night a bridge vanishes; the next a residential neighborhood goes up with nary a mention on American television.

"We don't care if we get killed," an Uzbek fighter named Khalev reassures me as he poses with his shiny AK. "What is important is to bomb the foreigner Taliban so they will come out and we can kill them." And the collateral damage? "It should not be mentioned as it would cause Americans to doubt themselves."

Ever since the Taliban defenders of Kunduz reneged on their surrender offer with a ferociously lethal ambush of their would-be conquerors, the Alliance has adopted a nationalist stance: Afghan Taliban will be welcomed into the warm bosom of indefinite imprisonment, while Pakistanis, Chechens, and other foreign volunteers will be executed *en masse*.

Donald Rumsfeld's obscene statement that the U.S. is happy to take no prisoners in Afghanistan is taken seriously by Afghans of all political persuasions. "As long as we are alive," I hear a Taliban commander inside Kunduz tell his Alliance counterpart over a military radio, "we will fight."

"You should surrender to prevent more killing," his Alliance counterpart reasons.

"Your killing or my killing?" the Taliban officer closes.

Sometimes the bombs hit the residential neighborhoods of this Northern Alliance-held city. It's intellectual calculus of the lowest sort. The per capita odds of you yourself getting hit by a bomb are tiny, akin to winning the lottery or getting that big promotion. And yet every night the bombs come again.

The important thing is to leave your windows open. It gets very cold at night, around 20 or 30 degrees, but there isn't any heat anyway. At first the ground shakes; then a rush of air punches the windows. A Swiss radio journalist is at the Red Crescent Hospital next door having shards of glass extracted from his body. "That's what happens when you don't leave the window open," his convoy mate, a writer for the British newspaper *The Guardian*, smirks. Twenty-four hours later the Brit is in the same hospital, unlikely to survive an encounter with Taliban P.O.W.s he was interviewing.

The journalists have reasons to be fatalistic: we're dropping like flies. Three killed, then four carjacked and killed by the Taliban near Jalalabad a week ago, then three more. None were killed in battle, Ernie Pyle-style. All were carjacked or mugged. The Alliance helps by turning us into targets; they force us into caravans of rented vehicles containing hundreds of thousands of dollars in cash, traveling across remote dustscapes, with no more control on human behavior than the estimated five million mines planted among the spindly trees alongside the road.

When the sun comes up nine and a half hours ahead of and a thousand years behind Ground Zero, the war commute begins. Tanks and trucks and Japanese rental cars with Dubai plates zoom west across the desert, dodging donkeys, potholes, piles of wheat drying on the asphalt—and every now and then, a group of refugees from Kunduz. The drama is purely theoretical; in practice the sight of teenage girls in brightly colored dresses, toting ridiculously tiny bags containing everything they own, becomes instantaneously mundane. Likewise the front itself, which has become such a local institution that it now has its own parking attendants for visiting journos.

Self-proclaimed experts on the differences between the various kinds of mines speculate on the F-16 circling the hamlet of Bangi, just outside Kunduz. "He's not going to drop," bets Lance from the BBC. "Once they drop they establish a straight line and get the hell out of there." If you squint, you can make out a Taliban bunker a half mile down the valley on a perfectly sunny day. "They've been trying to hit us all day," Lance notes. "They know we're here."

Lance is right. After a few hours photographing and sketching Alliance troops, the heat gets to me, and I hop into my car for the drive back to Taloqan. On the way home, I call my mom to wish her a happy Thanksgiving.

A few minutes after leaving Bangi, the Taliban score a coup; they take out the journalists' parking lot. Some guy from Finnish radio comes back in a pickup truck, bleeding from pebbles and rocks lodged somewhere inside him. And after that, all hell breaks loose when a Taliban commander drives down the road to surrender himself, a pile of guns, and a Ford Expedition.

There's a scramble for the keys to the SUV booty; 25 Northern Alliance soldiers are wounded and one is killed in the ensuing fracas. But the visceral thrill that normally pairs up with such brushes with death is oddly absent. In just 24 hours, the place where I was standing a few minutes earlier is pulverized by mortar shells, and the town I'm living in is

Journalist convoy becomes bogged down, rural Takhar Province. (Photo: Maryanne Patey.)

randomly bombed by Air Force dipshits. Mostly, though, it's a mind-numbingly dull existence. For one thing, I engaged in mere tourism where the locals are born pro. For another, the advantages of life over death aren't quite as apparent here as they are back home.

In the evening they send us back to T-town. "You should go home," Alliance commander General Mohammad Daoud informs the assembly of dehydrated writers and cameramen after another day when the main camera-ready action on the front has been an exchange of bodies.

"What are these guys dying of, old age?" someone asks. We want blood, Robert Capa, soldiers falling back dramatically, arms splayed. The closest we get is puffs of smoke in the distance where people and buildings used to be and a camel blown to smithereens by a mine. "We want to stay for the bombing," I tell Daoud. "We've been waiting for hours."

"If you stay after dark," he warns, "some of my troops will rob you. And maybe worse." There's something tantalizing about this possibility. For one thing, I'd have something to write about. For another, it might jump-start emotions and bowels locked solid by days of fending off stooped old ladies in burqas pulling at my clothes in Central Asia's ultimate form of aggressive panhandling. Maybe the sight of all of those guns— every other male carries at least one, too many of them pointed at me—might spark my sympathy for the millions who lie under graves of stones and green flags hanging limply from mangy sticks. More likely, some dumb fuck would shoot me just for the hell of it. I don't care to be Number 11, not tonight.

So I go home to a dinner of butter biscuits from Qatar with a side of Ashi-Mashi orange cola, and wait for the bombs to come.

6. All Things Fall Apart

TALOQAN, AFGHANISTAN, November 29

One week after the Taliban fled this dusty provincial capital to join their comrades defending nearby Kunduz, freedom was in the air. Eleven-year-old boys toting rocket launchers bigger than themselves milled about the central square, playing soccer, flying kites and shooting their AKs into the air. Women briefly lifted their burqas to take a clear look at the workman painting over the Taliban logo on the local school.

I wandered the streets feeling more like Mick Jagger than a citizen of the nation dropping bombs on the locals; a throng of men and boys followed me as I made my way to the market to buy Nescafé and flea powder. Due to Ramadan, the bazaar is quiet during the day, but the Shah Massoud restaurant springs to life at night. The local specialty is Afghan steak kebabs mixed with eggs (like the country itself, they're interesting but dangerous).

In a scene straight out of the Wild West, scowling gunmen sprawl over the tables, their weaponry laying about as they sing along to Indian movie music blasting from a loudspeaker and occasionally engage one another in fisticuffs. It's hard to believe that just a week ago most of these men were Talibs.

"Of course we will throw away our burqas," a young woman told me at the bazaar, "but we are afraid the Taliban will come back. If they do, they will punish anyone who removes their *burqas*."

There is understandable uncertainty in the air about whether "the current government," as locals call it, will stay in power. But it's more than that. Women as well as men dread a return to the "Mad Max"-like state of anarchy that characterized the early '90s, when the Northern Alliance last ruled this country.

From the April 1992 deposal of President Mohammad Najibullah until 1996, when the Taliban dragged him out of a U.N. compound and castrated, shot and hanged him, the Northern Alliance's Islamic State of Afghanistan was less a government than a state of institutionalized chaos. The highways were trolled by rapists and warlords, and the cities became so unsafe that few Afghans dared venture out after dark.

During this period, Afghanistan secured its role as the world's leading supplier of heroin. The Taliban put an end to all that, but at a terrible price—the rule of law found its pinnacle at 3 o'clock Friday afternoons when criminals were taken to the soccer stadium east of Kabul and subjected to amputation, stoning and execution.

The bad old days, it seems, may be coming back. At this point, the sole expression of government authority here is a lone traffic policeman standing at the Pakistani-style rotary in the middle of the main intersection. By yesterday, even he had repaired to a disused ammunition dump nearby where he could be found fast asleep, a lit cigarette dangling from his lips. Half of the male population—the heavily armed half—is cruising the streets looking for people to rob. And the drug trade has made a remarkable overnight comeback; pure opium paste is selling briskly a few blocks off the main drag.

The American bombing campaign, which continues to take a toll on Kunduz and much of Takhar Province, has heightened the sense that there are no longer any rules.

I confronted one of the customers at the opium joint: "Isn't that illegal in Afghanistan?"

"Nothing is illegal in Afghanistan," he replied. "You can do whatever you want and no one cares."

"That's not always true," I suggested, recalling week-old history.

"The Taliban would have cared," he responded, grinding the paste into fine dust and sprinkling it into a cigarette. "But you Americans have gotten rid of them, and now we are free."

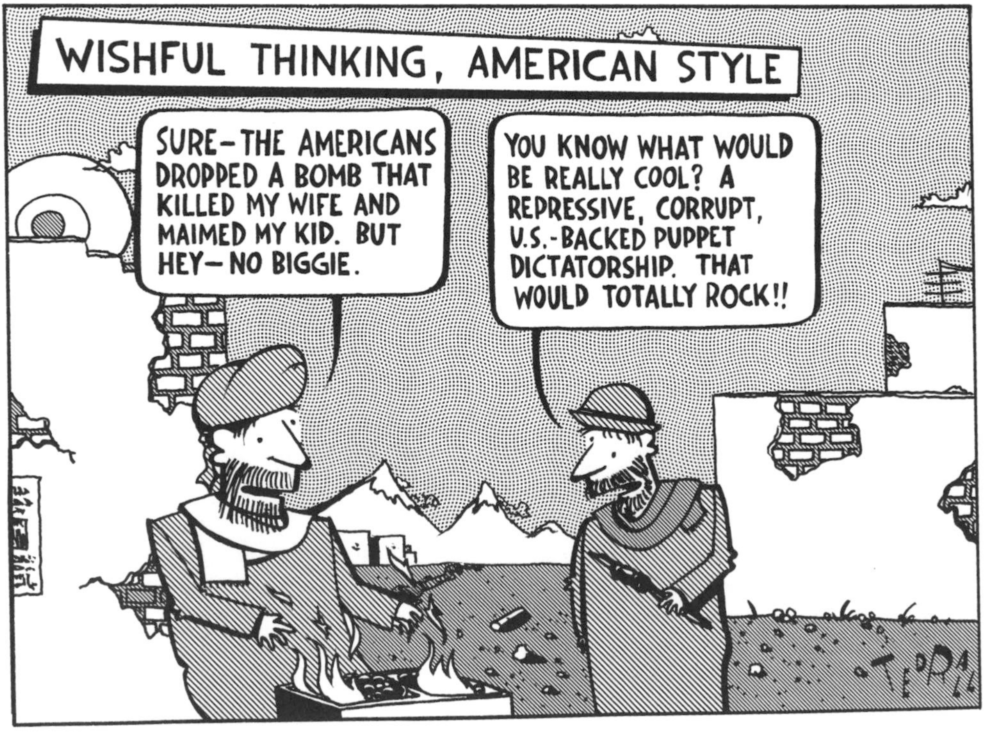
WISHFUL THINKING, AMERICAN STYLE
SURE—THE AMERICANS DROPPED A BOMB THAT KILLED MY WIFE AND MAIMED MY KID. BUT HEY—NO BIGGIE.
YOU KNOW WHAT WOULD BE REALLY COOL? A REPRESSIVE, CORRUPT, U.S.-BACKED PUPPET DICTATORSHIP. THAT WOULD TOTALLY ROCK!!
TED RALL

Rall writing a story in his Taloqan guest house. (Photo: Maryanne Patey.)

Certainly the Taliban's purist vision of Islam has taken a beating. Though people are faithfully fasting during Ramadan, nary a head turns in response to the mullahs' call to prayer. Alcoholic beverages have become the hottest consumer item in town.

"What? You didn't bring wine?" my guide and "fixer" asked me last night, as he geared up for a night of opium-induced haze.

"All the western journalists bring wine from Tajikistan," he scolded. Along with the collapse of legality and religiosity has come a wholesale plunge into the kind of societal cynicism that could mean real trouble if and when the new (and old) Northern Alliance gets its act together.

"In this country it's hard to tell the difference between life and death," the wine aficionado told me between bites of laghman noodles. "So we might as well live a little between all the dying."

33

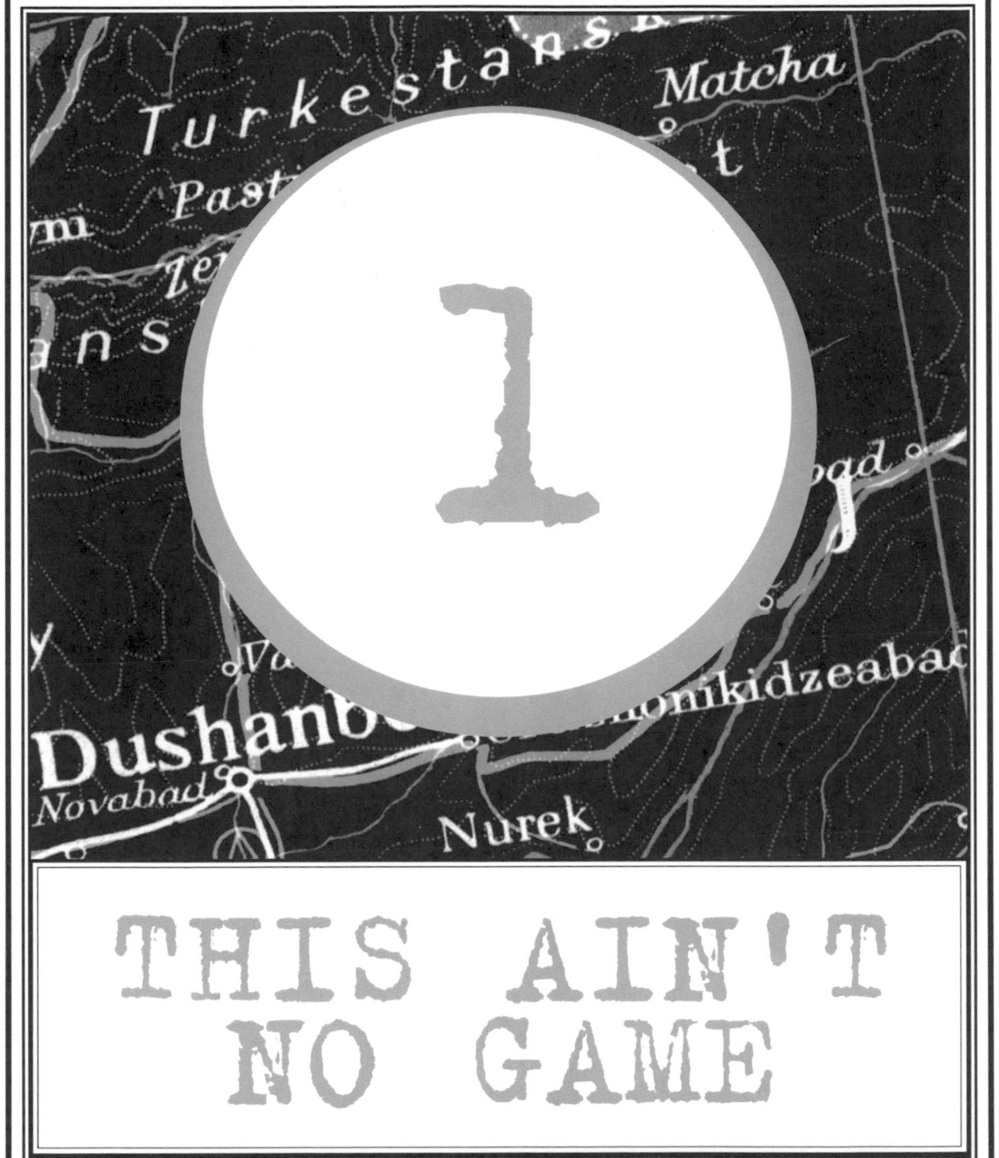
Matcha
Novabad
Nurek

1

THIS AIN'T NO GAME

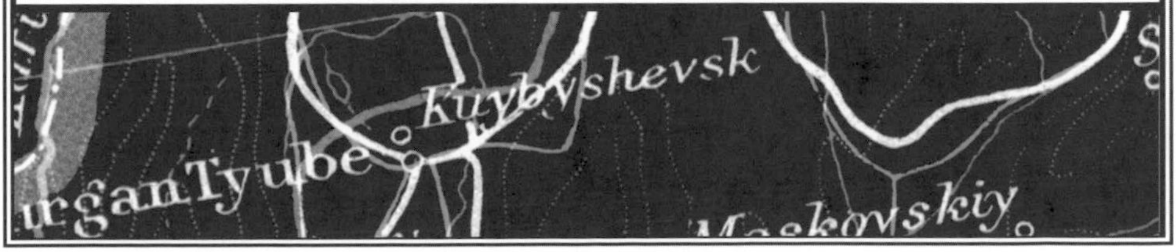
Kuybyshevsk

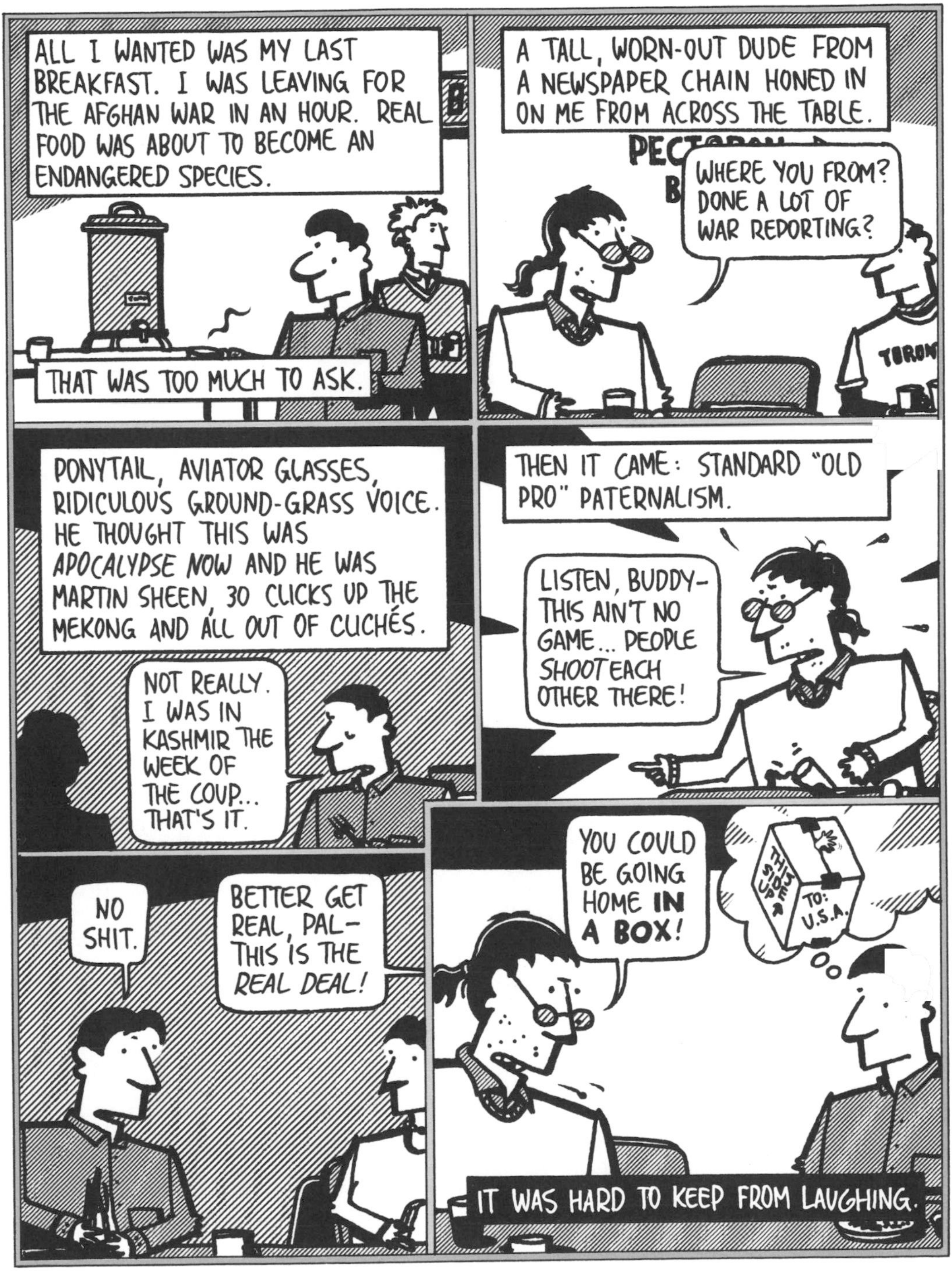
ALL I WANTED WAS MY LAST BREAKFAST. I WAS LEAVING FOR THE AFGHAN WAR IN AN HOUR. REAL FOOD WAS ABOUT TO BECOME AN ENDANGERED SPECIES.
THAT WAS TOO MUCH TO ASK.
A TALL, WORN-OUT DUDE FROM A NEWSPAPER CHAIN HONED IN ON ME FROM ACROSS THE TABLE.
WHERE YOU FROM? DONE A LOT OF WAR REPORTING?
PONYTAIL, AVIATOR GLASSES, RIDICULOUS GROUND-GRASS VOICE. HE THOUGHT THIS WAS *APOCALYPSE NOW* AND HE WAS MARTIN SHEEN, 30 CLICKS UP THE MEKONG AND ALL OUT OF CLICHÉS.
NOT REALLY. I WAS IN KASHMIR THE WEEK OF THE COUP... THAT'S IT.
THEN IT CAME: STANDARD "OLD PRO" PATERNALISM.
LISTEN, BUDDY- THIS AIN'T NO GAME... PEOPLE *SHOOT* EACH OTHER THERE!
NO SHIT.
BETTER GET REAL, PAL- THIS IS THE *REAL DEAL!*
YOU COULD BE GOING HOME **IN A BOX!**
THIS SIDE UP
TO: U.S.A.
IT WAS HARD TO KEEP FROM LAUGHING.

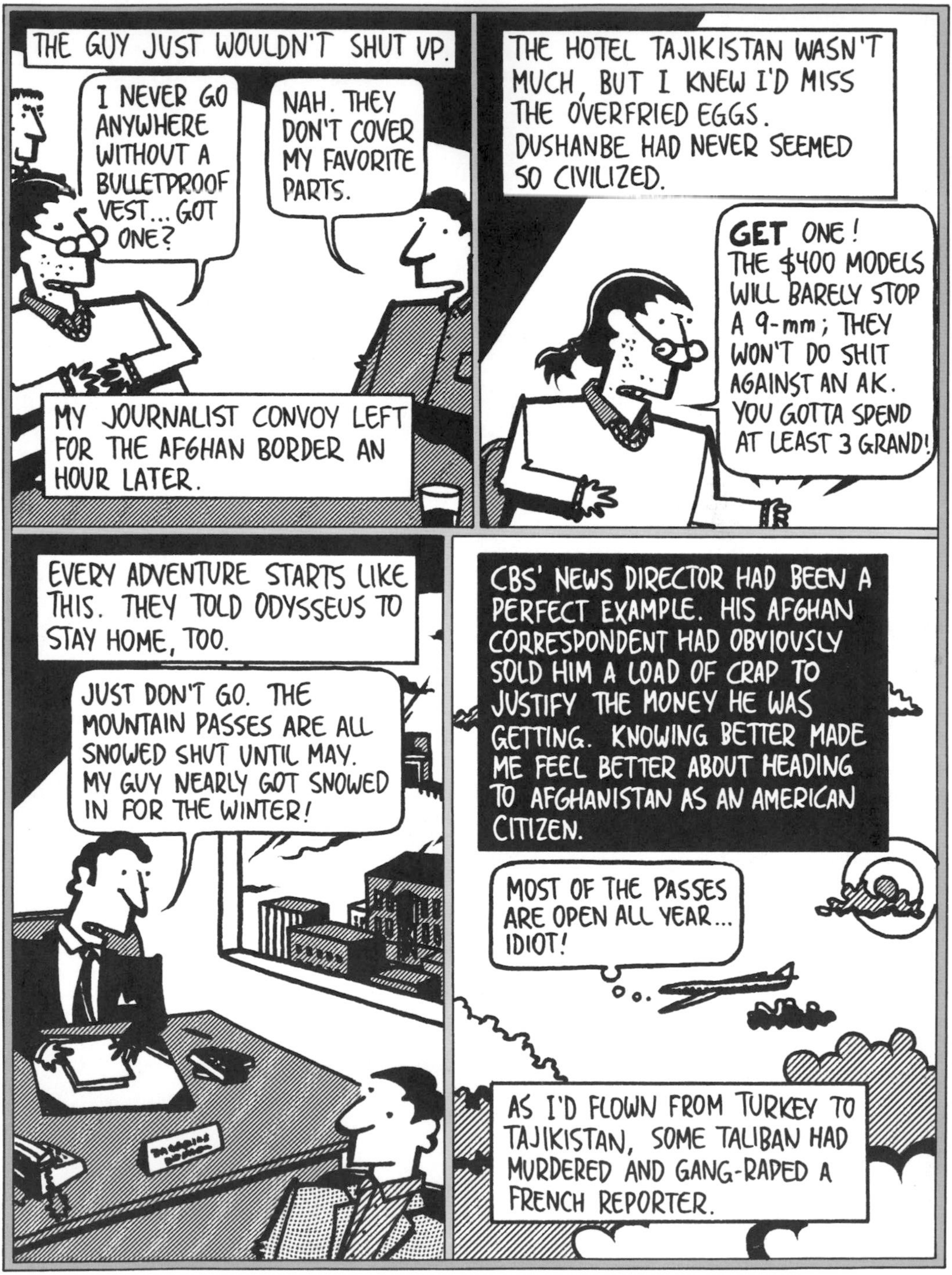
THE GUY JUST WOULDN'T SHUT UP.
I NEVER GO ANYWHERE WITHOUT A BULLETPROOF VEST... GOT ONE?
NAH. THEY DON'T COVER MY FAVORITE PARTS.
MY JOURNALIST CONVOY LEFT FOR THE AFGHAN BORDER AN HOUR LATER.
THE HOTEL TAJIKISTAN WASN'T MUCH, BUT I KNEW I'D MISS THE OVERFRIED EGGS. DUSHANBE HAD NEVER SEEMED SO CIVILIZED.
GET ONE! THE $400 MODELS WILL BARELY STOP A 9-mm; THEY WON'T DO SHIT AGAINST AN AK. YOU GOTTA SPEND AT LEAST 3 GRAND!
EVERY ADVENTURE STARTS LIKE THIS. THEY TOLD ODYSSEUS TO STAY HOME, TOO.
JUST DON'T GO. THE MOUNTAIN PASSES ARE ALL SNOWED SHUT UNTIL MAY. MY GUY NEARLY GOT SNOWED IN FOR THE WINTER!
CBS' NEWS DIRECTOR HAD BEEN A PERFECT EXAMPLE. HIS AFGHAN CORRESPONDENT HAD OBVIOUSLY SOLD HIM A LOAD OF CRAP TO JUSTIFY THE MONEY HE WAS GETTING. KNOWING BETTER MADE ME FEEL BETTER ABOUT HEADING TO AFGHANISTAN AS AN AMERICAN CITIZEN.
MOST OF THE PASSES ARE OPEN ALL YEAR... IDIOT!
AS I'D FLOWN FROM TURKEY TO TAJIKISTAN, SOME TALIBAN HAD MURDERED AND GANG-RAPED A FRENCH REPORTER.

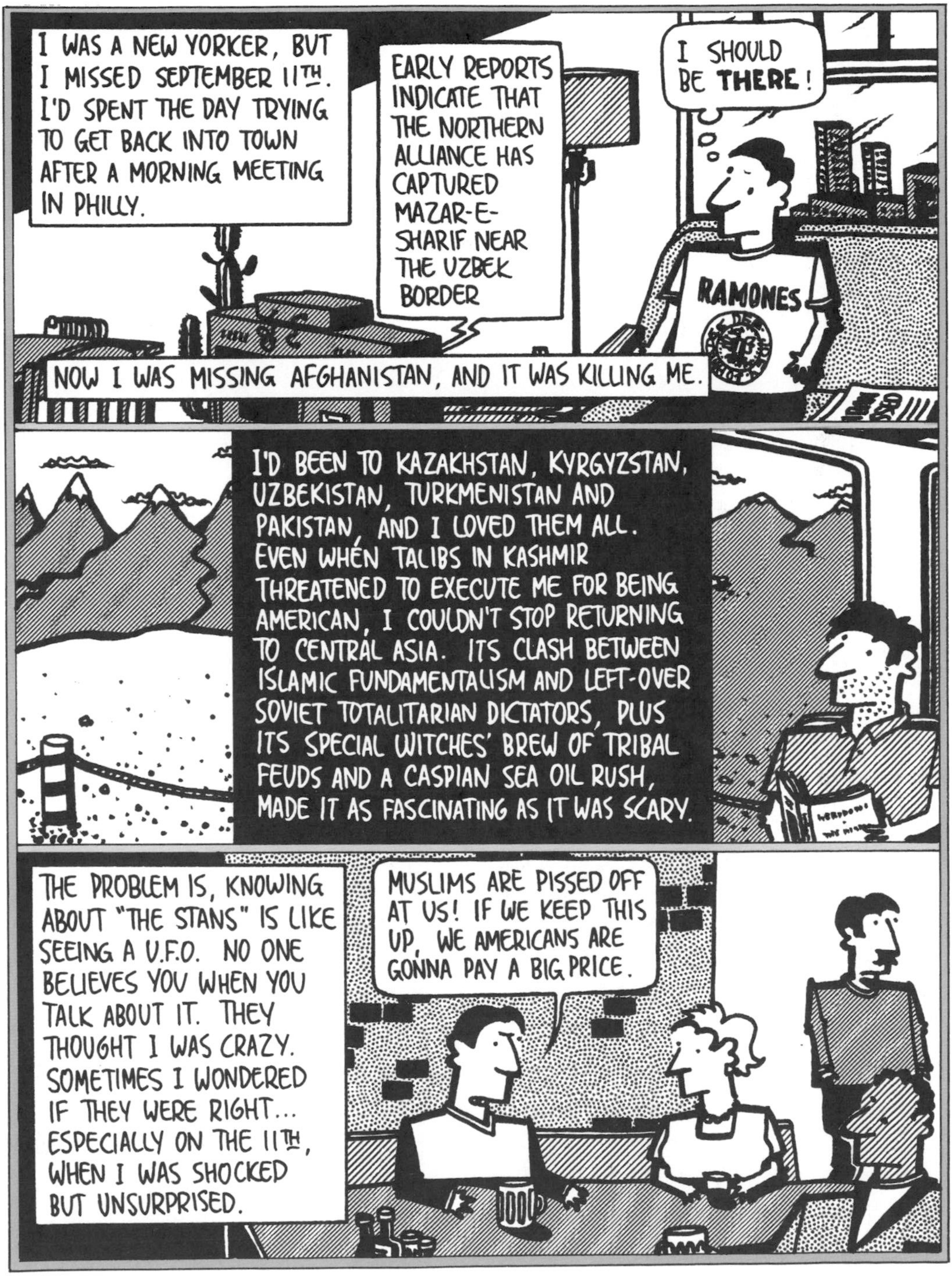
I WAS A NEW YORKER, BUT I MISSED SEPTEMBER 11TH. I'D SPENT THE DAY TRYING TO GET BACK INTO TOWN AFTER A MORNING MEETING IN PHILLY.
EARLY REPORTS INDICATE THAT THE NORTHERN ALLIANCE HAS CAPTURED MAZAR-E-SHARIF NEAR THE UZBEK BORDER
I SHOULD BE **THERE**!
RAMONES
NOW I WAS MISSING AFGHANISTAN, AND IT WAS KILLING ME.
I'D BEEN TO KAZAKHSTAN, KYRGYZSTAN, UZBEKISTAN, TURKMENISTAN AND PAKISTAN, AND I LOVED THEM ALL. EVEN WHEN TALIBS IN KASHMIR THREATENED TO EXECUTE ME FOR BEING AMERICAN, I COULDN'T STOP RETURNING TO CENTRAL ASIA. ITS CLASH BETWEEN ISLAMIC FUNDAMENTALISM AND LEFT-OVER SOVIET TOTALITARIAN DICTATORS, PLUS ITS SPECIAL WITCHES' BREW OF TRIBAL FEUDS AND A CASPIAN SEA OIL RUSH, MADE IT AS FASCINATING AS IT WAS SCARY.
THE PROBLEM IS, KNOWING ABOUT "THE STANS" IS LIKE SEEING A U.F.O. NO ONE BELIEVES YOU WHEN YOU TALK ABOUT IT. THEY THOUGHT I WAS CRAZY. SOMETIMES I WONDERED IF THEY WERE RIGHT... ESPECIALLY ON THE 11TH, WHEN I WAS SHOCKED BUT UNSURPRISED.
MUSLIMS ARE PISSED OFF AT US! IF WE KEEP THIS UP, WE AMERICANS ARE GONNA PAY A BIG PRICE.

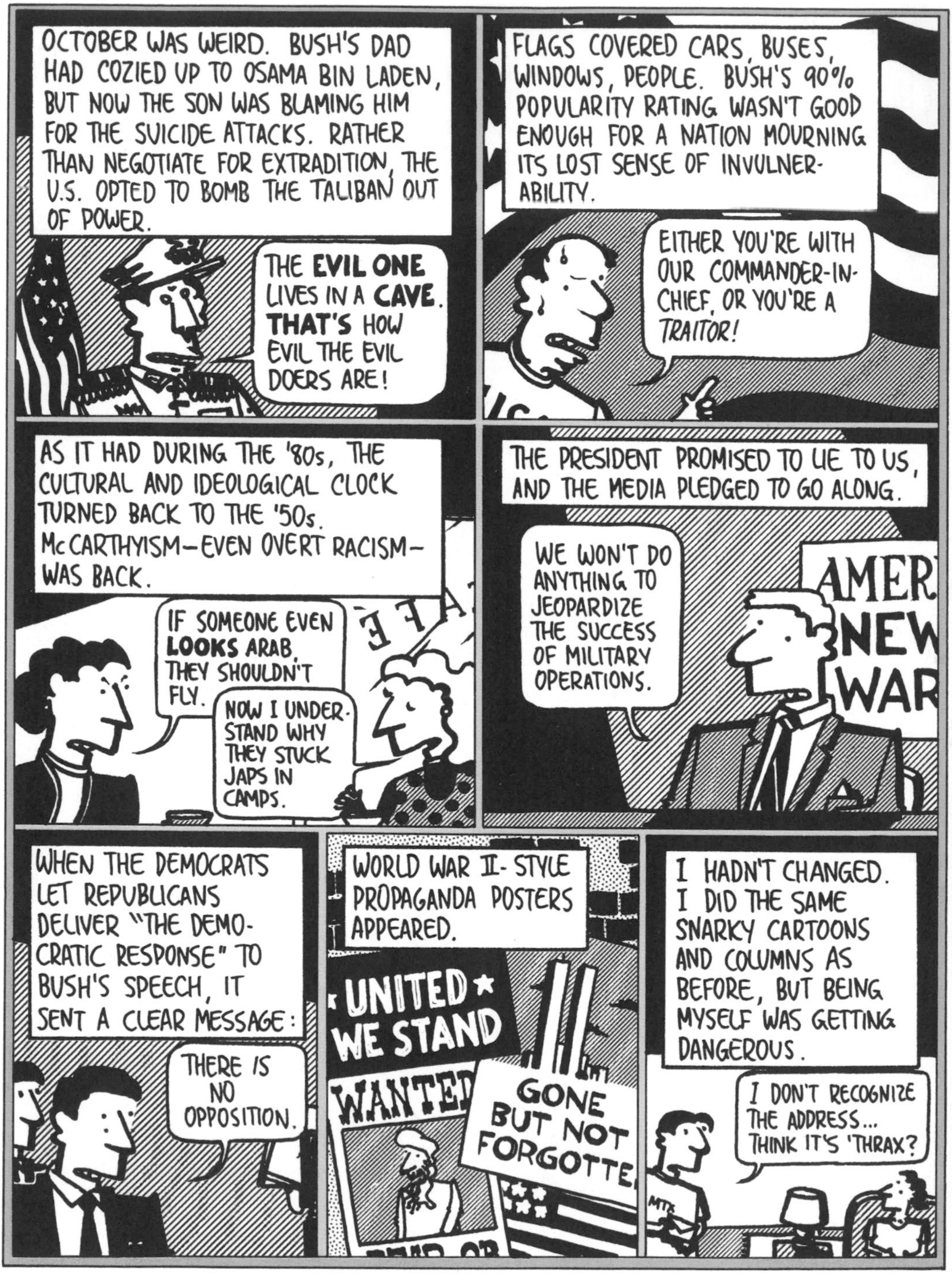
OCTOBER WAS WEIRD. BUSH'S DAD HAD COZIED UP TO OSAMA BIN LADEN, BUT NOW THE SON WAS BLAMING HIM FOR THE SUICIDE ATTACKS. RATHER THAN NEGOTIATE FOR EXTRADITION, THE U.S. OPTED TO BOMB THE TALIBAN OUT OF POWER.
THE EVIL ONE LIVES IN A CAVE. THAT'S HOW EVIL THE EVIL DOERS ARE!
FLAGS COVERED CARS, BUSES, WINDOWS, PEOPLE. BUSH'S 90% POPULARITY RATING WASN'T GOOD ENOUGH FOR A NATION MOURNING ITS LOST SENSE OF INVULNER-ABILITY.
EITHER YOU'RE WITH OUR COMMANDER-IN-CHIEF, OR YOU'RE A TRAITOR!
AS IT HAD DURING THE '80s, THE CULTURAL AND IDEOLOGICAL CLOCK TURNED BACK TO THE '50s. McCARTHYISM—EVEN OVERT RACISM—WAS BACK.
IF SOMEONE EVEN LOOKS ARAB, THEY SHOULDN'T FLY.
NOW I UNDER-STAND WHY THEY STUCK JAPS IN CAMPS.
THE PRESIDENT PROMISED TO LIE TO US, AND THE MEDIA PLEDGED TO GO ALONG.
WE WON'T DO ANYTHING TO JEOPARDIZE THE SUCCESS OF MILITARY OPERATIONS.
AMER NEW WAR
WHEN THE DEMOCRATS LET REPUBLICANS DELIVER "THE DEMO-CRATIC RESPONSE" TO BUSH'S SPEECH, IT SENT A CLEAR MESSAGE:
THERE IS NO OPPOSITION.
WORLD WAR II-STYLE PROPAGANDA POSTERS APPEARED.
UNITED WE STAND
WANTED
GONE BUT NOT FORGOTTE
I HADN'T CHANGED. I DID THE SAME SNARKY CARTOONS AND COLUMNS AS BEFORE, BUT BEING MYSELF WAS GETTING DANGEROUS.
I DON'T RECOGNIZE THE ADDRESS... THINK IT'S 'THRAX?

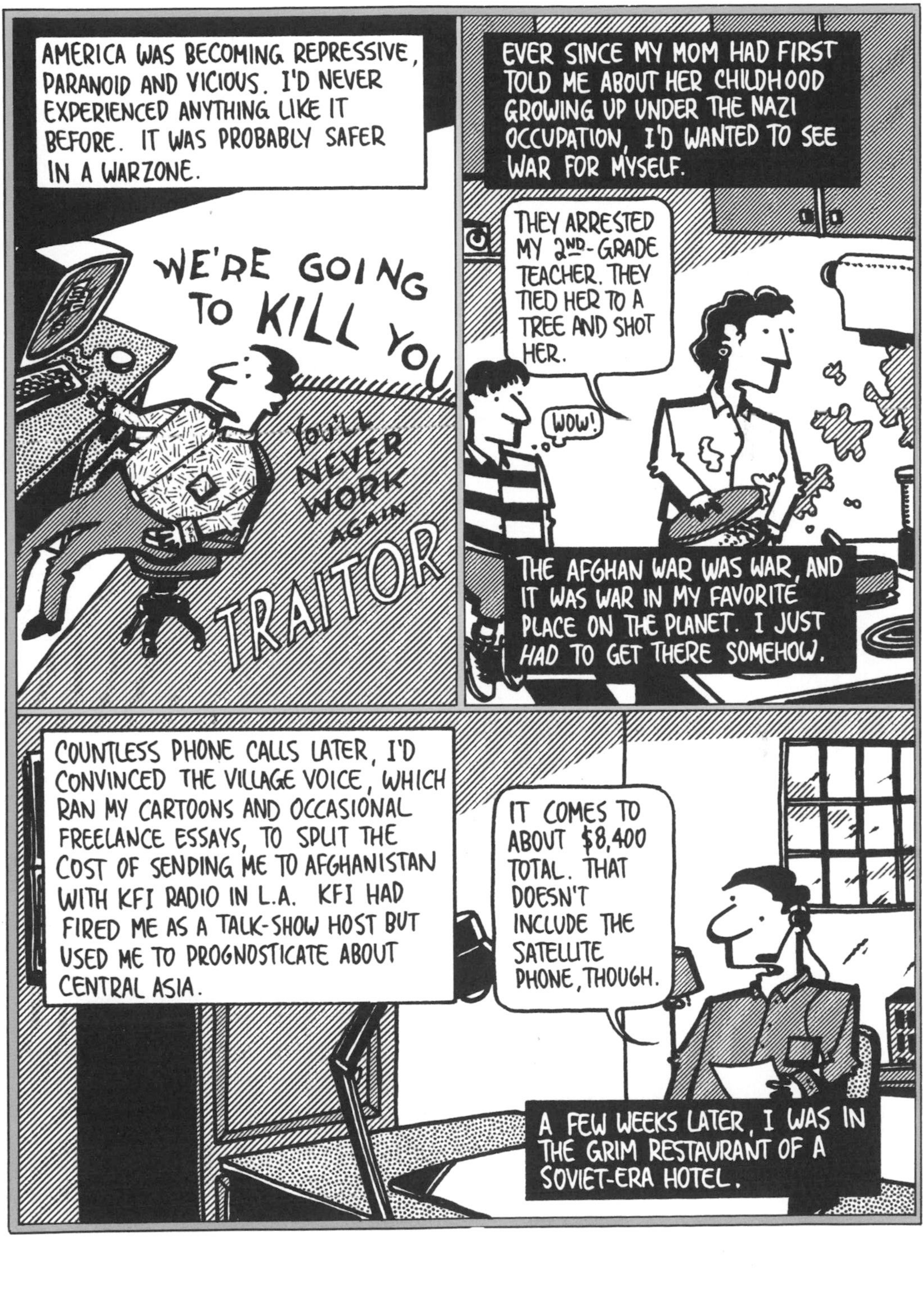
AMERICA WAS BECOMING REPRESSIVE, PARANOID AND VICIOUS. I'D NEVER EXPERIENCED ANYTHING LIKE IT BEFORE. IT WAS PROBABLY SAFER IN A WARZONE.
WE'RE GOING TO KILL YOU
YOU'LL NEVER WORK AGAIN
TRAITOR
EVER SINCE MY MOM HAD FIRST TOLD ME ABOUT HER CHILDHOOD GROWING UP UNDER THE NAZI OCCUPATION, I'D WANTED TO SEE WAR FOR MYSELF.
THEY ARRESTED MY 2ND-GRADE TEACHER. THEY TIED HER TO A TREE AND SHOT HER.
WOW!
THE AFGHAN WAR WAS WAR, AND IT WAS WAR IN MY FAVORITE PLACE ON THE PLANET. I JUST HAD TO GET THERE SOMEHOW.
COUNTLESS PHONE CALLS LATER, I'D CONVINCED THE VILLAGE VOICE, WHICH RAN MY CARTOONS AND OCCASIONAL FREELANCE ESSAYS, TO SPLIT THE COST OF SENDING ME TO AFGHANISTAN WITH KFI RADIO IN L.A. KFI HAD FIRED ME AS A TALK-SHOW HOST BUT USED ME TO PROGNOSTICATE ABOUT CENTRAL ASIA.
IT COMES TO ABOUT $8,400 TOTAL. THAT DOESN'T INCLUDE THE SATELLITE PHONE, THOUGH.
A FEW WEEKS LATER, I WAS IN THE GRIM RESTAURANT OF A SOVIET-ERA HOTEL.

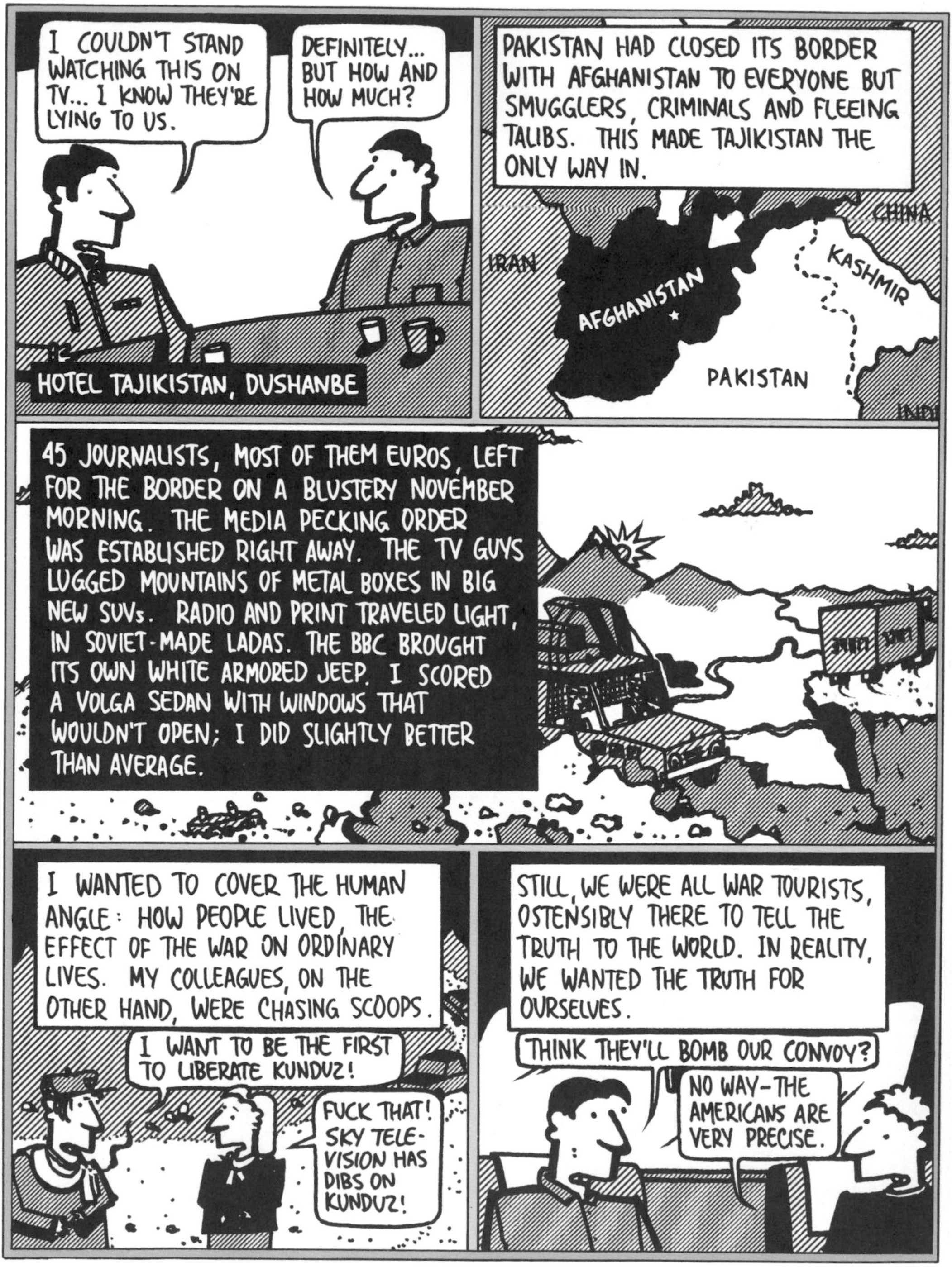
I COULDN'T STAND WATCHING THIS ON TV... I KNOW THEY'RE LYING TO US.
DEFINITELY... BUT HOW AND HOW MUCH?
HOTEL TAJIKISTAN, DUSHANBE
PAKISTAN HAD CLOSED ITS BORDER WITH AFGHANISTAN TO EVERYONE BUT SMUGGLERS, CRIMINALS AND FLEEING TALIBS. THIS MADE TAJIKISTAN THE ONLY WAY IN.
CHINA
IRAN
KASHMIR
AFGHANISTAN
PAKISTAN
45 JOURNALISTS, MOST OF THEM EUROS, LEFT FOR THE BORDER ON A BLUSTERY NOVEMBER MORNING. THE MEDIA PECKING ORDER WAS ESTABLISHED RIGHT AWAY. THE TV GUYS LUGGED MOUNTAINS OF METAL BOXES IN BIG NEW SUVs. RADIO AND PRINT TRAVELED LIGHT, IN SOVIET-MADE LADAS. THE BBC BROUGHT ITS OWN WHITE ARMORED JEEP. I SCORED A VOLGA SEDAN WITH WINDOWS THAT WOULDN'T OPEN; I DID SLIGHTLY BETTER THAN AVERAGE.
I WANTED TO COVER THE HUMAN ANGLE: HOW PEOPLE LIVED, THE EFFECT OF THE WAR ON ORDINARY LIVES. MY COLLEAGUES, ON THE OTHER HAND, WERE CHASING SCOOPS.
I WANT TO BE THE FIRST TO LIBERATE KUNDUZ!
FUCK THAT! SKY TELEVISION HAS DIBS ON KUNDUZ!
STILL, WE WERE ALL WAR TOURISTS, OSTENSIBLY THERE TO TELL THE TRUTH TO THE WORLD. IN REALITY, WE WANTED THE TRUTH FOR OURSELVES.
THINK THEY'LL BOMB OUR CONVOY?
NO WAY—THE AMERICANS ARE VERY PRECISE.

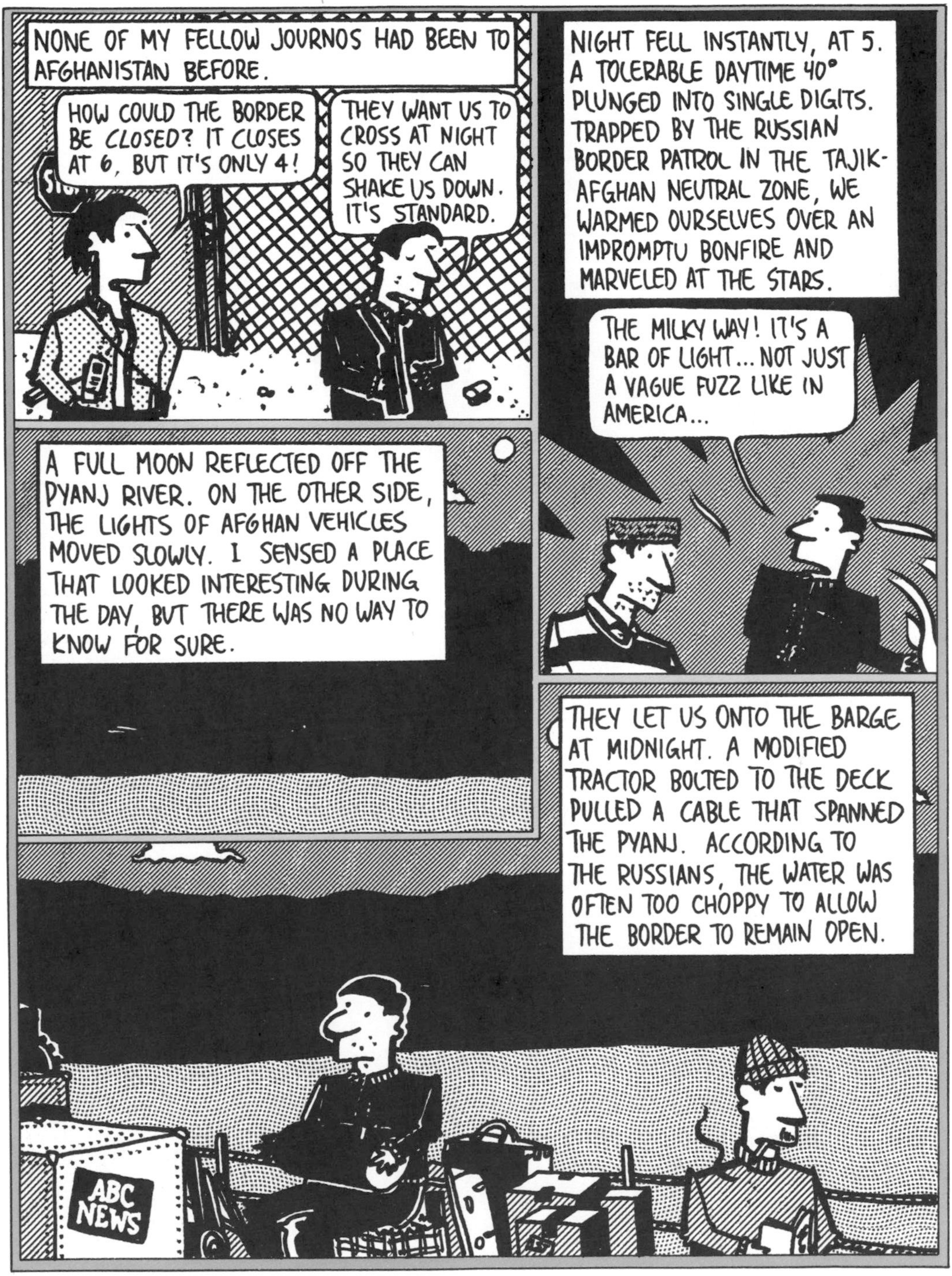
NONE OF MY FELLOW JOURNOS HAD BEEN TO AFGHANISTAN BEFORE.
HOW COULD THE BORDER BE CLOSED? IT CLOSES AT 6, BUT IT'S ONLY 4!
THEY WANT US TO CROSS AT NIGHT SO THEY CAN SHAKE US DOWN. IT'S STANDARD.
NIGHT FELL INSTANTLY, AT 5. A TOLERABLE DAYTIME 40° PLUNGED INTO SINGLE DIGITS. TRAPPED BY THE RUSSIAN BORDER PATROL IN THE TAJIK-AFGHAN NEUTRAL ZONE, WE WARMED OURSELVES OVER AN IMPROMPTU BONFIRE AND MARVELED AT THE STARS.
THE MILKY WAY! IT'S A BAR OF LIGHT... NOT JUST A VAGUE FUZZ LIKE IN AMERICA...
A FULL MOON REFLECTED OFF THE PYANJ RIVER. ON THE OTHER SIDE, THE LIGHTS OF AFGHAN VEHICLES MOVED SLOWLY. I SENSED A PLACE THAT LOOKED INTERESTING DURING THE DAY, BUT THERE WAS NO WAY TO KNOW FOR SURE.
THEY LET US ONTO THE BARGE AT MIDNIGHT. A MODIFIED TRACTOR BOLTED TO THE DECK PULLED A CABLE THAT SPANNED THE PYANJ. ACCORDING TO THE RUSSIANS, THE WATER WAS OFTEN TOO CHOPPY TO ALLOW THE BORDER TO REMAIN OPEN.
ABC NEWS

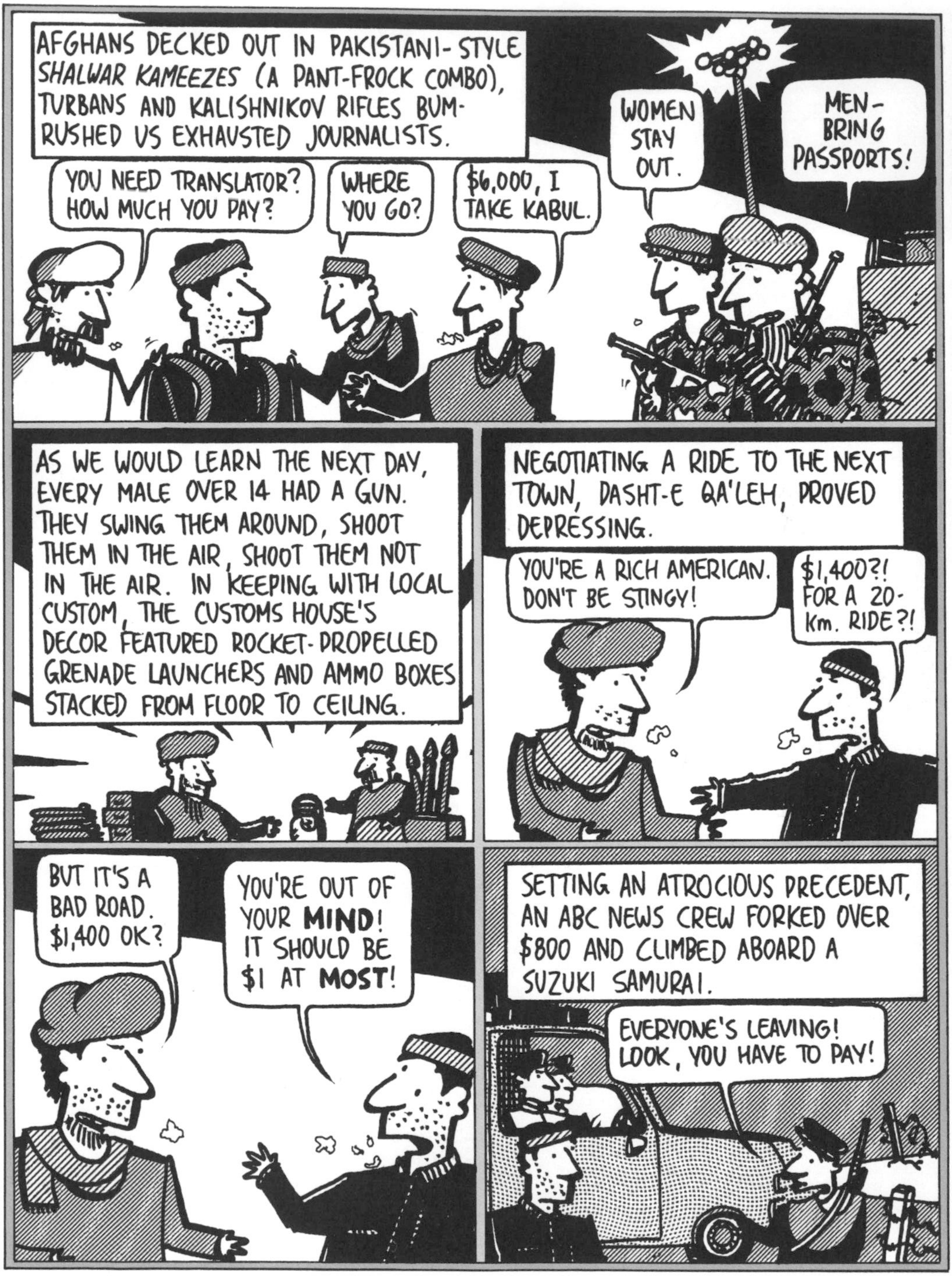
AFGHANS DECKED OUT IN PAKISTANI-STYLE SHALWAR KAMEEZES (A PANT-FROCK COMBO), TURBANS AND KALISHNIKOV RIFLES BUM-RUSHED US EXHAUSTED JOURNALISTS.
YOU NEED TRANSLATOR? HOW MUCH YOU PAY?
WHERE YOU GO?
$6,000, I TAKE KABUL.
WOMEN STAY OUT.
MEN- BRING PASSPORTS!
AS WE WOULD LEARN THE NEXT DAY, EVERY MALE OVER 14 HAD A GUN. THEY SWING THEM AROUND, SHOOT THEM IN THE AIR, SHOOT THEM NOT IN THE AIR. IN KEEPING WITH LOCAL CUSTOM, THE CUSTOMS HOUSE'S DECOR FEATURED ROCKET-PROPELLED GRENADE LAUNCHERS AND AMMO BOXES STACKED FROM FLOOR TO CEILING.
NEGOTIATING A RIDE TO THE NEXT TOWN, DASHT-E QA'LEH, PROVED DEPRESSING.
YOU'RE A RICH AMERICAN. DON'T BE STINGY!
$1,400?! FOR A 20-Km. RIDE?!
BUT IT'S A BAD ROAD. $1,400 OK?
YOU'RE OUT OF YOUR MIND! IT SHOULD BE $1 AT MOST!
SETTING AN ATROCIOUS PRECEDENT, AN ABC NEWS CREW FORKED OVER $800 AND CLIMBED ABOARD A SUZUKI SAMURAI.
EVERYONE'S LEAVING! LOOK, YOU HAVE TO PAY!

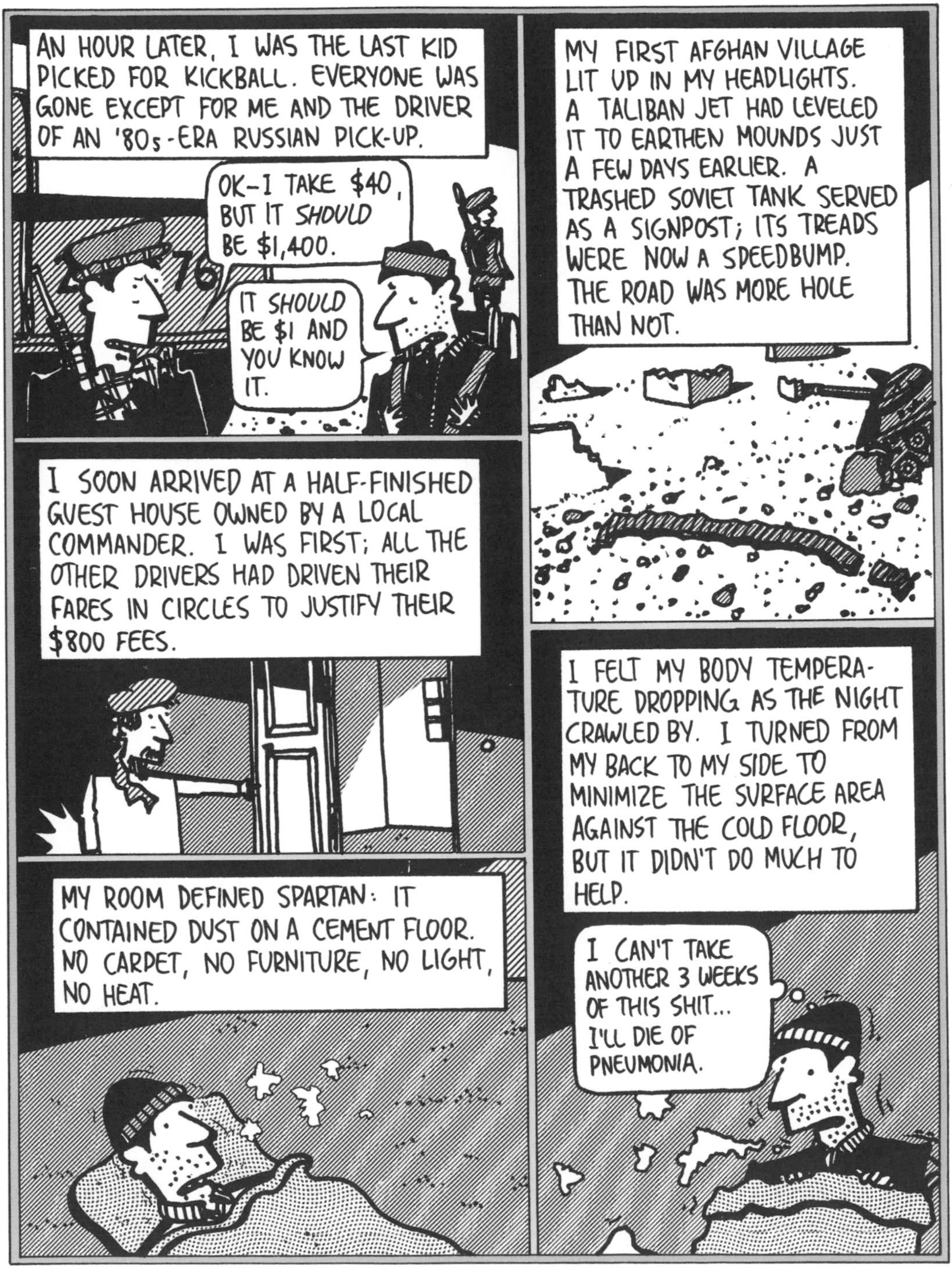
AN HOUR LATER, I WAS THE LAST KID PICKED FOR KICKBALL. EVERYONE WAS GONE EXCEPT FOR ME AND THE DRIVER OF AN '80s-ERA RUSSIAN PICK-UP.
OK–I TAKE $40, BUT IT SHOULD BE $1,400.
IT SHOULD BE $1 AND YOU KNOW IT.
MY FIRST AFGHAN VILLAGE LIT UP IN MY HEADLIGHTS. A TALIBAN JET HAD LEVELED IT TO EARTHEN MOUNDS JUST A FEW DAYS EARLIER. A TRASHED SOVIET TANK SERVED AS A SIGNPOST; ITS TREADS WERE NOW A SPEEDBUMP. THE ROAD WAS MORE HOLE THAN NOT.
I SOON ARRIVED AT A HALF-FINISHED GUEST HOUSE OWNED BY A LOCAL COMMANDER. I WAS FIRST; ALL THE OTHER DRIVERS HAD DRIVEN THEIR FARES IN CIRCLES TO JUSTIFY THEIR $800 FEES.
MY ROOM DEFINED SPARTAN: IT CONTAINED DUST ON A CEMENT FLOOR. NO CARPET, NO FURNITURE, NO LIGHT, NO HEAT.
I FELT MY BODY TEMPERATURE DROPPING AS THE NIGHT CRAWLED BY. I TURNED FROM MY BACK TO MY SIDE TO MINIMIZE THE SURFACE AREA AGAINST THE COLD FLOOR, BUT IT DIDN'T DO MUCH TO HELP.
I CAN'T TAKE ANOTHER 3 WEEKS OF THIS SHIT... I'LL DIE OF PNEUMONIA.

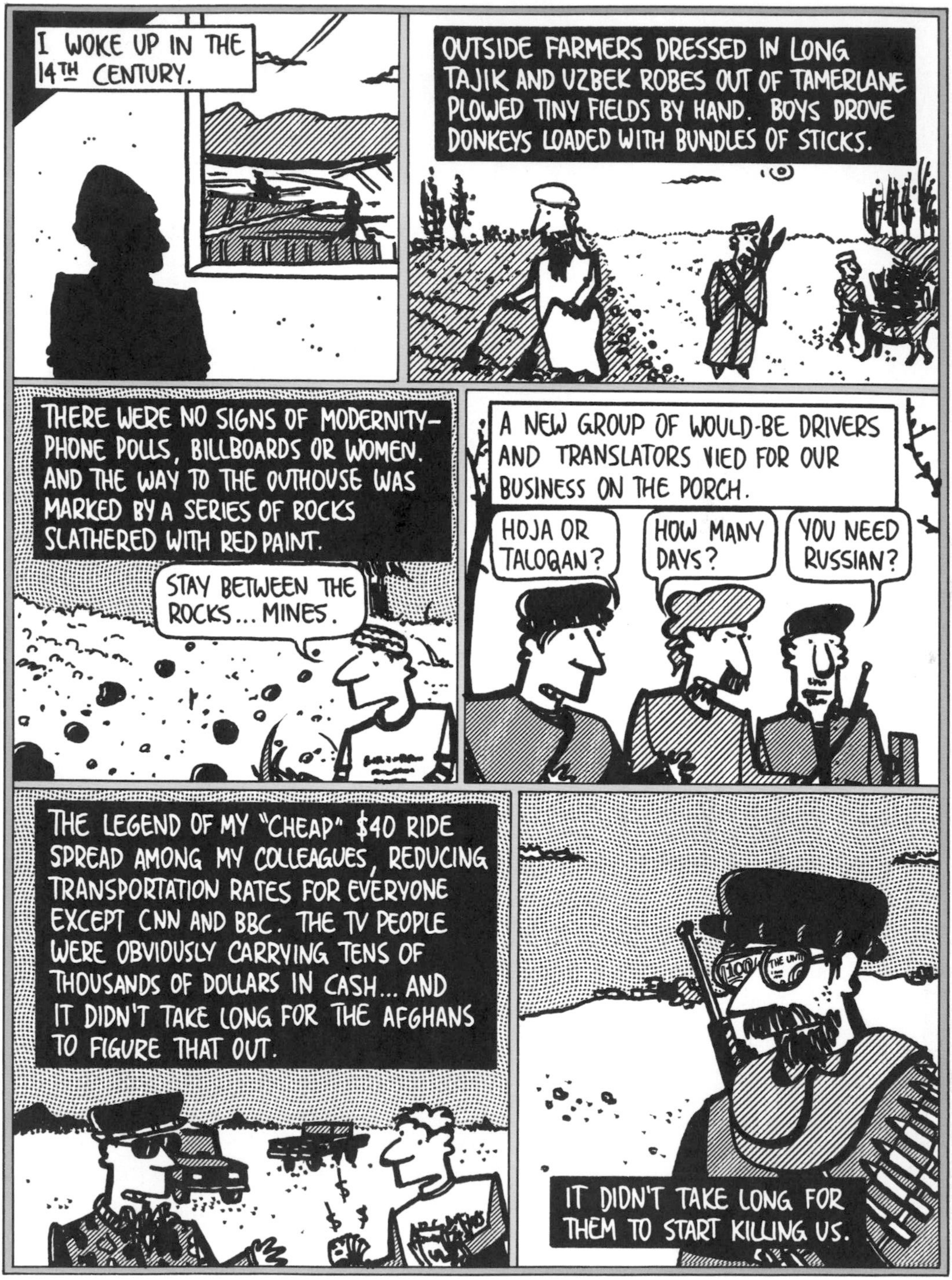
I WOKE UP IN THE 14TH CENTURY.
OUTSIDE FARMERS DRESSED IN LONG TAJIK AND UZBEK ROBES OUT OF TAMERLANE PLOWED TINY FIELDS BY HAND. BOYS DROVE DONKEYS LOADED WITH BUNDLES OF STICKS.
THERE WERE NO SIGNS OF MODERNITY- PHONE POLLS, BILLBOARDS OR WOMEN. AND THE WAY TO THE OUTHOUSE WAS MARKED BY A SERIES OF ROCKS SLATHERED WITH RED PAINT.
STAY BETWEEN THE ROCKS... MINES.
A NEW GROUP OF WOULD-BE DRIVERS AND TRANSLATORS VIED FOR OUR BUSINESS ON THE PORCH.
HOJA OR TALOQAN?
HOW MANY DAYS?
YOU NEED RUSSIAN?
THE LEGEND OF MY "CHEAP" $40 RIDE SPREAD AMONG MY COLLEAGUES, REDUCING TRANSPORTATION RATES FOR EVERYONE EXCEPT CNN AND BBC. THE TV PEOPLE WERE OBVIOUSLY CARRYING TENS OF THOUSANDS OF DOLLARS IN CASH... AND IT DIDN'T TAKE LONG FOR THE AFGHANS TO FIGURE THAT OUT.
IT DIDN'T TAKE LONG FOR THEM TO START KILLING US.

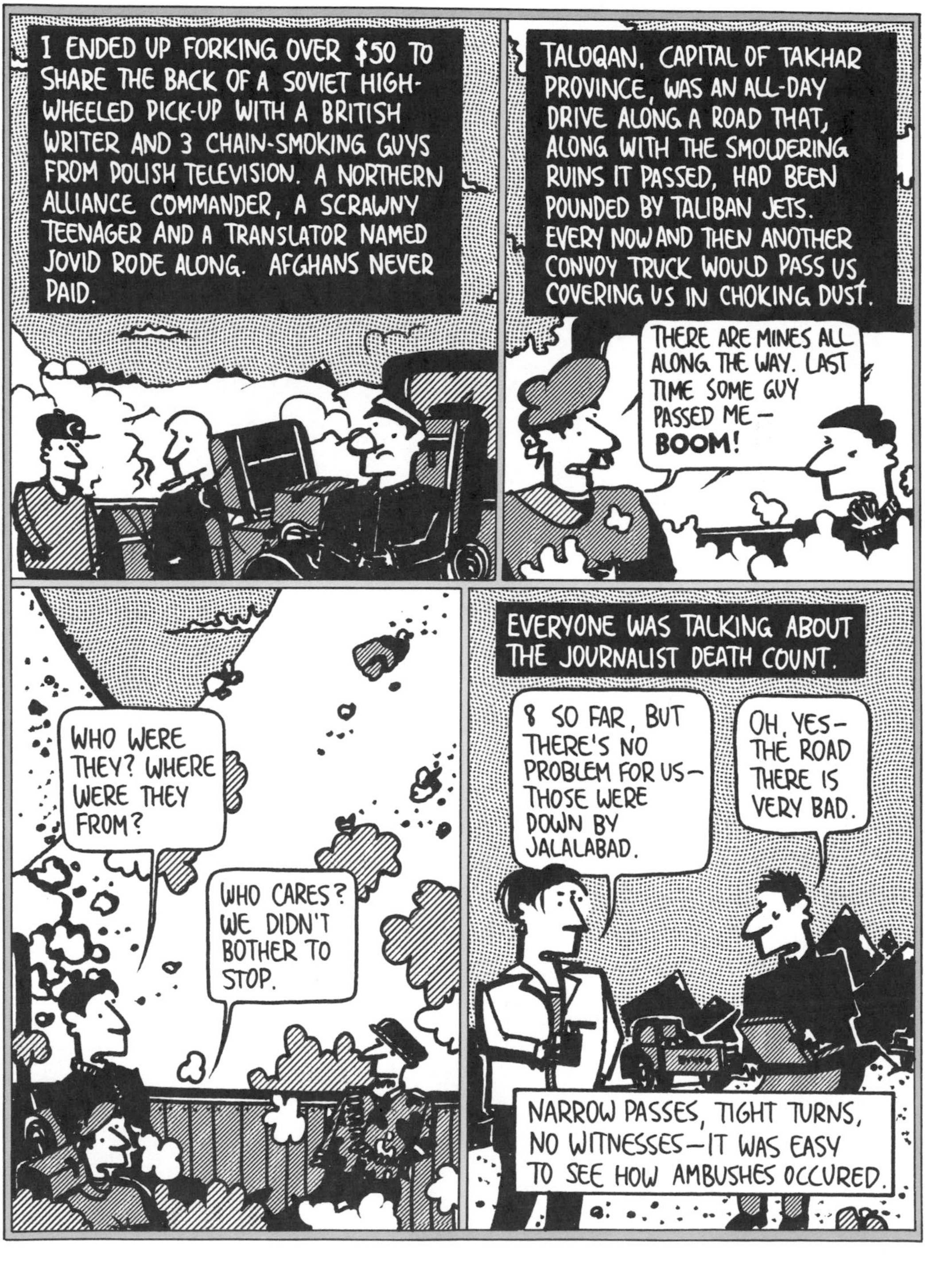
I ENDED UP FORKING OVER $50 TO SHARE THE BACK OF A SOVIET HIGH-WHEELED PICK-UP WITH A BRITISH WRITER AND 3 CHAIN-SMOKING GUYS FROM POLISH TELEVISION. A NORTHERN ALLIANCE COMMANDER, A SCRAWNY TEENAGER AND A TRANSLATOR NAMED JOVID RODE ALONG. AFGHANS NEVER PAID.
TALOQAN, CAPITAL OF TAKHAR PROVINCE, WAS AN ALL-DAY DRIVE ALONG A ROAD THAT, ALONG WITH THE SMOLDERING RUINS IT PASSED, HAD BEEN POUNDED BY TALIBAN JETS. EVERY NOW AND THEN ANOTHER CONVOY TRUCK WOULD PASS US COVERING US IN CHOKING DUST.
THERE ARE MINES ALL ALONG THE WAY. LAST TIME SOME GUY PASSED ME— BOOM!
WHO WERE THEY? WHERE WERE THEY FROM?
WHO CARES? WE DIDN'T BOTHER TO STOP.
EVERYONE WAS TALKING ABOUT THE JOURNALIST DEATH COUNT.
8 SO FAR, BUT THERE'S NO PROBLEM FOR US— THOSE WERE DOWN BY JALALABAD.
OH, YES— THE ROAD THERE IS VERY BAD.
NARROW PASSES, TIGHT TURNS, NO WITNESSES—IT WAS EASY TO SEE HOW AMBUSHES OCCURED.

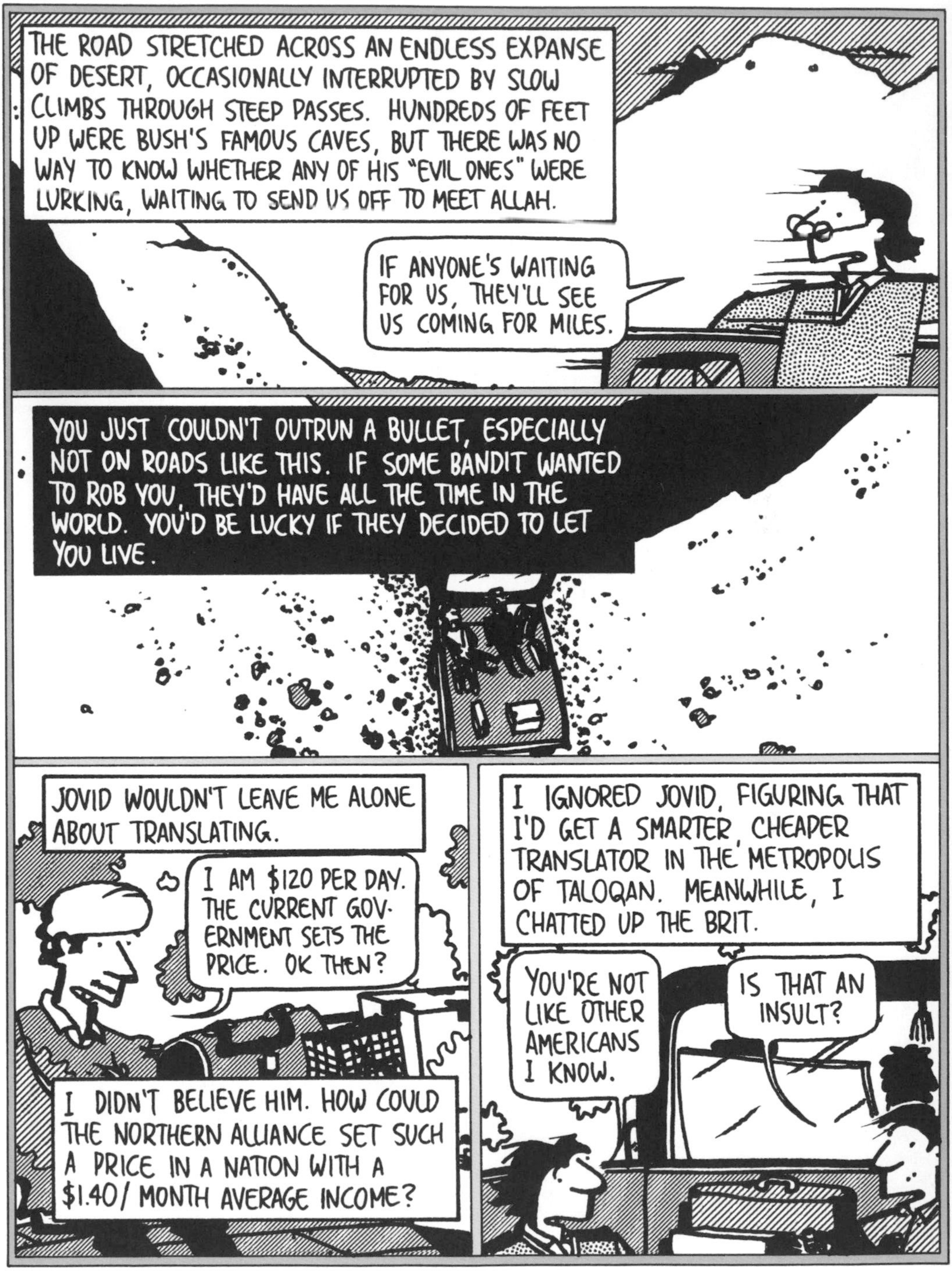
THE ROAD STRETCHED ACROSS AN ENDLESS EXPANSE OF DESERT, OCCASIONALLY INTERRUPTED BY SLOW CLIMBS THROUGH STEEP PASSES. HUNDREDS OF FEET UP WERE BUSH'S FAMOUS CAVES, BUT THERE WAS NO WAY TO KNOW WHETHER ANY OF HIS "EVIL ONES" WERE LURKING, WAITING TO SEND US OFF TO MEET ALLAH.
IF ANYONE'S WAITING FOR US, THEY'LL SEE US COMING FOR MILES.
YOU JUST COULDN'T OUTRUN A BULLET, ESPECIALLY NOT ON ROADS LIKE THIS. IF SOME BANDIT WANTED TO ROB YOU, THEY'D HAVE ALL THE TIME IN THE WORLD. YOU'D BE LUCKY IF THEY DECIDED TO LET YOU LIVE.
JOVID WOULDN'T LEAVE ME ALONE ABOUT TRANSLATING.
I AM $120 PER DAY. THE CURRENT GOV-ERNMENT SETS THE PRICE. OK THEN?
I DIDN'T BELIEVE HIM. HOW COULD THE NORTHERN ALLIANCE SET SUCH A PRICE IN A NATION WITH A $1.40/ MONTH AVERAGE INCOME?
I IGNORED JOVID, FIGURING THAT I'D GET A SMARTER, CHEAPER TRANSLATOR IN THE METROPOLIS OF TALOQAN. MEANWHILE, I CHATTED UP THE BRIT.
YOU'RE NOT LIKE OTHER AMERICANS I KNOW.
IS THAT AN INSULT?

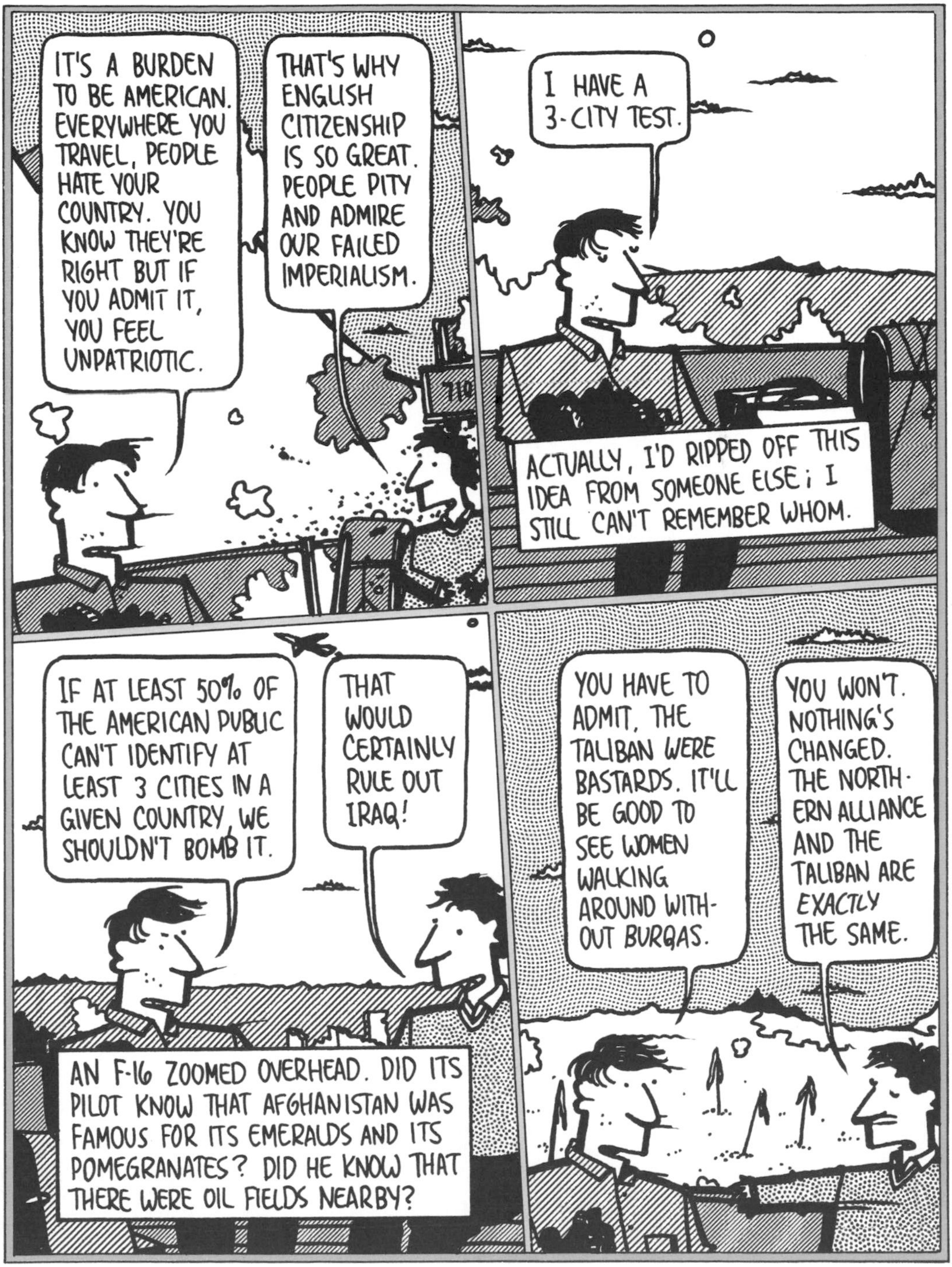
IT'S A BURDEN TO BE AMERICAN. EVERYWHERE YOU TRAVEL, PEOPLE HATE YOUR COUNTRY. YOU KNOW THEY'RE RIGHT BUT IF YOU ADMIT IT, YOU FEEL UNPATRIOTIC.
THAT'S WHY ENGLISH CITIZENSHIP IS SO GREAT. PEOPLE PITY AND ADMIRE OUR FAILED IMPERIALISM.
710
I HAVE A 3-CITY TEST.
ACTUALLY, I'D RIPPED OFF THIS IDEA FROM SOMEONE ELSE; I STILL CAN'T REMEMBER WHOM.
IF AT LEAST 50% OF THE AMERICAN PUBLIC CAN'T IDENTIFY AT LEAST 3 CITIES IN A GIVEN COUNTRY, WE SHOULDN'T BOMB IT.
THAT WOULD CERTAINLY RULE OUT IRAQ!
AN F-16 ZOOMED OVERHEAD. DID ITS PILOT KNOW THAT AFGHANISTAN WAS FAMOUS FOR ITS EMERALDS AND ITS POMEGRANATES? DID HE KNOW THAT THERE WERE OIL FIELDS NEARBY?
YOU HAVE TO ADMIT, THE TALIBAN WERE BASTARDS. IT'LL BE GOOD TO SEE WOMEN WALKING AROUND WITHOUT BURQAS.
YOU WON'T. NOTHING'S CHANGED. THE NORTHERN ALLIANCE AND THE TALIBAN ARE EXACTLY THE SAME.

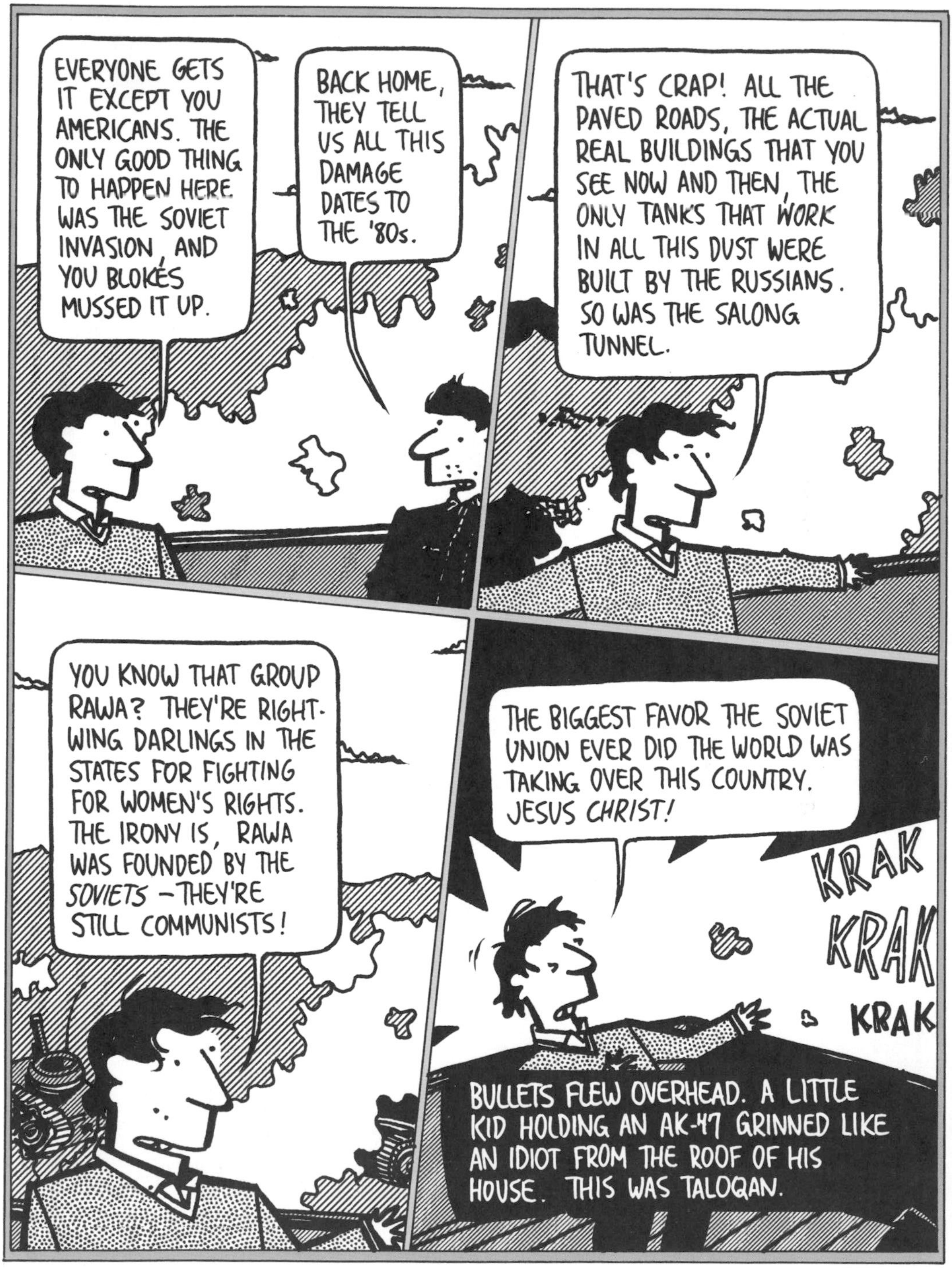
EVERYONE GETS IT EXCEPT YOU AMERICANS. THE ONLY GOOD THING TO HAPPEN HERE WAS THE SOVIET INVASION, AND YOU BLOKES MUSSED IT UP.
BACK HOME, THEY TELL US ALL THIS DAMAGE DATES TO THE '80s.
THAT'S CRAP! ALL THE PAVED ROADS, THE ACTUAL REAL BUILDINGS THAT YOU SEE NOW AND THEN, THE ONLY TANKS THAT WORK IN ALL THIS DUST WERE BUILT BY THE RUSSIANS. SO WAS THE SALONG TUNNEL.
YOU KNOW THAT GROUP RAWA? THEY'RE RIGHT-WING DARLINGS IN THE STATES FOR FIGHTING FOR WOMEN'S RIGHTS. THE IRONY IS, RAWA WAS FOUNDED BY THE SOVIETS – THEY'RE STILL COMMUNISTS!
THE BIGGEST FAVOR THE SOVIET UNION EVER DID THE WORLD WAS TAKING OVER THIS COUNTRY. JESUS CHRIST!
KRAK
KRAK
KRAK
BULLETS FLEW OVERHEAD. A LITTLE KID HOLDING AN AK-47 GRINNED LIKE AN IDIOT FROM THE ROOF OF HIS HOUSE. THIS WAS TALOQAN.

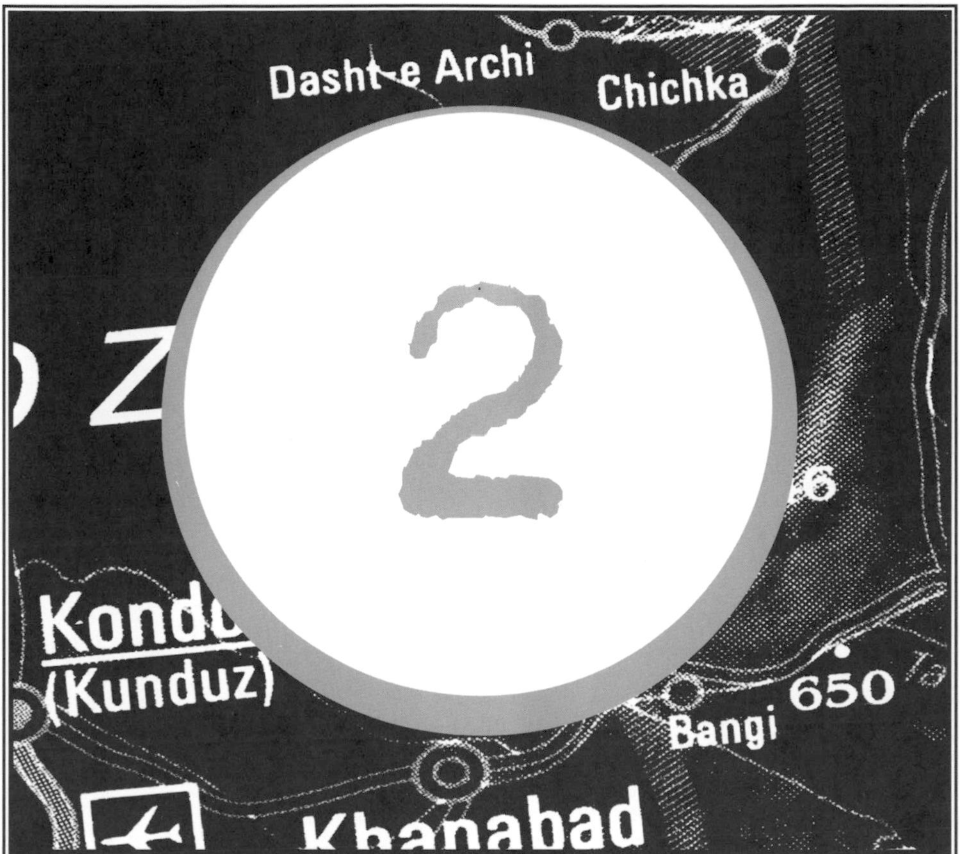
Dasht-e Archi
Chichka
(Kunduz)
Bangi
650

2

COMMUTER WAR

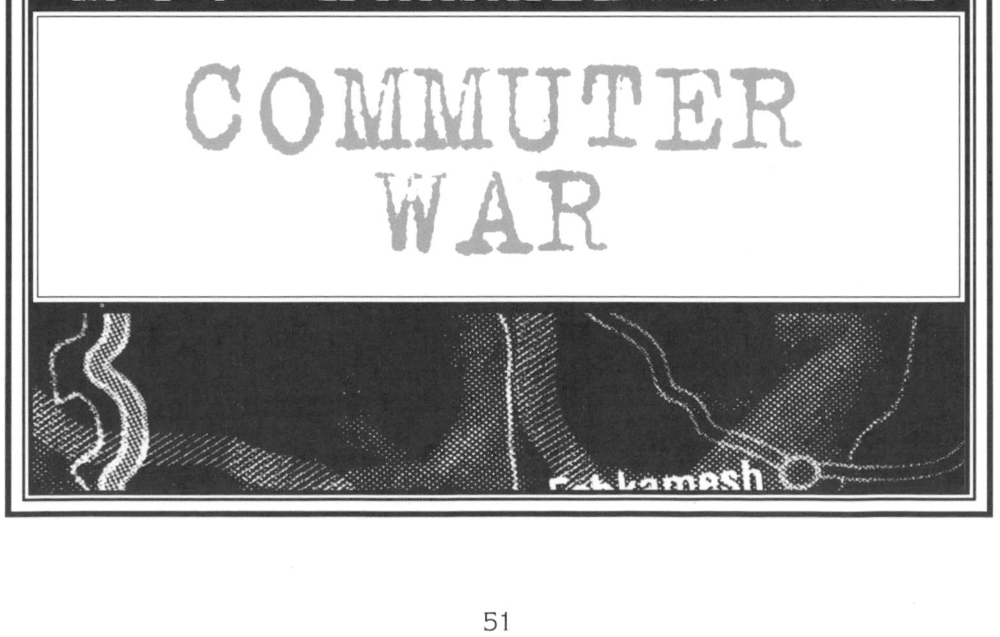

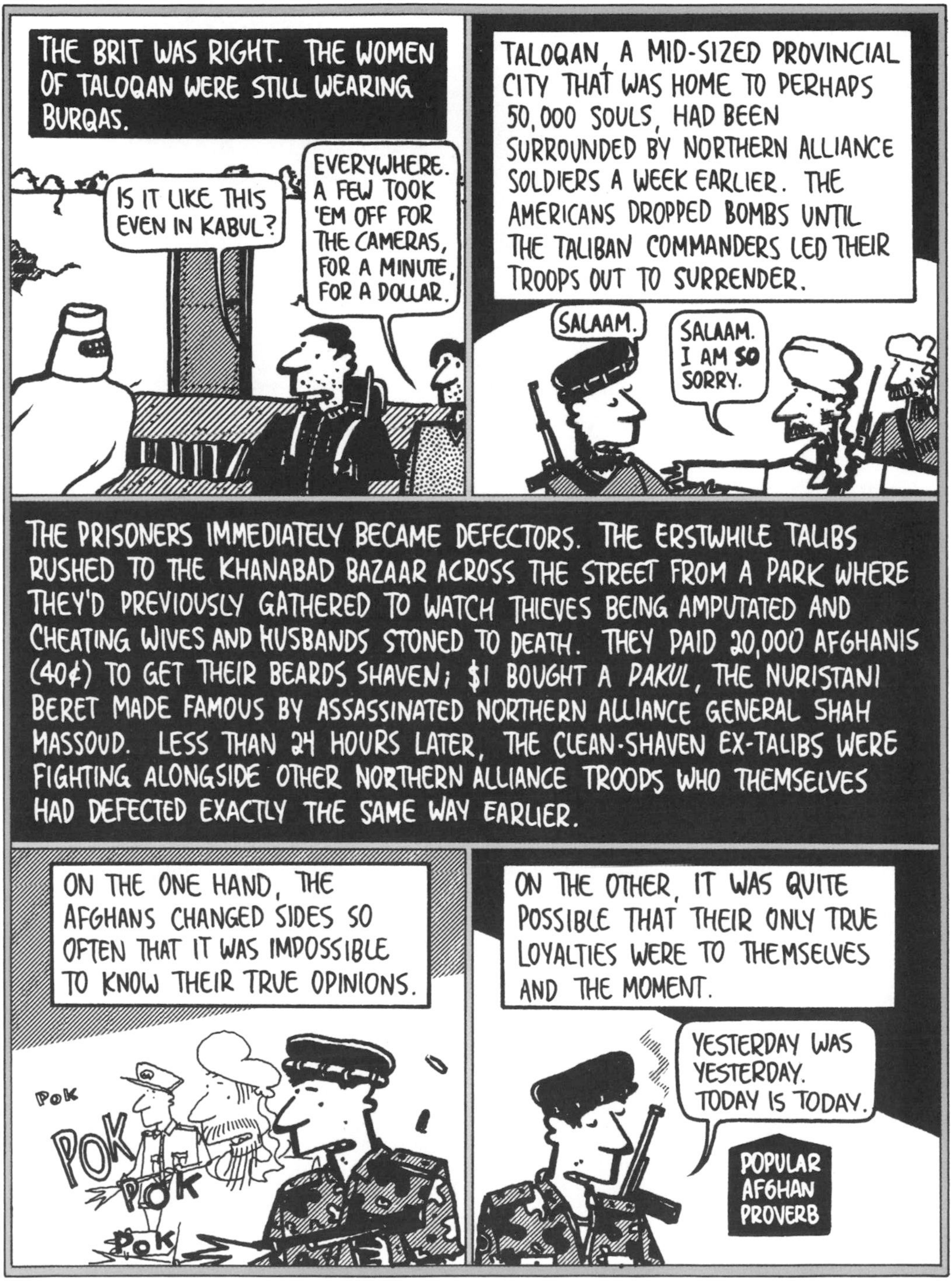
THE BRIT WAS RIGHT. THE WOMEN OF TALOQAN WERE STILL WEARING BURQAS.
IS IT LIKE THIS EVEN IN KABUL?
EVERYWHERE. A FEW TOOK 'EM OFF FOR THE CAMERAS, FOR A MINUTE, FOR A DOLLAR.
TALOQAN, A MID-SIZED PROVINCIAL CITY THAT WAS HOME TO PERHAPS 50,000 SOULS, HAD BEEN SURROUNDED BY NORTHERN ALLIANCE SOLDIERS A WEEK EARLIER. THE AMERICANS DROPPED BOMBS UNTIL THE TALIBAN COMMANDERS LED THEIR TROOPS OUT TO SURRENDER.
SALAAM.
SALAAM. I AM **SO** SORRY.
THE PRISONERS IMMEDIATELY BECAME DEFECTORS. THE ERSTWHILE TALIBS RUSHED TO THE KHANABAD BAZAAR ACROSS THE STREET FROM A PARK WHERE THEY'D PREVIOUSLY GATHERED TO WATCH THIEVES BEING AMPUTATED AND CHEATING WIVES AND HUSBANDS STONED TO DEATH. THEY PAID 20,000 AFGHANIS (40¢) TO GET THEIR BEARDS SHAVEN; $1 BOUGHT A *PAKUL*, THE NURISTANI BERET MADE FAMOUS BY ASSASSINATED NORTHERN ALLIANCE GENERAL SHAH MASSOUD. LESS THAN 24 HOURS LATER, THE CLEAN-SHAVEN EX-TALIBS WERE FIGHTING ALONGSIDE OTHER NORTHERN ALLIANCE TROOPS WHO THEMSELVES HAD DEFECTED EXACTLY THE SAME WAY EARLIER.
ON THE ONE HAND, THE AFGHANS CHANGED SIDES SO OFTEN THAT IT WAS IMPOSSIBLE TO KNOW THEIR TRUE OPINIONS.
POK
POK
POK
POK
ON THE OTHER, IT WAS QUITE POSSIBLE THAT THEIR ONLY TRUE LOYALTIES WERE TO THEMSELVES AND THE MOMENT.
YESTERDAY WAS YESTERDAY. TODAY IS TODAY.
POPULAR AFGHAN PROVERB

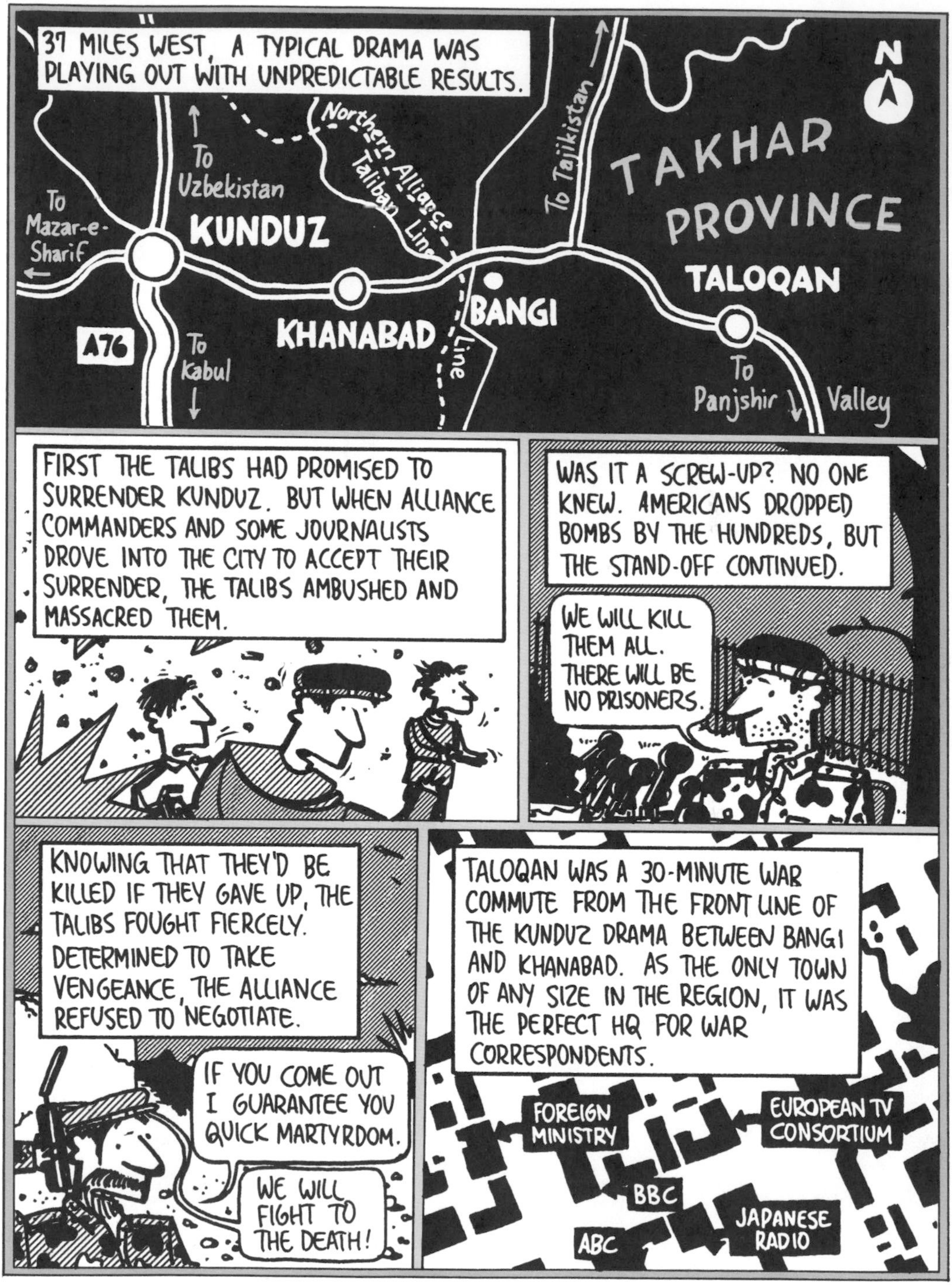

37 MILES WEST, A TYPICAL DRAMA WAS PLAYING OUT WITH UNPREDICTABLE RESULTS.
N
To Uzbekistan
Northern Alliance
Taliban Line
To Tajikistan
TAKHAR PROVINCE
To Mazar-e-Sharif
KUNDUZ
TALOQAN
BANGI
A76
To Kabul
KHANABAD
Line
To Panjshir Valley
FIRST THE TALIBS HAD PROMISED TO SURRENDER KUNDUZ. BUT WHEN ALLIANCE COMMANDERS AND SOME JOURNALISTS DROVE INTO THE CITY TO ACCEPT THEIR SURRENDER, THE TALIBS AMBUSHED AND MASSACRED THEM.
WAS IT A SCREW-UP? NO ONE KNEW. AMERICANS DROPPED BOMBS BY THE HUNDREDS, BUT THE STAND-OFF CONTINUED.
WE WILL KILL THEM ALL. THERE WILL BE NO PRISONERS.
KNOWING THAT THEY'D BE KILLED IF THEY GAVE UP, THE TALIBS FOUGHT FIERCELY. DETERMINED TO TAKE VENGEANCE, THE ALLIANCE REFUSED TO NEGOTIATE.
IF YOU COME OUT I GUARANTEE YOU QUICK MARTYRDOM.
WE WILL FIGHT TO THE DEATH!
TALOQAN WAS A 30-MINUTE WAR COMMUTE FROM THE FRONT LINE OF THE KUNDUZ DRAMA BETWEEN BANGI AND KHANABAD. AS THE ONLY TOWN OF ANY SIZE IN THE REGION, IT WAS THE PERFECT HQ FOR WAR CORRESPONDENTS.
FOREIGN MINISTRY
EUROPEAN TV CONSORTIUM
BBC
JAPANESE RADIO
ABC

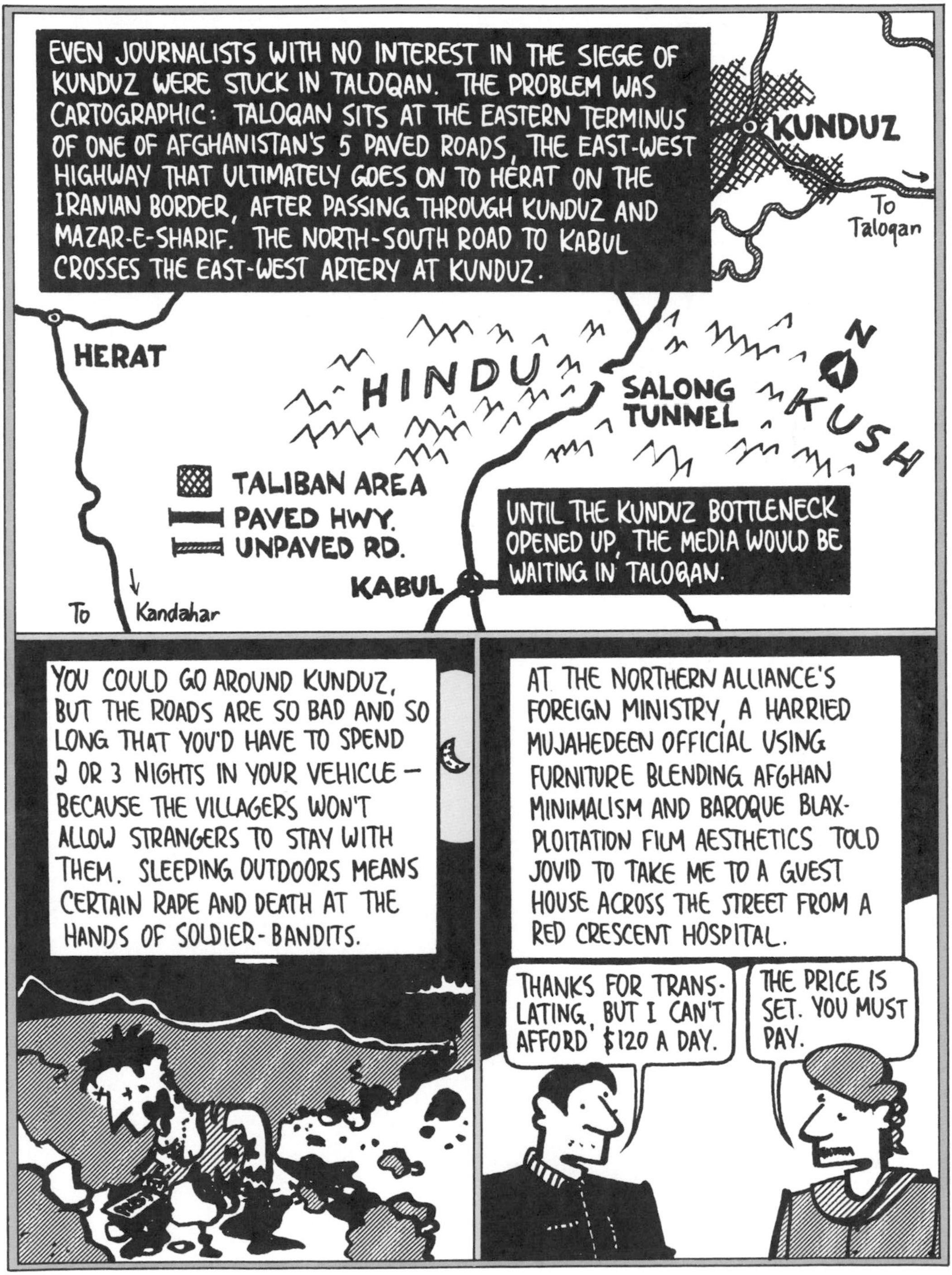
EVEN JOURNALISTS WITH NO INTEREST IN THE SIEGE OF KUNDUZ WERE STUCK IN TALOQAN. THE PROBLEM WAS CARTOGRAPHIC: TALOQAN SITS AT THE EASTERN TERMINUS OF ONE OF AFGHANISTAN'S 5 PAVED ROADS, THE EAST-WEST HIGHWAY THAT ULTIMATELY GOES ON TO HÉRAT ON THE IRANIAN BORDER, AFTER PASSING THROUGH KUNDUZ AND MAZAR-E-SHARIF. THE NORTH-SOUTH ROAD TO KABUL CROSSES THE EAST-WEST ARTERY AT KUNDUZ.
KUNDUZ
To Taloqan
HERAT
HINDU KUSH
SALONG TUNNEL
N
TALIBAN AREA
PAVED HWY.
UNPAVED RD.
KABUL
To Kandahar
UNTIL THE KUNDUZ BOTTLENECK OPENED UP, THE MEDIA WOULD BE WAITING IN TALOQAN.
YOU COULD GO AROUND KUNDUZ, BUT THE ROADS ARE SO BAD AND SO LONG THAT YOU'D HAVE TO SPEND 2 OR 3 NIGHTS IN YOUR VEHICLE— BECAUSE THE VILLAGERS WON'T ALLOW STRANGERS TO STAY WITH THEM. SLEEPING OUTDOORS MEANS CERTAIN RAPE AND DEATH AT THE HANDS OF SOLDIER-BANDITS.
AT THE NORTHERN ALLIANCE'S FOREIGN MINISTRY, A HARRIED MUJAHEDEEN OFFICIAL USING FURNITURE BLENDING AFGHAN MINIMALISM AND BAROQUE BLAX-PLOITATION FILM AESTHETICS TOLD JOVID TO TAKE ME TO A GUEST HOUSE ACROSS THE STREET FROM A RED CRESCENT HOSPITAL.
THANKS FOR TRANS-LATING, BUT I CAN'T AFFORD $120 A DAY.
THE PRICE IS SET. YOU MUST PAY.

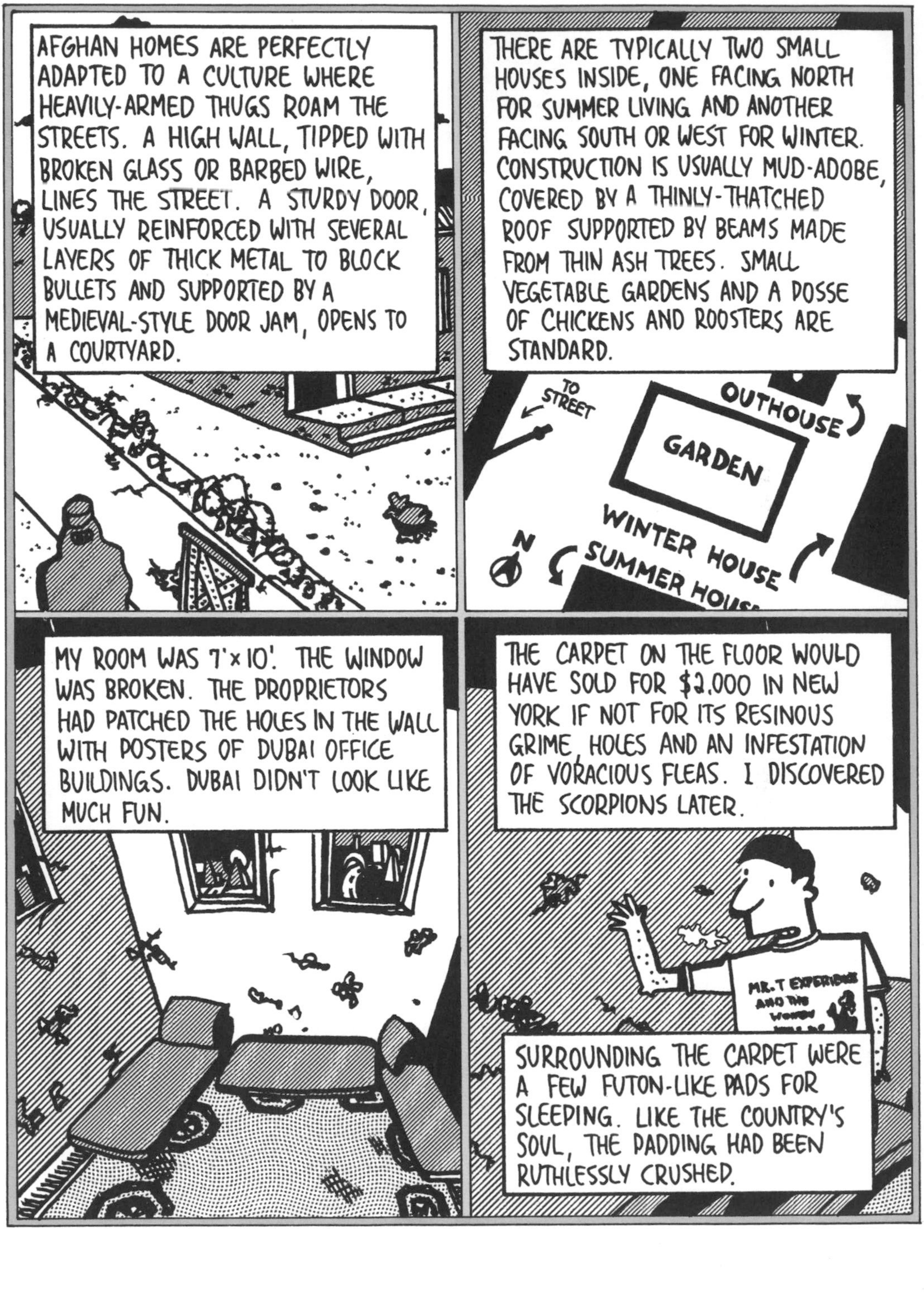
AFGHAN HOMES ARE PERFECTLY ADAPTED TO A CULTURE WHERE HEAVILY-ARMED THUGS ROAM THE STREETS. A HIGH WALL, TIPPED WITH BROKEN GLASS OR BARBED WIRE, LINES THE STREET. A STURDY DOOR, USUALLY REINFORCED WITH SEVERAL LAYERS OF THICK METAL TO BLOCK BULLETS AND SUPPORTED BY A MEDIEVAL-STYLE DOOR JAM, OPENS TO A COURTYARD.
THERE ARE TYPICALLY TWO SMALL HOUSES INSIDE, ONE FACING NORTH FOR SUMMER LIVING AND ANOTHER FACING SOUTH OR WEST FOR WINTER. CONSTRUCTION IS USUALLY MUD-ADOBE, COVERED BY A THINLY-THATCHED ROOF SUPPORTED BY BEAMS MADE FROM THIN ASH TREES. SMALL VEGETABLE GARDENS AND A POSSE OF CHICKENS AND ROOSTERS ARE STANDARD.
TO STREET
OUTHOUSE
GARDEN
WINTER HOUSE
SUMMER HOUSE
N
MY ROOM WAS 7'×10'. THE WINDOW WAS BROKEN. THE PROPRIETORS HAD PATCHED THE HOLES IN THE WALL WITH POSTERS OF DUBAI OFFICE BUILDINGS. DUBAI DIDN'T LOOK LIKE MUCH FUN.
THE CARPET ON THE FLOOR WOULD HAVE SOLD FOR $2,000 IN NEW YORK IF NOT FOR ITS RESINOUS GRIME, HOLES AND AN INFESTATION OF VORACIOUS FLEAS. I DISCOVERED THE SCORPIONS LATER.
SURROUNDING THE CARPET WERE A FEW FUTON-LIKE PADS FOR SLEEPING. LIKE THE COUNTRY'S SOUL, THE PADDING HAD BEEN RUTHLESSLY CRUSHED.

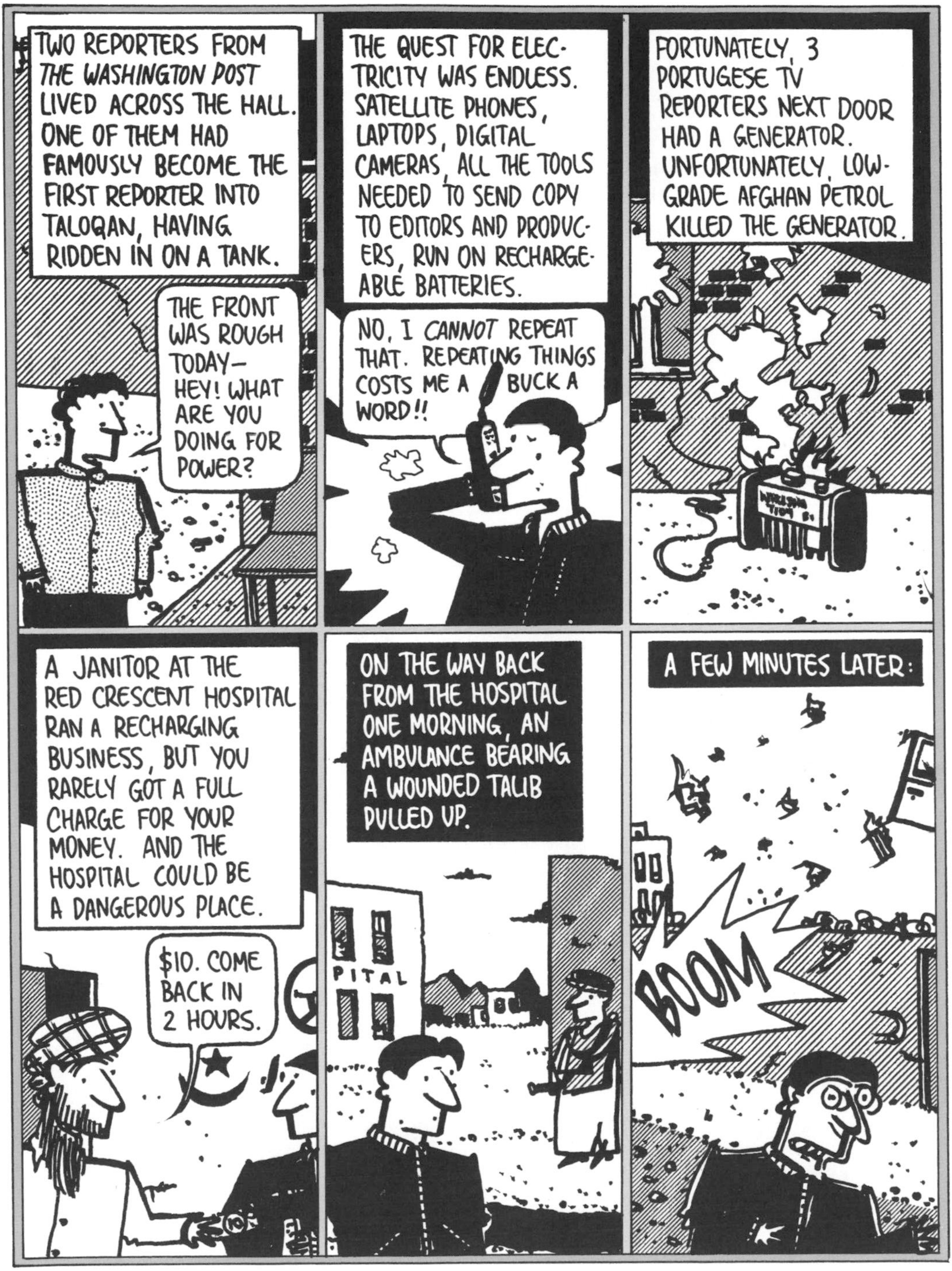
TWO REPORTERS FROM *THE WASHINGTON POST* LIVED ACROSS THE HALL. ONE OF THEM HAD FAMOUSLY BECOME THE FIRST REPORTER INTO TALOQAN, HAVING RIDDEN IN ON A TANK.
THE FRONT WAS ROUGH TODAY— HEY! WHAT ARE YOU DOING FOR POWER?
THE QUEST FOR ELECTRICITY WAS ENDLESS. SATELLITE PHONES, LAPTOPS, DIGITAL CAMERAS, ALL THE TOOLS NEEDED TO SEND COPY TO EDITORS AND PRODUCERS, RUN ON RECHARGEABLE BATTERIES.
NO, I *CANNOT* REPEAT THAT. REPEATING THINGS COSTS ME A BUCK A WORD!!
FORTUNATELY, 3 PORTUGESE TV REPORTERS NEXT DOOR HAD A GENERATOR. UNFORTUNATELY, LOW-GRADE AFGHAN PETROL KILLED THE GENERATOR.
A JANITOR AT THE RED CRESCENT HOSPITAL RAN A RECHARGING BUSINESS, BUT YOU RARELY GOT A FULL CHARGE FOR YOUR MONEY. AND THE HOSPITAL COULD BE A DANGEROUS PLACE.
$10. COME BACK IN 2 HOURS.
ON THE WAY BACK FROM THE HOSPITAL ONE MORNING, AN AMBULANCE BEARING A WOUNDED TALIB PULLED UP.
PITAL
A FEW MINUTES LATER:
BOOM

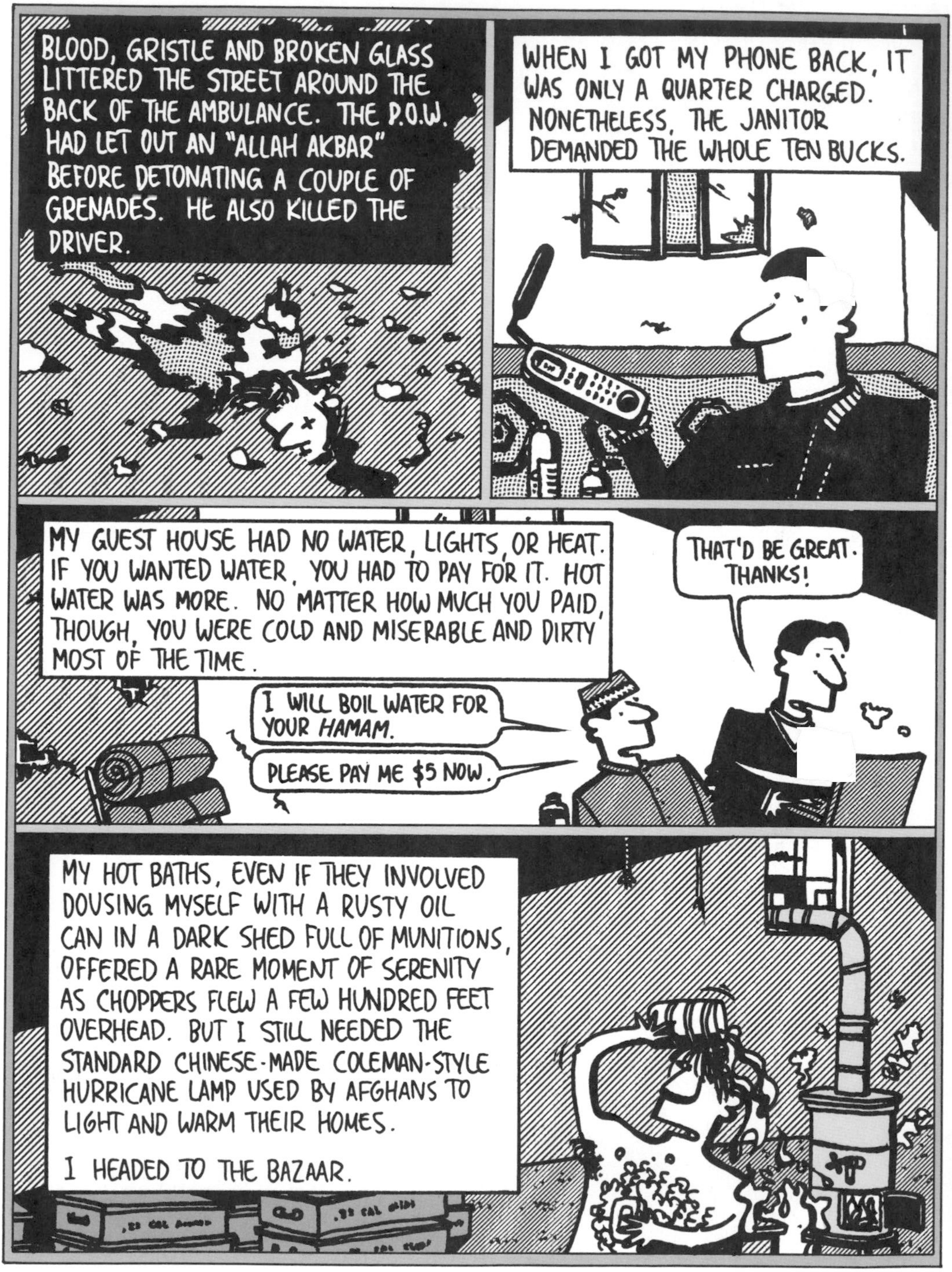
BLOOD, GRISTLE AND BROKEN GLASS LITTERED THE STREET AROUND THE BACK OF THE AMBULANCE. THE P.O.W. HAD LET OUT AN "ALLAH AKBAR" BEFORE DETONATING A COUPLE OF GRENADES. HE ALSO KILLED THE DRIVER.
WHEN I GOT MY PHONE BACK, IT WAS ONLY A QUARTER CHARGED. NONETHELESS, THE JANITOR DEMANDED THE WHOLE TEN BUCKS.
MY GUEST HOUSE HAD NO WATER, LIGHTS, OR HEAT. IF YOU WANTED WATER, YOU HAD TO PAY FOR IT. HOT WATER WAS MORE. NO MATTER HOW MUCH YOU PAID, THOUGH, YOU WERE COLD AND MISERABLE AND DIRTY MOST OF THE TIME.
I WILL BOIL WATER FOR YOUR *HAMAM*.
PLEASE PAY ME $5 NOW.
THAT'D BE GREAT. THANKS!
MY HOT BATHS, EVEN IF THEY INVOLVED DOUSING MYSELF WITH A RUSTY OIL CAN IN A DARK SHED FULL OF MUNITIONS, OFFERED A RARE MOMENT OF SERENITY AS CHOPPERS FLEW A FEW HUNDRED FEET OVERHEAD. BUT I STILL NEEDED THE STANDARD CHINESE-MADE COLEMAN-STYLE HURRICANE LAMP USED BY AFGHANS TO LIGHT AND WARM THEIR HOMES.
I HEADED TO THE BAZAAR.

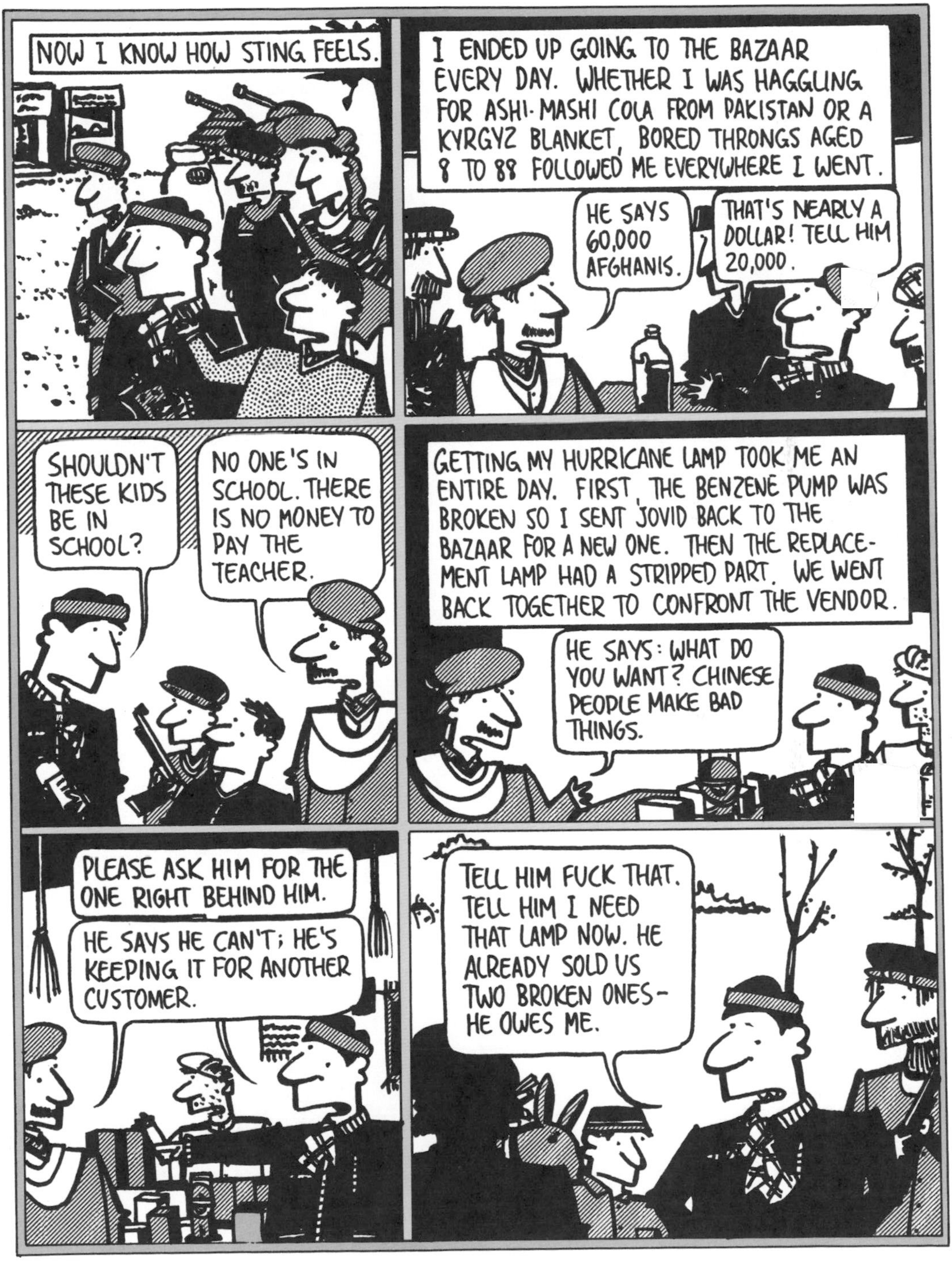
NOW I KNOW HOW STING FEELS.
I ENDED UP GOING TO THE BAZAAR EVERY DAY. WHETHER I WAS HAGGLING FOR ASHI-MASHI COLA FROM PAKISTAN OR A KYRGYZ BLANKET, BORED THRONGS AGED 8 TO 88 FOLLOWED ME EVERYWHERE I WENT.
HE SAYS 60,000 AFGHANIS.
THAT'S NEARLY A DOLLAR! TELL HIM 20,000.
SHOULDN'T THESE KIDS BE IN SCHOOL?
NO ONE'S IN SCHOOL. THERE IS NO MONEY TO PAY THE TEACHER.
GETTING MY HURRICANE LAMP TOOK ME AN ENTIRE DAY. FIRST, THE BENZENE PUMP WAS BROKEN SO I SENT JOVID BACK TO THE BAZAAR FOR A NEW ONE. THEN THE REPLACEMENT LAMP HAD A STRIPPED PART. WE WENT BACK TOGETHER TO CONFRONT THE VENDOR.
HE SAYS: WHAT DO YOU WANT? CHINESE PEOPLE MAKE BAD THINGS.
PLEASE ASK HIM FOR THE ONE RIGHT BEHIND HIM.
HE SAYS HE CAN'T; HE'S KEEPING IT FOR ANOTHER CUSTOMER.
TELL HIM FUCK THAT. TELL HIM I NEED THAT LAMP NOW. HE ALREADY SOLD US TWO BROKEN ONES- HE OWES ME.

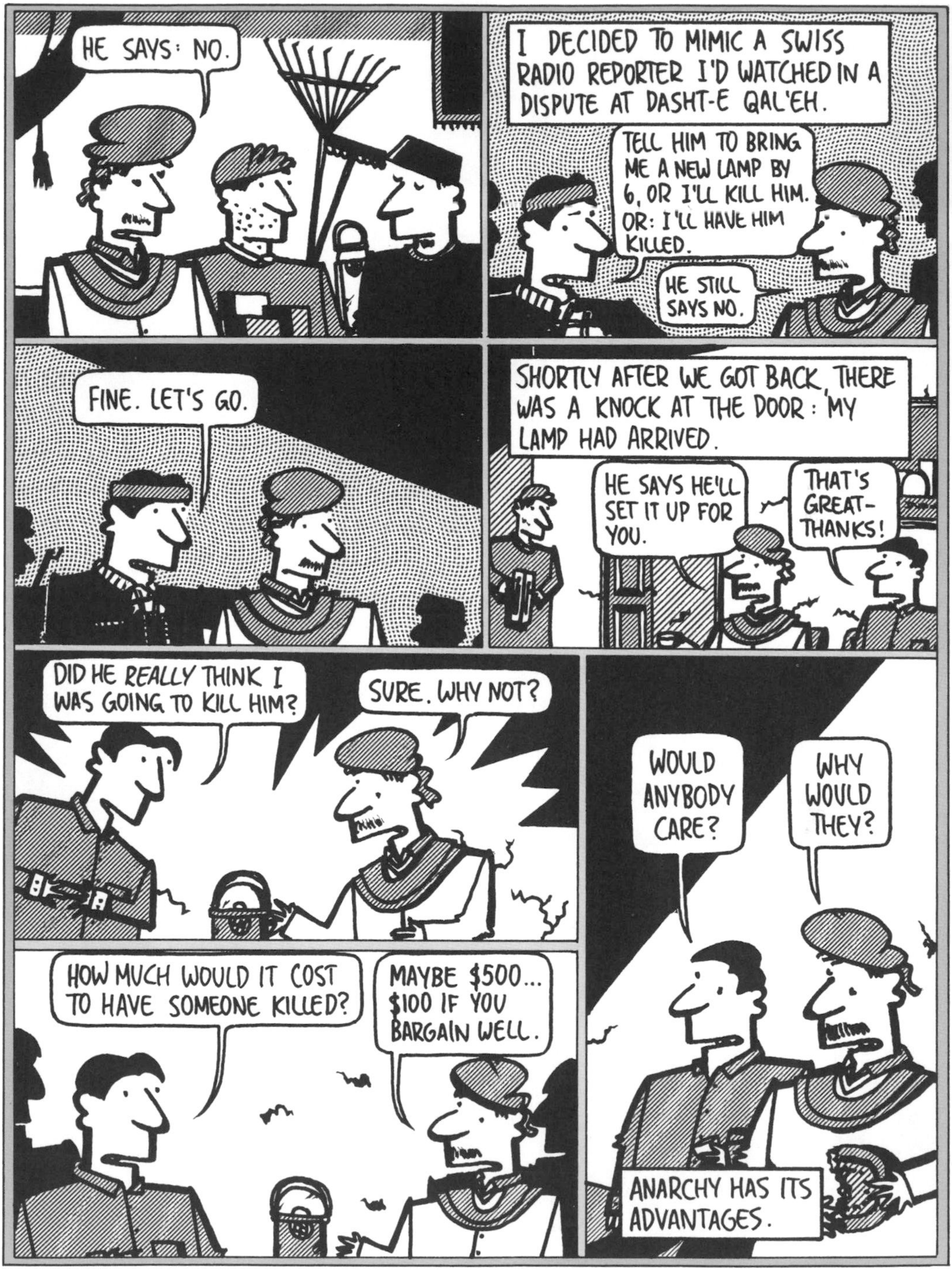
HE SAYS: NO.
I DECIDED TO MIMIC A SWISS RADIO REPORTER I'D WATCHED IN A DISPUTE AT DASHT-E QAL'EH.
TELL HIM TO BRING ME A NEW LAMP BY 6, OR I'LL KILL HIM. OR: I'LL HAVE HIM KILLED.
HE STILL SAYS NO.
FINE. LET'S GO.
SHORTLY AFTER WE GOT BACK, THERE WAS A KNOCK AT THE DOOR: MY LAMP HAD ARRIVED.
HE SAYS HE'LL SET IT UP FOR YOU.
THAT'S GREAT-THANKS!
DID HE REALLY THINK I WAS GOING TO KILL HIM?
SURE. WHY NOT?
HOW MUCH WOULD IT COST TO HAVE SOMEONE KILLED?
MAYBE $500... $100 IF YOU BARGAIN WELL.
WOULD ANYBODY CARE?
WHY WOULD THEY?
ANARCHY HAS ITS ADVANTAGES.

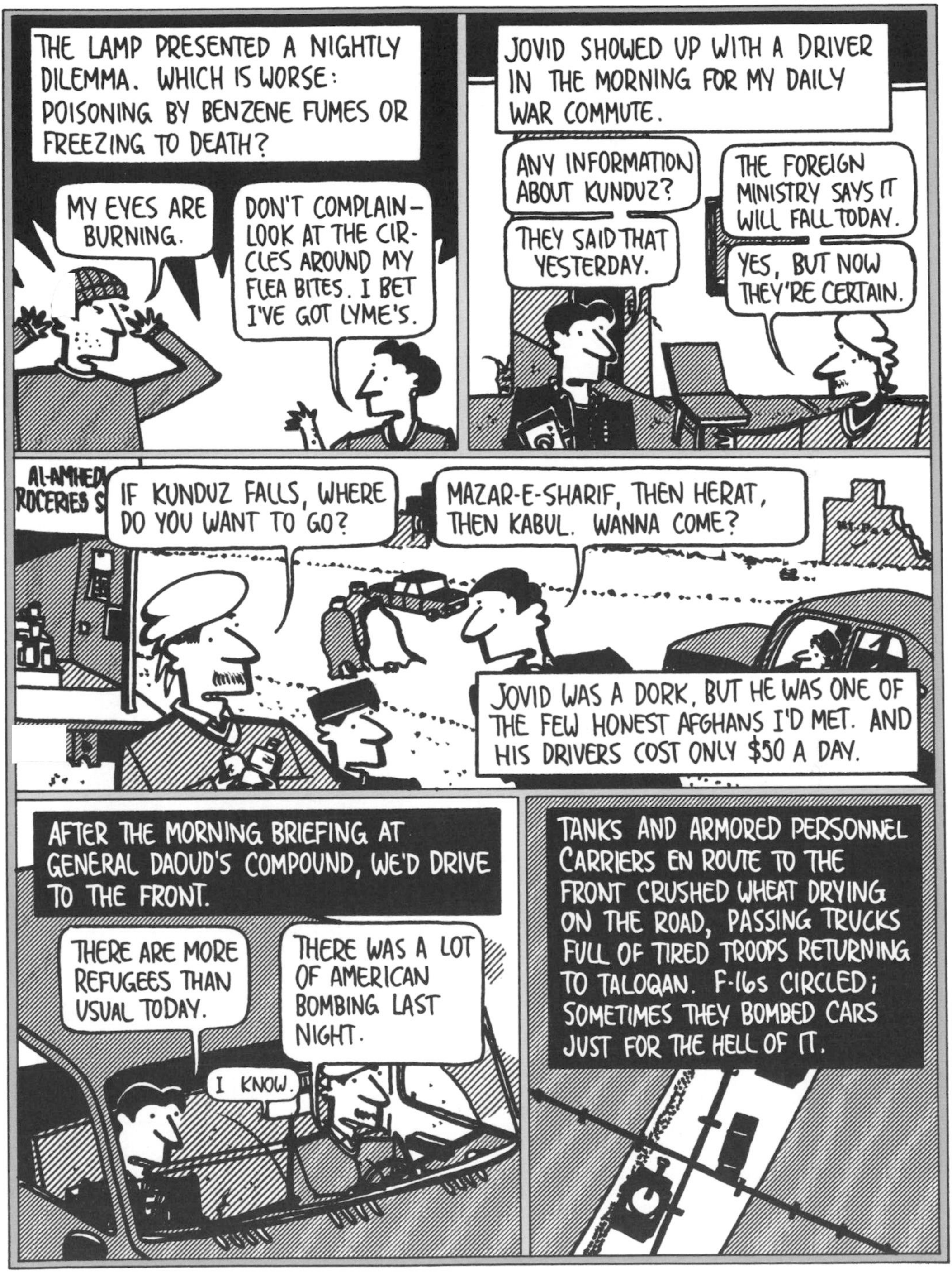
THE LAMP PRESENTED A NIGHTLY DILEMMA. WHICH IS WORSE: POISONING BY BENZENE FUMES OR FREEZING TO DEATH?
MY EYES ARE BURNING.
DON'T COMPLAIN— LOOK AT THE CIRCLES AROUND MY FLEA BITES. I BET I'VE GOT LYME'S.
JOVID SHOWED UP WITH A DRIVER IN THE MORNING FOR MY DAILY WAR COMMUTE.
ANY INFORMATION ABOUT KUNDUZ?
THE FOREIGN MINISTRY SAYS IT WILL FALL TODAY.
THEY SAID THAT YESTERDAY.
YES, BUT NOW THEY'RE CERTAIN.
AL-AHMEDI GROCERIES S
IF KUNDUZ FALLS, WHERE DO YOU WANT TO GO?
MAZAR-E-SHARIF, THEN HERAT, THEN KABUL. WANNA COME?
JOVID WAS A DORK, BUT HE WAS ONE OF THE FEW HONEST AFGHANS I'D MET. AND HIS DRIVERS COST ONLY $50 A DAY.
AFTER THE MORNING BRIEFING AT GENERAL DAOUD'S COMPOUND, WE'D DRIVE TO THE FRONT.
THERE ARE MORE REFUGEES THAN USUAL TODAY.
THERE WAS A LOT OF AMERICAN BOMBING LAST NIGHT.
I KNOW.
TANKS AND ARMORED PERSONNEL CARRIERS EN ROUTE TO THE FRONT CRUSHED WHEAT DRYING ON THE ROAD, PASSING TRUCKS FULL OF TIRED TROOPS RETURNING TO TALOQAN. F-16s CIRCLED; SOMETIMES THEY BOMBED CARS JUST FOR THE HELL OF IT.

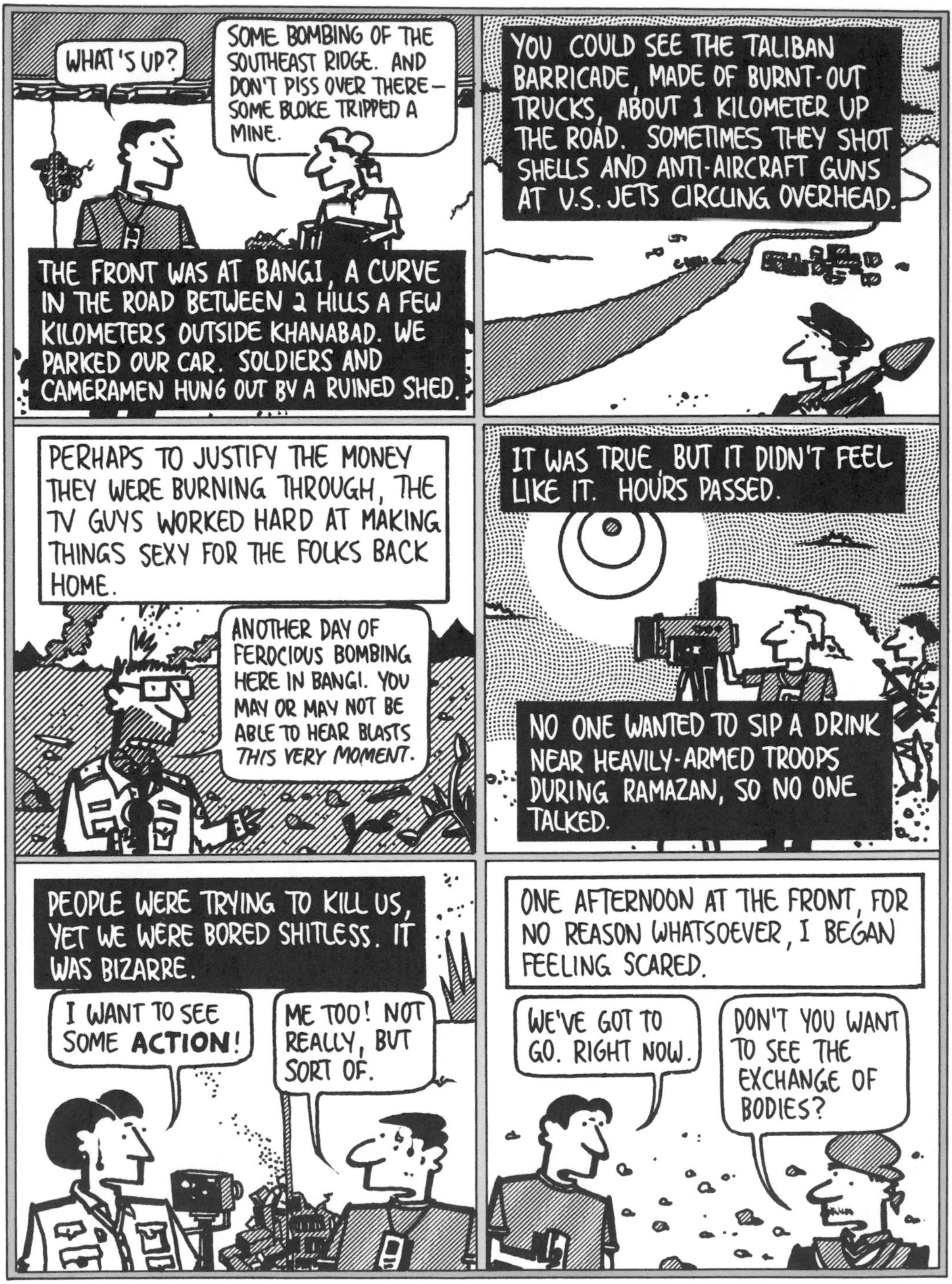
WHAT'S UP?
SOME BOMBING OF THE SOUTHEAST RIDGE. AND DON'T PISS OVER THERE— SOME BLOKE TRIPPED A MINE.
THE FRONT WAS AT BANGI, A CURVE IN THE ROAD BETWEEN 2 HILLS A FEW KILOMETERS OUTSIDE KHANABAD. WE PARKED OUR CAR. SOLDIERS AND CAMERAMEN HUNG OUT BY A RUINED SHED.
YOU COULD SEE THE TALIBAN BARRICADE, MADE OF BURNT-OUT TRUCKS, ABOUT 1 KILOMETER UP THE ROAD. SOMETIMES THEY SHOT SHELLS AND ANTI-AIRCRAFT GUNS AT U.S. JETS CIRCLING OVERHEAD.
PERHAPS TO JUSTIFY THE MONEY THEY WERE BURNING THROUGH, THE TV GUYS WORKED HARD AT MAKING THINGS SEXY FOR THE FOLKS BACK HOME.
ANOTHER DAY OF FEROCIOUS BOMBING HERE IN BANGI. YOU MAY OR MAY NOT BE ABLE TO HEAR BLASTS *THIS VERY MOMENT*.
IT WAS TRUE, BUT IT DIDN'T FEEL LIKE IT. HOURS PASSED.
NO ONE WANTED TO SIP A DRINK NEAR HEAVILY-ARMED TROOPS DURING RAMAZAN, SO NO ONE TALKED.
PEOPLE WERE TRYING TO KILL US, YET WE WERE BORED SHITLESS. IT WAS BIZARRE.
I WANT TO SEE SOME **ACTION**!
ME TOO! NOT REALLY, BUT SORT OF.
ONE AFTERNOON AT THE FRONT, FOR NO REASON WHATSOEVER, I BEGAN FEELING SCARED.
WE'VE GOT TO GO. RIGHT NOW.
DON'T YOU WANT TO SEE THE EXCHANGE OF BODIES?

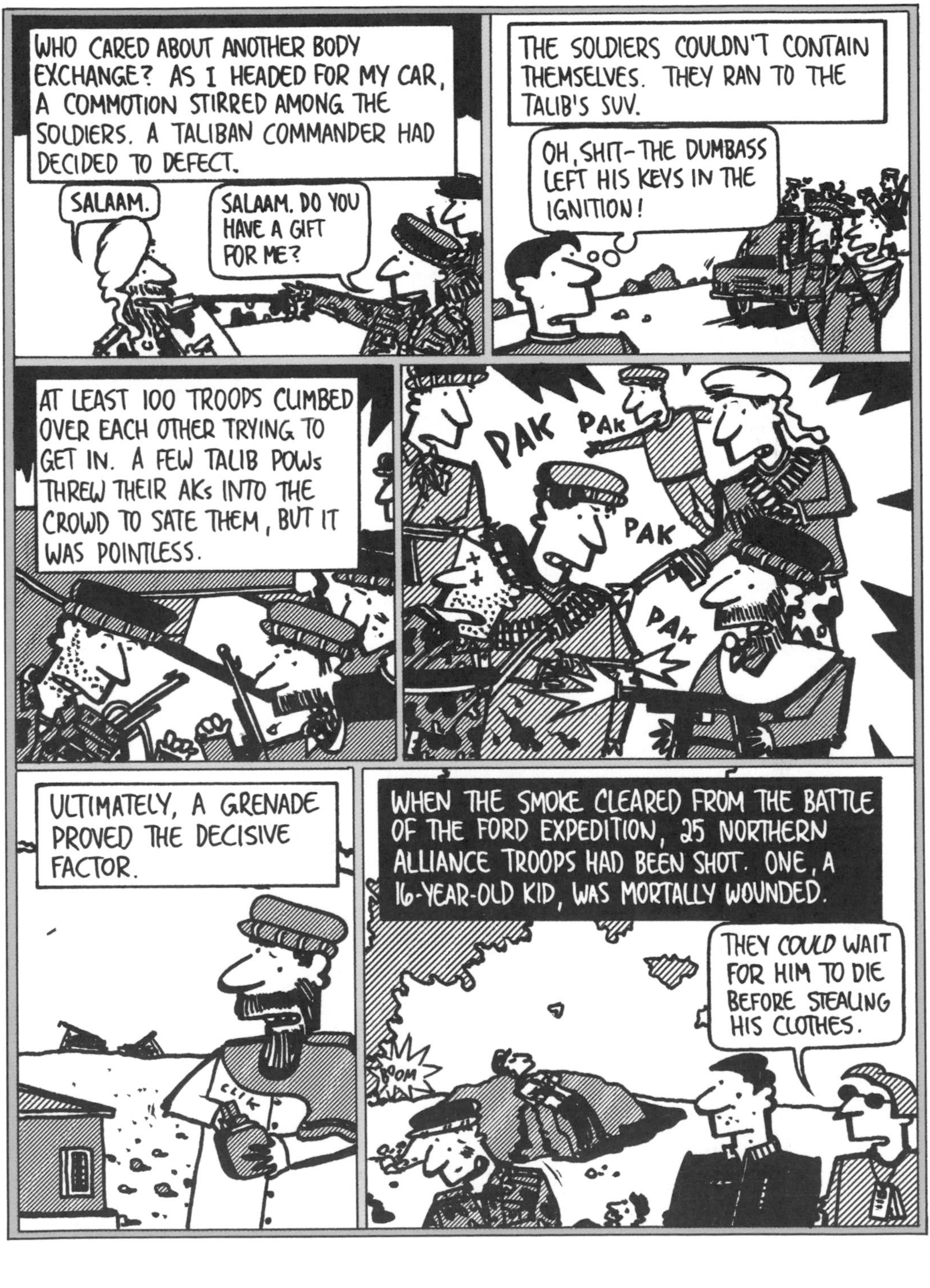
WHO CARED ABOUT ANOTHER BODY EXCHANGE? AS I HEADED FOR MY CAR, A COMMOTION STIRRED AMONG THE SOLDIERS. A TALIBAN COMMANDER HAD DECIDED TO DEFECT.
SALAAM.
SALAAM. DO YOU HAVE A GIFT FOR ME?
THE SOLDIERS COULDN'T CONTAIN THEMSELVES. THEY RAN TO THE TALIB'S SUV.
OH, SHIT—THE DUMBASS LEFT HIS KEYS IN THE IGNITION!
AT LEAST 100 TROOPS CLIMBED OVER EACH OTHER TRYING TO GET IN. A FEW TALIB POWs THREW THEIR AKs INTO THE CROWD TO SATE THEM, BUT IT WAS POINTLESS.
PAK
PAK
PAK
PAK
ULTIMATELY, A GRENADE PROVED THE DECISIVE FACTOR.
CLIK
WHEN THE SMOKE CLEARED FROM THE BATTLE OF THE FORD EXPEDITION, 25 NORTHERN ALLIANCE TROOPS HAD BEEN SHOT. ONE, A 16-YEAR-OLD KID, WAS MORTALLY WOUNDED.
THEY *COULD* WAIT FOR HIM TO DIE BEFORE STEALING HIS CLOTHES.
BOOM

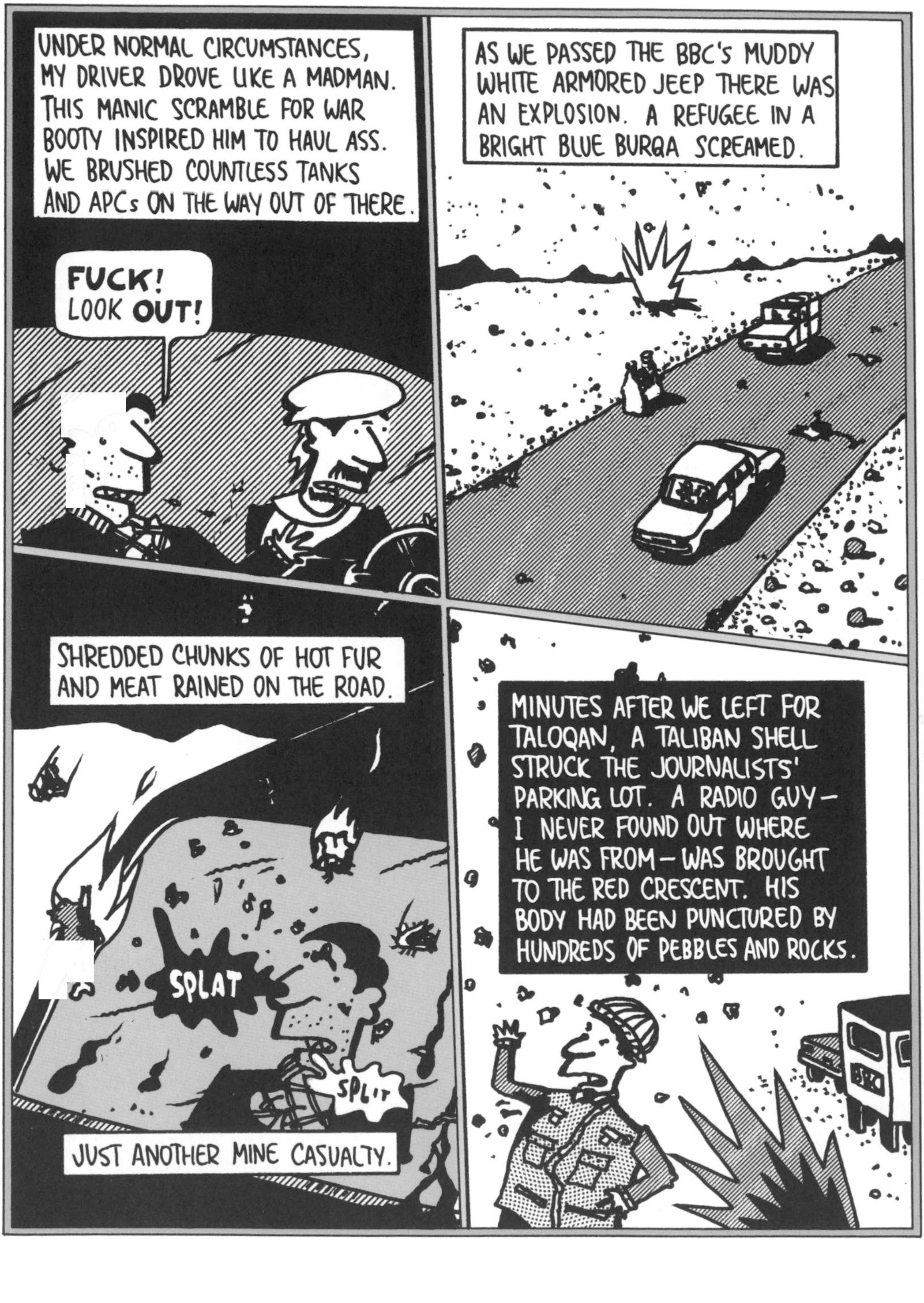
UNDER NORMAL CIRCUMSTANCES, MY DRIVER DROVE LIKE A MADMAN. THIS MANIC SCRAMBLE FOR WAR BOOTY INSPIRED HIM TO HAUL ASS. WE BRUSHED COUNTLESS TANKS AND APCs ON THE WAY OUT OF THERE.
FUCK! LOOK OUT!
AS WE PASSED THE BBC's MUDDY WHITE ARMORED JEEP THERE WAS AN EXPLOSION. A REFUGEE IN A BRIGHT BLUE BURQA SCREAMED.
SHREDDED CHUNKS OF HOT FUR AND MEAT RAINED ON THE ROAD.
SPLAT
SPLIT
JUST ANOTHER MINE CASUALTY.
MINUTES AFTER WE LEFT FOR TALOQAN, A TALIBAN SHELL STRUCK THE JOURNALISTS' PARKING LOT. A RADIO GUY— I NEVER FOUND OUT WHERE HE WAS FROM—WAS BROUGHT TO THE RED CRESCENT. HIS BODY HAD BEEN PUNCTURED BY HUNDREDS OF PEBBLES AND ROCKS.

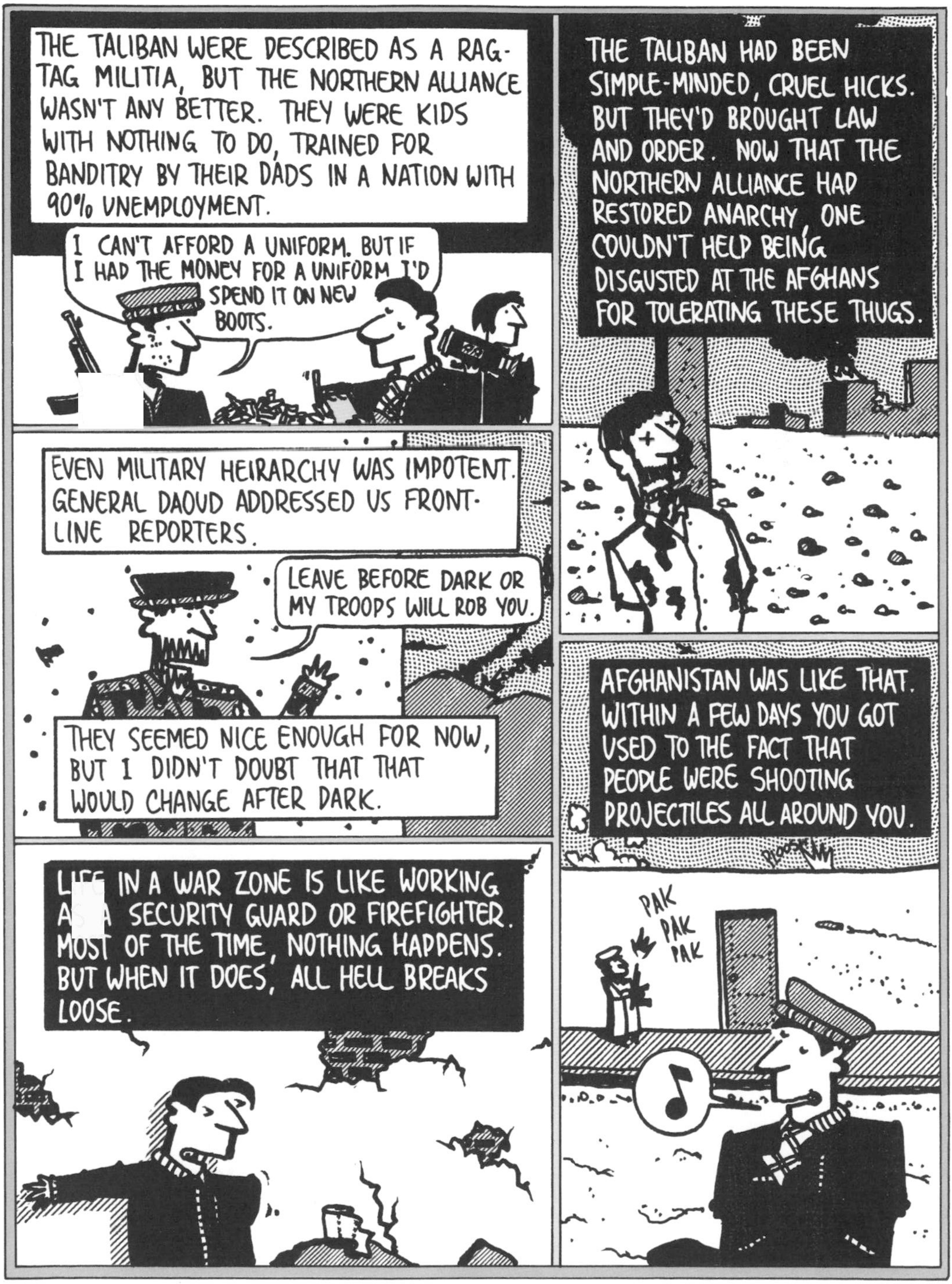
THE TALIBAN WERE DESCRIBED AS A RAG-TAG MILITIA, BUT THE NORTHERN ALLIANCE WASN'T ANY BETTER. THEY WERE KIDS WITH NOTHING TO DO, TRAINED FOR BANDITRY BY THEIR DADS IN A NATION WITH 90% UNEMPLOYMENT.
I CAN'T AFFORD A UNIFORM. BUT IF I HAD THE MONEY FOR A UNIFORM I'D SPEND IT ON NEW BOOTS.
THE TALIBAN HAD BEEN SIMPLE-MINDED, CRUEL HICKS. BUT THEY'D BROUGHT LAW AND ORDER. NOW THAT THE NORTHERN ALLIANCE HAD RESTORED ANARCHY, ONE COULDN'T HELP BEING DISGUSTED AT THE AFGHANS FOR TOLERATING THESE THUGS.
EVEN MILITARY HEIRARCHY WAS IMPOTENT. GENERAL DAOUD ADDRESSED US FRONT-LINE REPORTERS.
LEAVE BEFORE DARK OR MY TROOPS WILL ROB YOU.
THEY SEEMED NICE ENOUGH FOR NOW, BUT I DIDN'T DOUBT THAT THAT WOULD CHANGE AFTER DARK.
AFGHANISTAN WAS LIKE THAT. WITHIN A FEW DAYS YOU GOT USED TO THE FACT THAT PEOPLE WERE SHOOTING PROJECTILES ALL AROUND YOU.
LIFE IN A WAR ZONE IS LIKE WORKING AS A SECURITY GUARD OR FIREFIGHTER. MOST OF THE TIME, NOTHING HAPPENS. BUT WHEN IT DOES, ALL HELL BREAKS LOOSE.
PAK PAK PAK

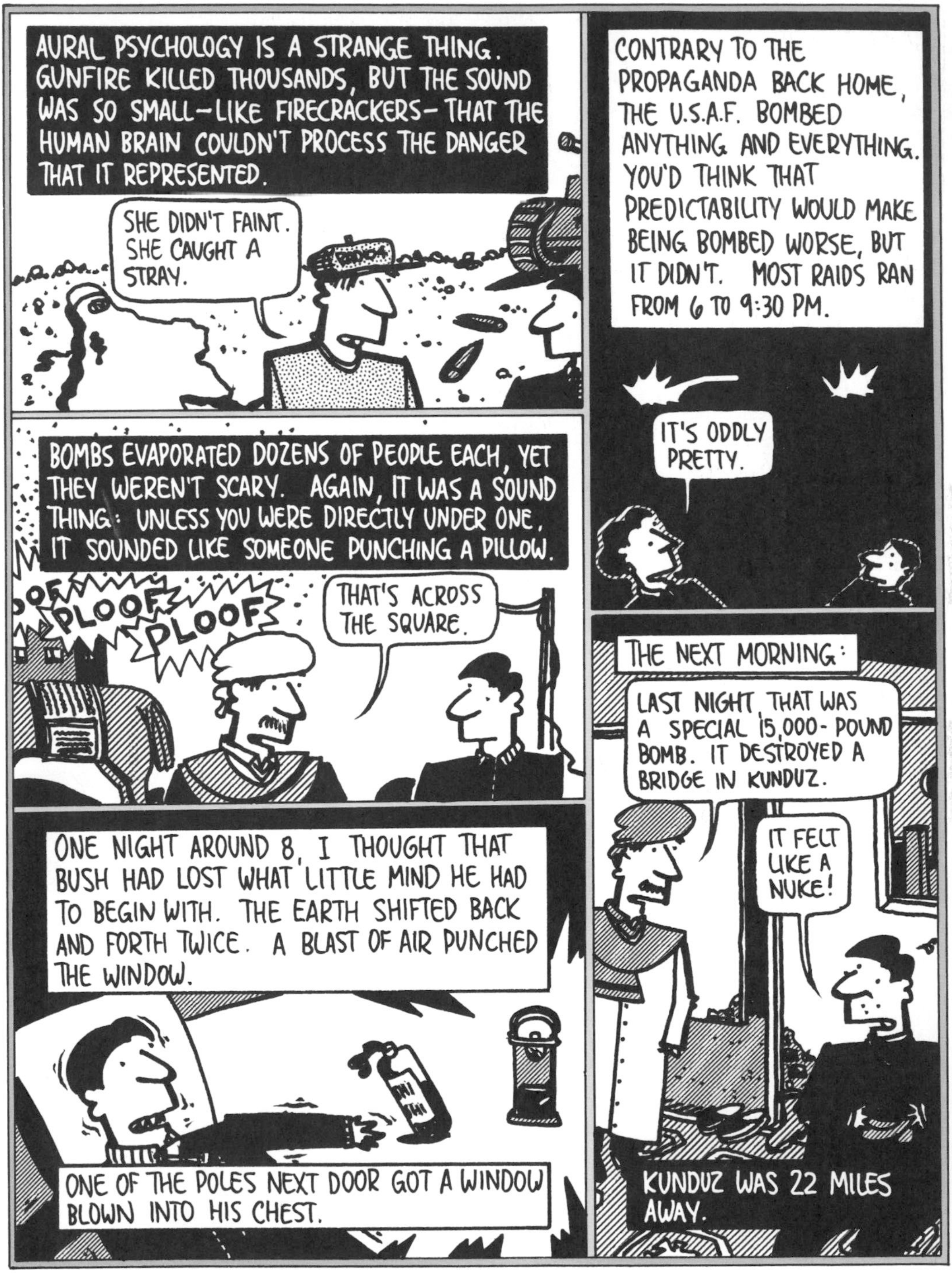
AURAL PSYCHOLOGY IS A STRANGE THING. GUNFIRE KILLED THOUSANDS, BUT THE SOUND WAS SO SMALL—LIKE FIRECRACKERS—THAT THE HUMAN BRAIN COULDN'T PROCESS THE DANGER THAT IT REPRESENTED.
SHE DIDN'T FAINT. SHE CAUGHT A STRAY.
CONTRARY TO THE PROPAGANDA BACK HOME, THE U.S.A.F. BOMBED ANYTHING AND EVERYTHING. YOU'D THINK THAT PREDICTABILITY WOULD MAKE BEING BOMBED WORSE, BUT IT DIDN'T. MOST RAIDS RAN FROM 6 TO 9:30 PM.
IT'S ODDLY PRETTY.
BOMBS EVAPORATED DOZENS OF PEOPLE EACH, YET THEY WEREN'T SCARY. AGAIN, IT WAS A SOUND THING: UNLESS YOU WERE DIRECTLY UNDER ONE, IT SOUNDED LIKE SOMEONE PUNCHING A PILLOW.
PLOOF
PLOOF
THAT'S ACROSS THE SQUARE.
THE NEXT MORNING:
LAST NIGHT, THAT WAS A SPECIAL 15,000-POUND BOMB. IT DESTROYED A BRIDGE IN KUNDUZ.
IT FELT LIKE A NUKE!
KUNDUZ WAS 22 MILES AWAY.
ONE NIGHT AROUND 8, I THOUGHT THAT BUSH HAD LOST WHAT LITTLE MIND HE HAD TO BEGIN WITH. THE EARTH SHIFTED BACK AND FORTH TWICE. A BLAST OF AIR PUNCHED THE WINDOW.
ONE OF THE POLES NEXT DOOR GOT A WINDOW BLOWN INTO HIS CHEST.

I'D ALWAYS WONDERED HOW PEOPLE SURVIVED MASS BOMBINGS, LIKE DURING THE BLITZ, WITHOUT LOSING THEIR MINDS. NOW, I THINK I KNOW.

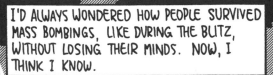

IT'S LIKE A NATURE SPECIAL I SAW. THOUSANDS OF WILDEBEEST MIGRATE ACROSS THE AFRICAN PLAINS. THEIR ROUTE TAKES THEM ACROSS A RIVER INFESTED WITH HUGE CROCODILES. I DON'T KNOW WHY THEY DON'T SIMPLY GO AROUND THE RIVER. MAYBE THEY CAN'T; MAYBE THEY DON'T THINK ABOUT IT.

ANYWAY, IF YOU BELIEVE THE NARRATOR, THE WILDEBEEST ENGAGE IN A COLD CALCULUS. SOME OF THEM WILL GET EATEN, BUT THE VAST MAJORITY WON'T. IT'LL SUCK FOR THE VICTIMS, BUT THE ODDS OF YOU YOURSELF AS AN INDIVIDUAL WILDEBEEST MAKING IT ARE EXCELLENT. SO YOU ALL HOP IN, IGNORING THE CHURNING BLOODY WATER AROUND YOU... UNLESS, OF COURSE, YOU YOURSELF ARE THE SOURCE OF THAT BLOOD.

BOMBING IS LIKE THAT. EVEN WHEN THEY'RE COMING EVERY 30 SECONDS, CHANCES ARE THAT YOU'LL LIVE TO SEE MORNING. THERE ARE SO MANY PEOPLE TO BOMB AND RELATIVELY SO FEW BOMBS TO HIT THEM WITH. WHY BOTHER TO LEAVE?

BOMBING LOTTO: IT'S A COPING MECHANISM FOR INSANITY.

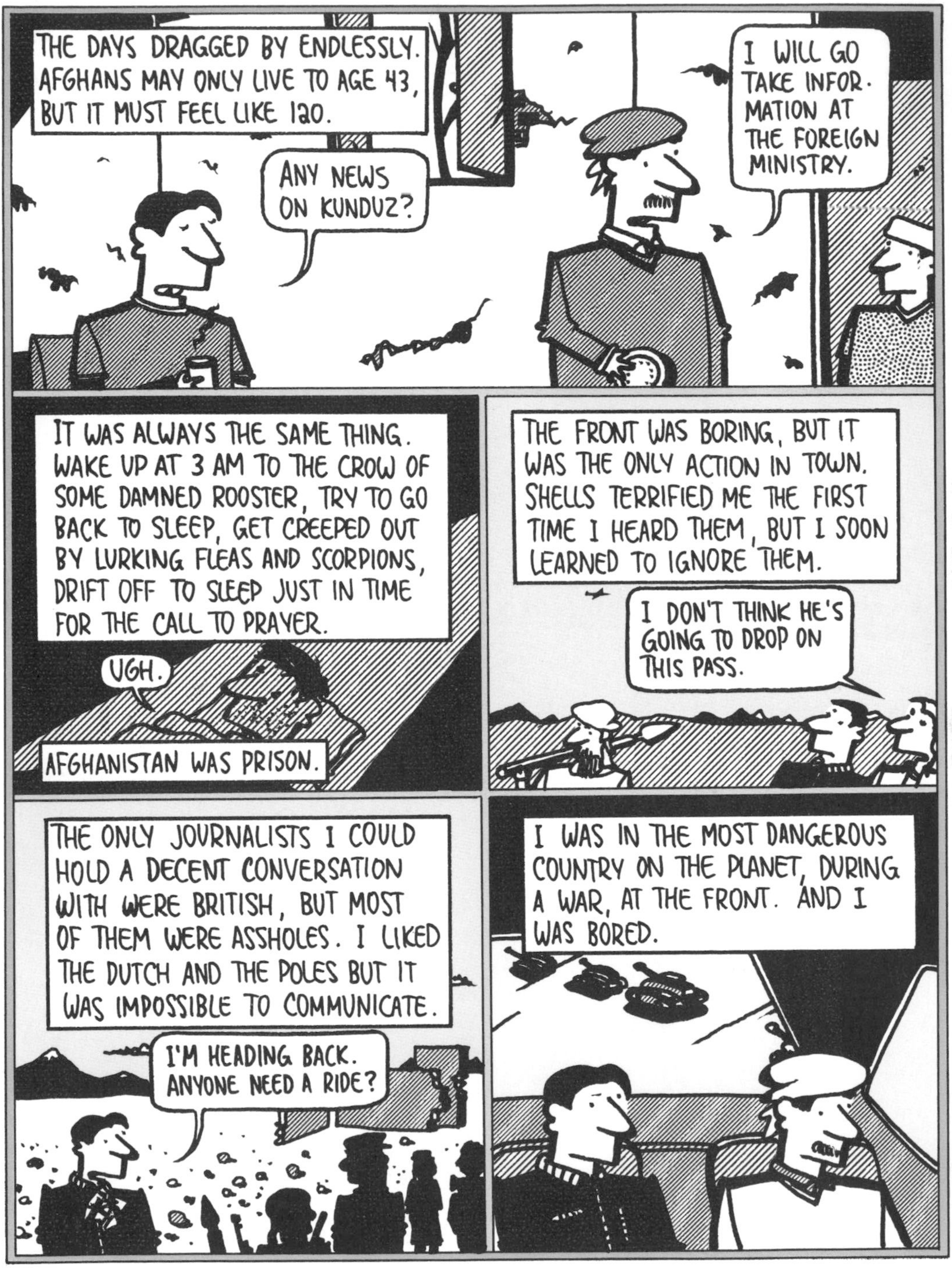
THE DAYS DRAGGED BY ENDLESSLY. AFGHANS MAY ONLY LIVE TO AGE 43, BUT IT MUST FEEL LIKE 120.
ANY NEWS ON KUNDUZ?
I WILL GO TAKE INFOR-MATION AT THE FOREIGN MINISTRY.
IT WAS ALWAYS THE SAME THING. WAKE UP AT 3 AM TO THE CROW OF SOME DAMNED ROOSTER, TRY TO GO BACK TO SLEEP, GET CREEPED OUT BY LURKING FLEAS AND SCORPIONS, DRIFT OFF TO SLEEP JUST IN TIME FOR THE CALL TO PRAYER.
UGH.
AFGHANISTAN WAS PRISON.
THE FRONT WAS BORING, BUT IT WAS THE ONLY ACTION IN TOWN. SHELLS TERRIFIED ME THE FIRST TIME I HEARD THEM, BUT I SOON LEARNED TO IGNORE THEM.
I DON'T THINK HE'S GOING TO DROP ON THIS PASS.
THE ONLY JOURNALISTS I COULD HOLD A DECENT CONVERSATION WITH WERE BRITISH, BUT MOST OF THEM WERE ASSHOLES. I LIKED THE DUTCH AND THE POLES BUT IT WAS IMPOSSIBLE TO COMMUNICATE.
I'M HEADING BACK. ANYONE NEED A RIDE?
I WAS IN THE MOST DANGEROUS COUNTRY ON THE PLANET, DURING A WAR, AT THE FRONT. AND I WAS BORED.

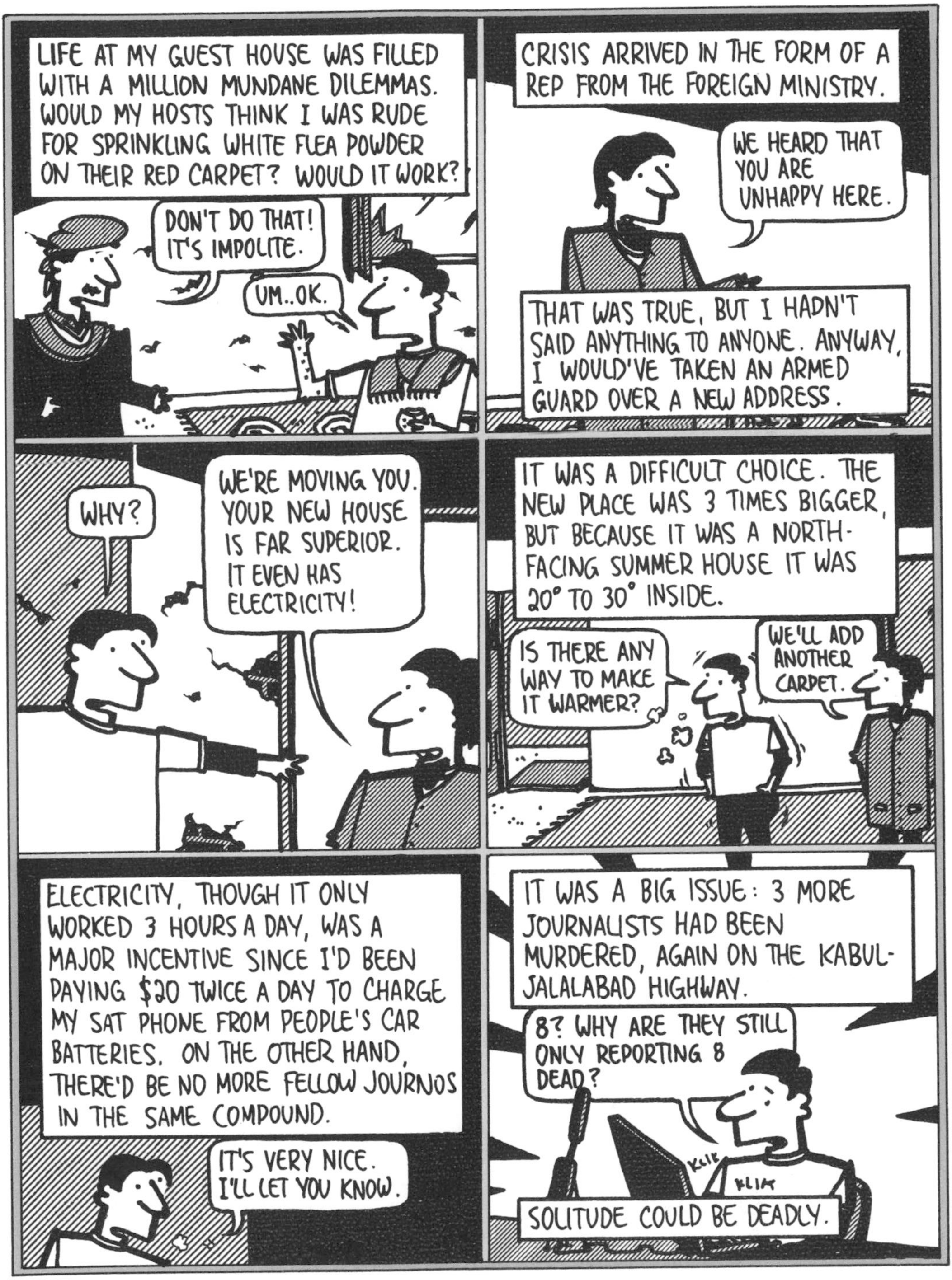
LIFE AT MY GUEST HOUSE WAS FILLED WITH A MILLION MUNDANE DILEMMAS. WOULD MY HOSTS THINK I WAS RUDE FOR SPRINKLING WHITE FLEA POWDER ON THEIR RED CARPET? WOULD IT WORK?
DON'T DO THAT! IT'S IMPOLITE.
UM..OK.
CRISIS ARRIVED IN THE FORM OF A REP FROM THE FOREIGN MINISTRY.
WE HEARD THAT YOU ARE UNHAPPY HERE.
THAT WAS TRUE, BUT I HADN'T SAID ANYTHING TO ANYONE. ANYWAY, I WOULD'VE TAKEN AN ARMED GUARD OVER A NEW ADDRESS.
WHY?
WE'RE MOVING YOU. YOUR NEW HOUSE IS FAR SUPERIOR. IT EVEN HAS ELECTRICITY!
IT WAS A DIFFICULT CHOICE. THE NEW PLACE WAS 3 TIMES BIGGER, BUT BECAUSE IT WAS A NORTH-FACING SUMMER HOUSE IT WAS 20° TO 30° INSIDE.
IS THERE ANY WAY TO MAKE IT WARMER?
WE'LL ADD ANOTHER CARPET.
ELECTRICITY, THOUGH IT ONLY WORKED 3 HOURS A DAY, WAS A MAJOR INCENTIVE SINCE I'D BEEN PAYING $20 TWICE A DAY TO CHARGE MY SAT PHONE FROM PEOPLE'S CAR BATTERIES. ON THE OTHER HAND, THERE'D BE NO MORE FELLOW JOURNOS IN THE SAME COMPOUND.
IT'S VERY NICE. I'LL LET YOU KNOW.
IT WAS A BIG ISSUE: 3 MORE JOURNALISTS HAD BEEN MURDERED, AGAIN ON THE KABUL-JALALABAD HIGHWAY.
8? WHY ARE THEY STILL ONLY REPORTING 8 DEAD?
KLIK
KLIK
SOLITUDE COULD BE DEADLY.

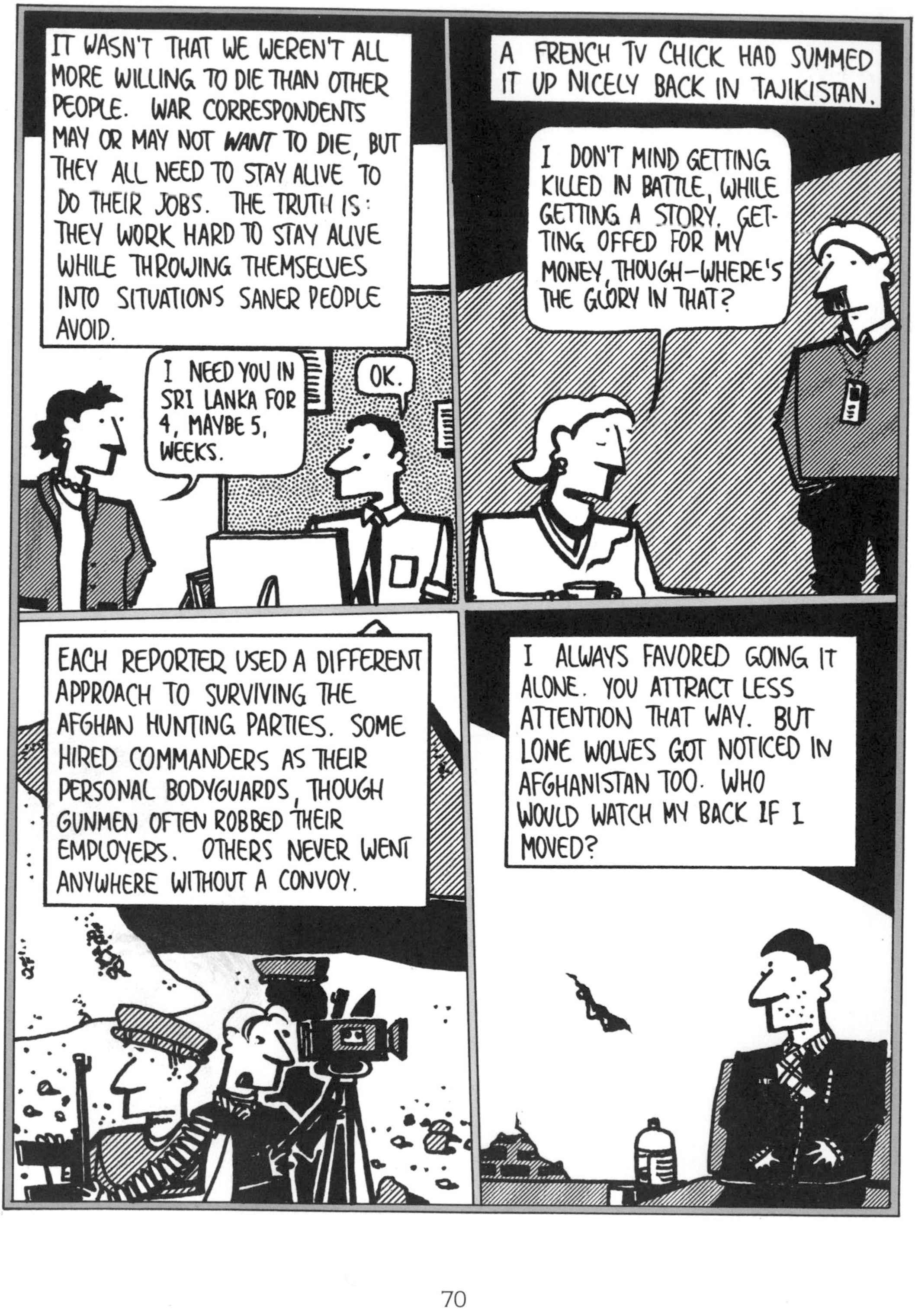
IT WASN'T THAT WE WEREN'T ALL MORE WILLING TO DIE THAN OTHER PEOPLE. WAR CORRESPONDENTS MAY OR MAY NOT WANT TO DIE, BUT THEY ALL NEED TO STAY ALIVE TO DO THEIR JOBS. THE TRUTH IS: THEY WORK HARD TO STAY ALIVE WHILE THROWING THEMSELVES INTO SITUATIONS SANER PEOPLE AVOID.
I NEED YOU IN SRI LANKA FOR 4, MAYBE 5, WEEKS.
OK.
A FRENCH TV CHICK HAD SUMMED IT UP NICELY BACK IN TAJIKISTAN.
I DON'T MIND GETTING KILLED IN BATTLE, WHILE GETTING A STORY. GETTING OFFED FOR MY MONEY, THOUGH—WHERE'S THE GLORY IN THAT?
EACH REPORTER USED A DIFFERENT APPROACH TO SURVIVING THE AFGHAN HUNTING PARTIES. SOME HIRED COMMANDERS AS THEIR PERSONAL BODYGUARDS, THOUGH GUNMEN OFTEN ROBBED THEIR EMPLOYERS. OTHERS NEVER WENT ANYWHERE WITHOUT A CONVOY.
I ALWAYS FAVORED GOING IT ALONE. YOU ATTRACT LESS ATTENTION THAT WAY. BUT LONE WOLVES GOT NOTICED IN AFGHANISTAN TOO. WHO WOULD WATCH MY BACK IF I MOVED?

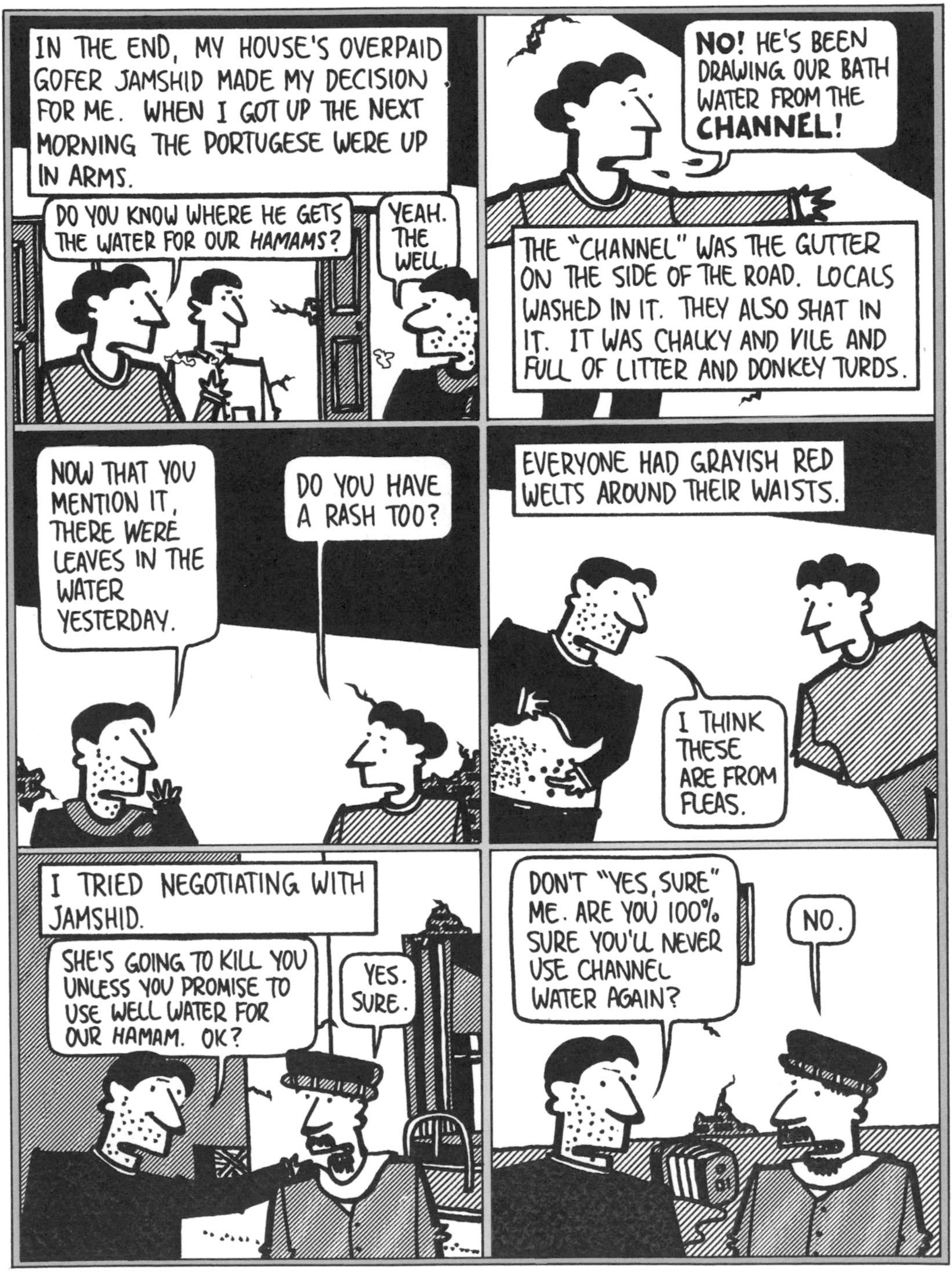
IN THE END, MY HOUSE'S OVERPAID GOFER JAMSHID MADE MY DECISION FOR ME. WHEN I GOT UP THE NEXT MORNING THE PORTUGESE WERE UP IN ARMS.
DO YOU KNOW WHERE HE GETS THE WATER FOR OUR *HAMAMS*?
YEAH. THE WELL.
NO! HE'S BEEN DRAWING OUR BATH WATER FROM THE **CHANNEL!**
THE "CHANNEL" WAS THE GUTTER ON THE SIDE OF THE ROAD. LOCALS WASHED IN IT. THEY ALSO SHAT IN IT. IT WAS CHALKY AND VILE AND FULL OF LITTER AND DONKEY TURDS.
NOW THAT YOU MENTION IT, THERE WERE LEAVES IN THE WATER YESTERDAY.
DO YOU HAVE A RASH TOO?
EVERYONE HAD GRAYISH RED WELTS AROUND THEIR WAISTS.
I THINK THESE ARE FROM FLEAS.
I TRIED NEGOTIATING WITH JAMSHID.
SHE'S GOING TO KILL YOU UNLESS YOU PROMISE TO USE WELL WATER FOR OUR HAMAM. OK?
YES. SURE.
DON'T "YES, SURE" ME. ARE YOU 100% SURE YOU'LL NEVER USE CHANNEL WATER AGAIN?
NO.

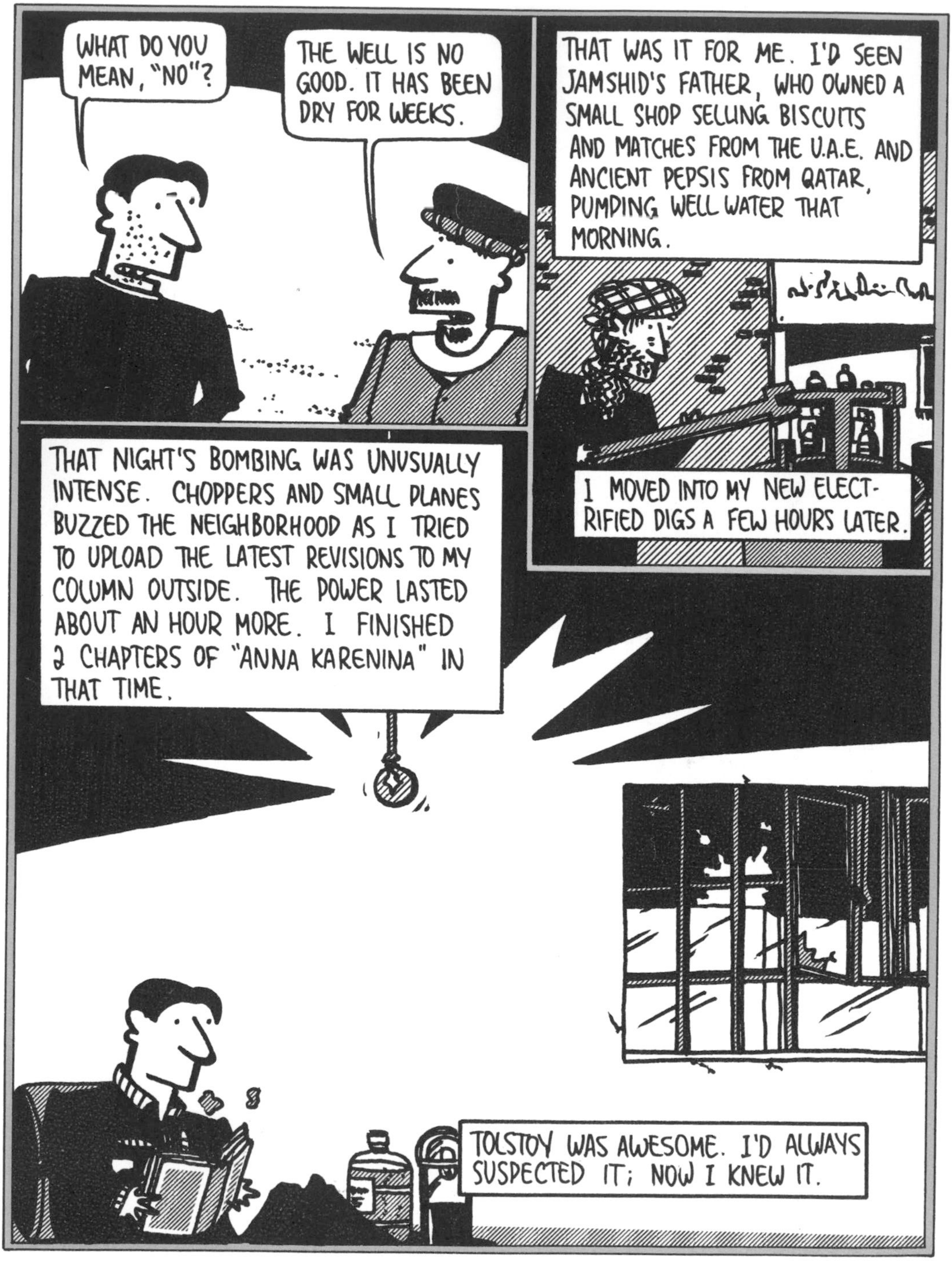
WHAT DO YOU MEAN, "NO"?
THE WELL IS NO GOOD. IT HAS BEEN DRY FOR WEEKS.
THAT WAS IT FOR ME. I'D SEEN JAMSHID'S FATHER, WHO OWNED A SMALL SHOP SELLING BISCUITS AND MATCHES FROM THE U.A.E. AND ANCIENT PEPSIS FROM QATAR, PUMPING WELL WATER THAT MORNING.
I MOVED INTO MY NEW ELECTRIFIED DIGS A FEW HOURS LATER.
THAT NIGHT'S BOMBING WAS UNUSUALLY INTENSE. CHOPPERS AND SMALL PLANES BUZZED THE NEIGHBORHOOD AS I TRIED TO UPLOAD THE LATEST REVISIONS TO MY COLUMN OUTSIDE. THE POWER LASTED ABOUT AN HOUR MORE. I FINISHED 2 CHAPTERS OF "ANNA KARENINA" IN THAT TIME.
TOLSTOY WAS AWESOME. I'D ALWAYS SUSPECTED IT; NOW I KNEW IT.

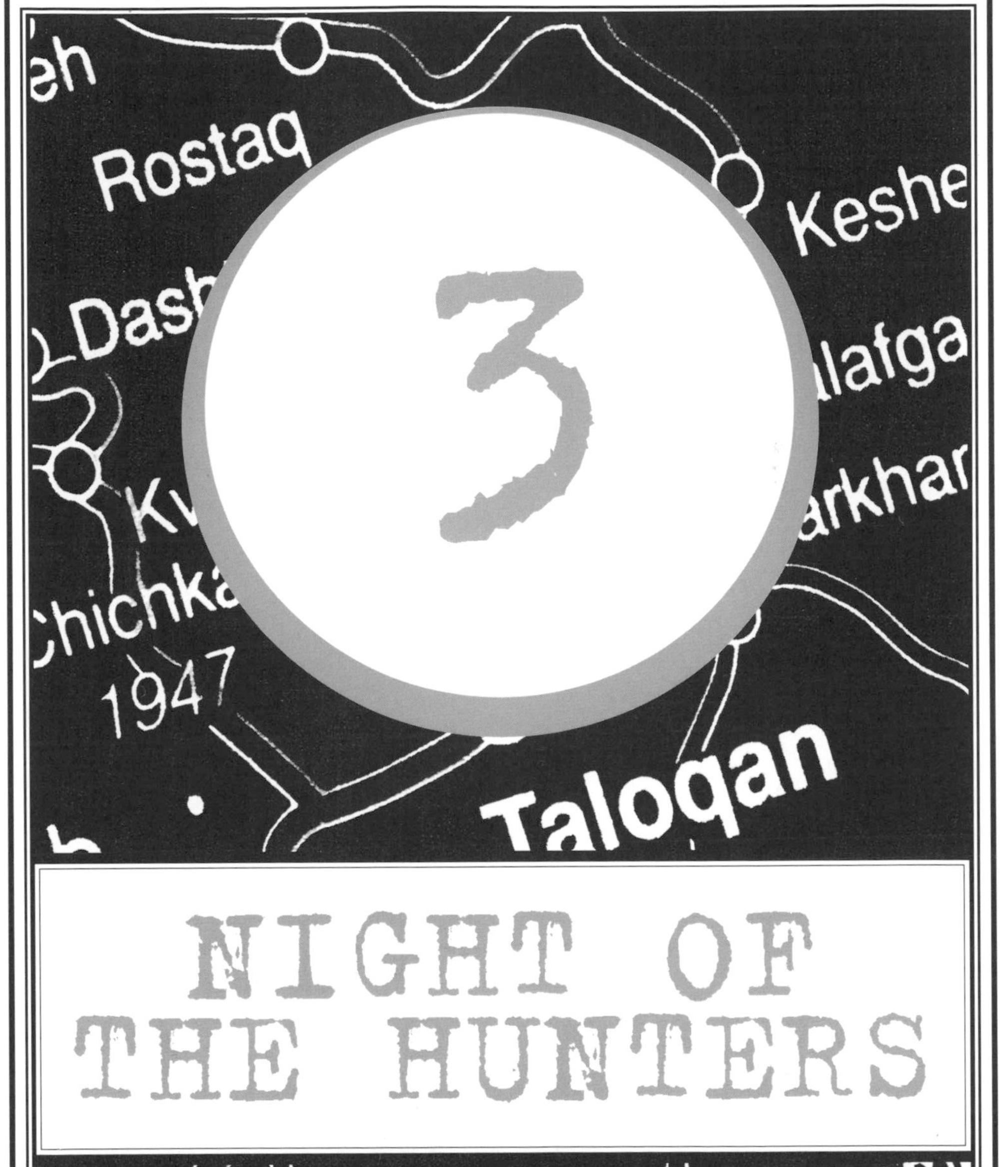
eh
Rostaq
Keshe
Dash
alafga
arkhar
Kv
Chichka
1947
Taloqan

3

NIGHT OF THE HUNTERS

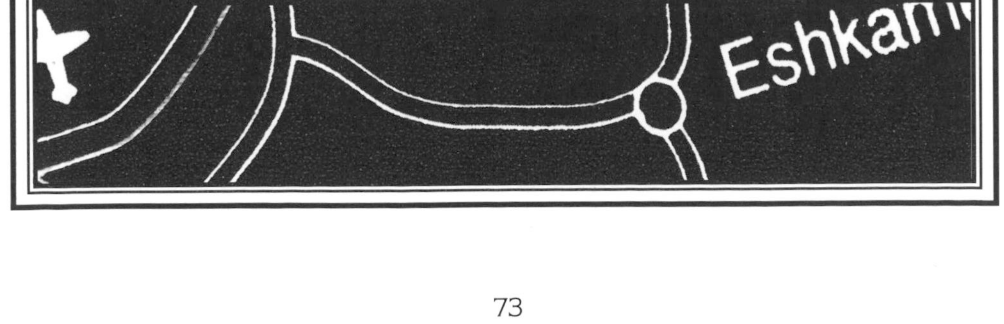
Eshkam

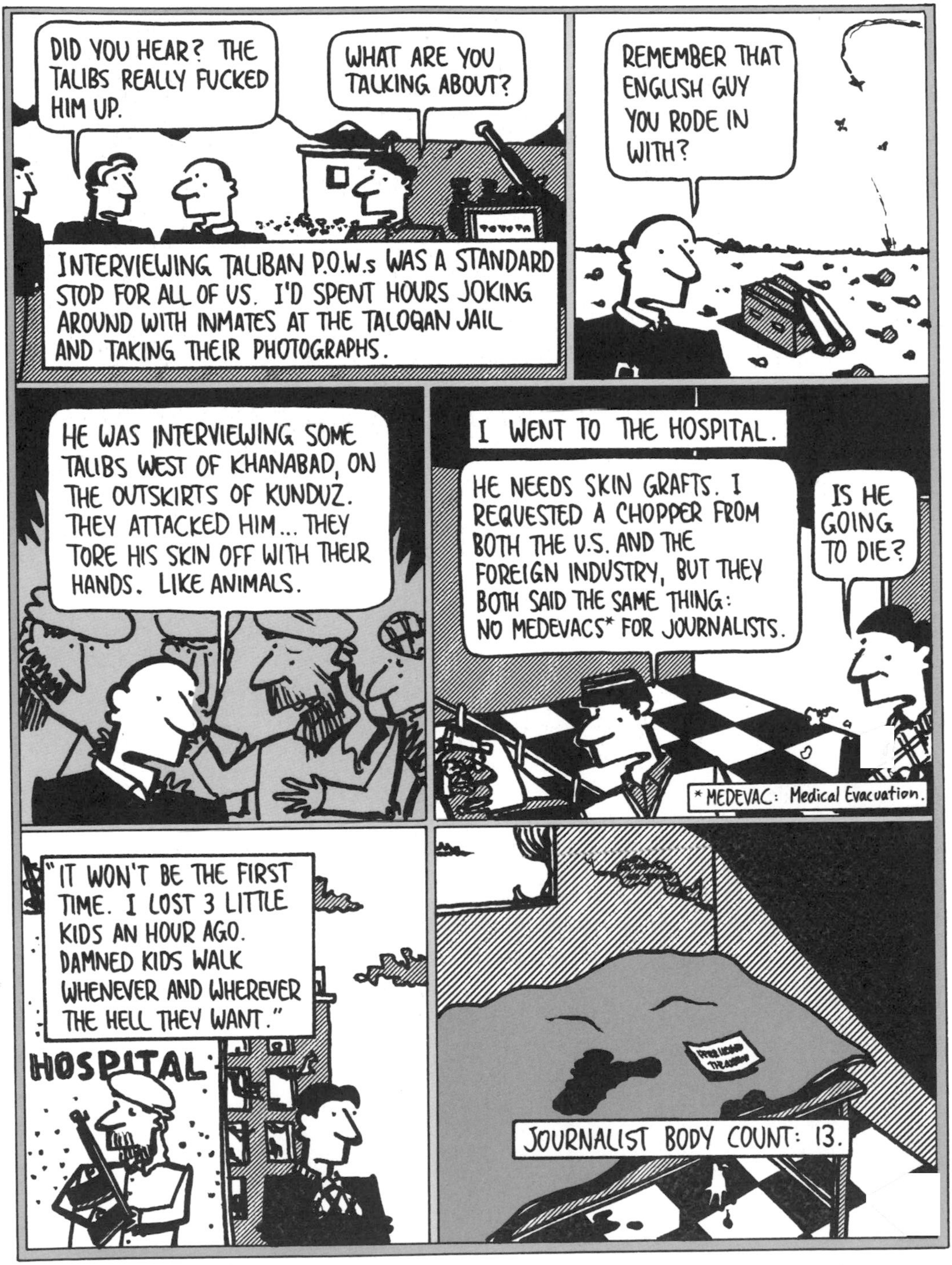
DID YOU HEAR? THE TALIBS REALLY FUCKED HIM UP.
WHAT ARE YOU TALKING ABOUT?
INTERVIEWING TALIBAN P.O.W.s WAS A STANDARD STOP FOR ALL OF US. I'D SPENT HOURS JOKING AROUND WITH INMATES AT THE TALOQAN JAIL AND TAKING THEIR PHOTOGRAPHS.
REMEMBER THAT ENGLISH GUY YOU RODE IN WITH?
HE WAS INTERVIEWING SOME TALIBS WEST OF KHANABAD, ON THE OUTSKIRTS OF KUNDUZ. THEY ATTACKED HIM... THEY TORE HIS SKIN OFF WITH THEIR HANDS. LIKE ANIMALS.
I WENT TO THE HOSPITAL.
HE NEEDS SKIN GRAFTS. I REQUESTED A CHOPPER FROM BOTH THE U.S. AND THE FOREIGN INDUSTRY, BUT THEY BOTH SAID THE SAME THING: NO MEDEVACS* FOR JOURNALISTS.
IS HE GOING TO DIE?
*MEDEVAC: Medical Evacuation.
"IT WON'T BE THE FIRST TIME. I LOST 3 LITTLE KIDS AN HOUR AGO. DAMNED KIDS WALK WHENEVER AND WHEREVER THE HELL THEY WANT."
HOSPITAL
JOURNALIST BODY COUNT: 13.

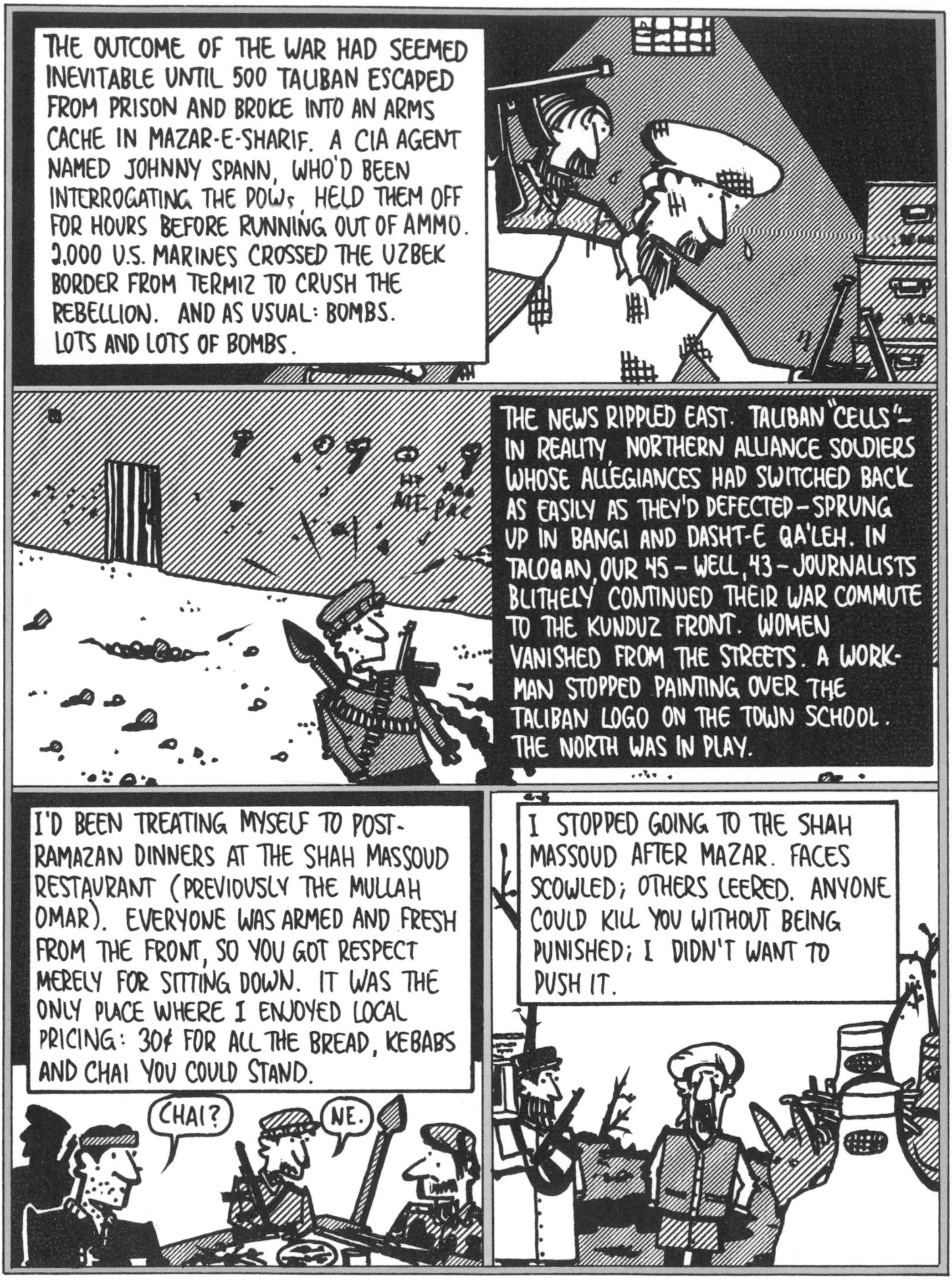
THE OUTCOME OF THE WAR HAD SEEMED INEVITABLE UNTIL 500 TALIBAN ESCAPED FROM PRISON AND BROKE INTO AN ARMS CACHE IN MAZAR-E-SHARIF. A CIA AGENT NAMED JOHNNY SPANN, WHO'D BEEN INTERROGATING THE POWs, HELD THEM OFF FOR HOURS BEFORE RUNNING OUT OF AMMO. 2,000 U.S. MARINES CROSSED THE UZBEK BORDER FROM TERMIZ TO CRUSH THE REBELLION. AND AS USUAL: BOMBS. LOTS AND LOTS OF BOMBS.
THE NEWS RIPPLED EAST. TALIBAN "CELLS"—IN REALITY, NORTHERN ALLIANCE SOLDIERS WHOSE ALLEGIANCES HAD SWITCHED BACK AS EASILY AS THEY'D DEFECTED—SPRUNG UP IN BANGI AND DASHT-E QA'LEH. IN TALOQAN, OUR 45—WELL, 43—JOURNALISTS BLITHELY CONTINUED THEIR WAR COMMUTE TO THE KUNDUZ FRONT. WOMEN VANISHED FROM THE STREETS. A WORKMAN STOPPED PAINTING OVER THE TALIBAN LOGO ON THE TOWN SCHOOL. THE NORTH WAS IN PLAY.
I'D BEEN TREATING MYSELF TO POST-RAMAZAN DINNERS AT THE SHAH MASSOUD RESTAURANT (PREVIOUSLY THE MULLAH OMAR). EVERYONE WAS ARMED AND FRESH FROM THE FRONT, SO YOU GOT RESPECT MERELY FOR SITTING DOWN. IT WAS THE ONLY PLACE WHERE I ENJOYED LOCAL PRICING: 30¢ FOR ALL THE BREAD, KEBABS AND CHAI YOU COULD STAND.
CHAI?
NE.
I STOPPED GOING TO THE SHAH MASSOUD AFTER MAZAR. FACES SCOWLED; OTHERS LEERED. ANYONE COULD KILL YOU WITHOUT BEING PUNISHED; I DIDN'T WANT TO PUSH IT.

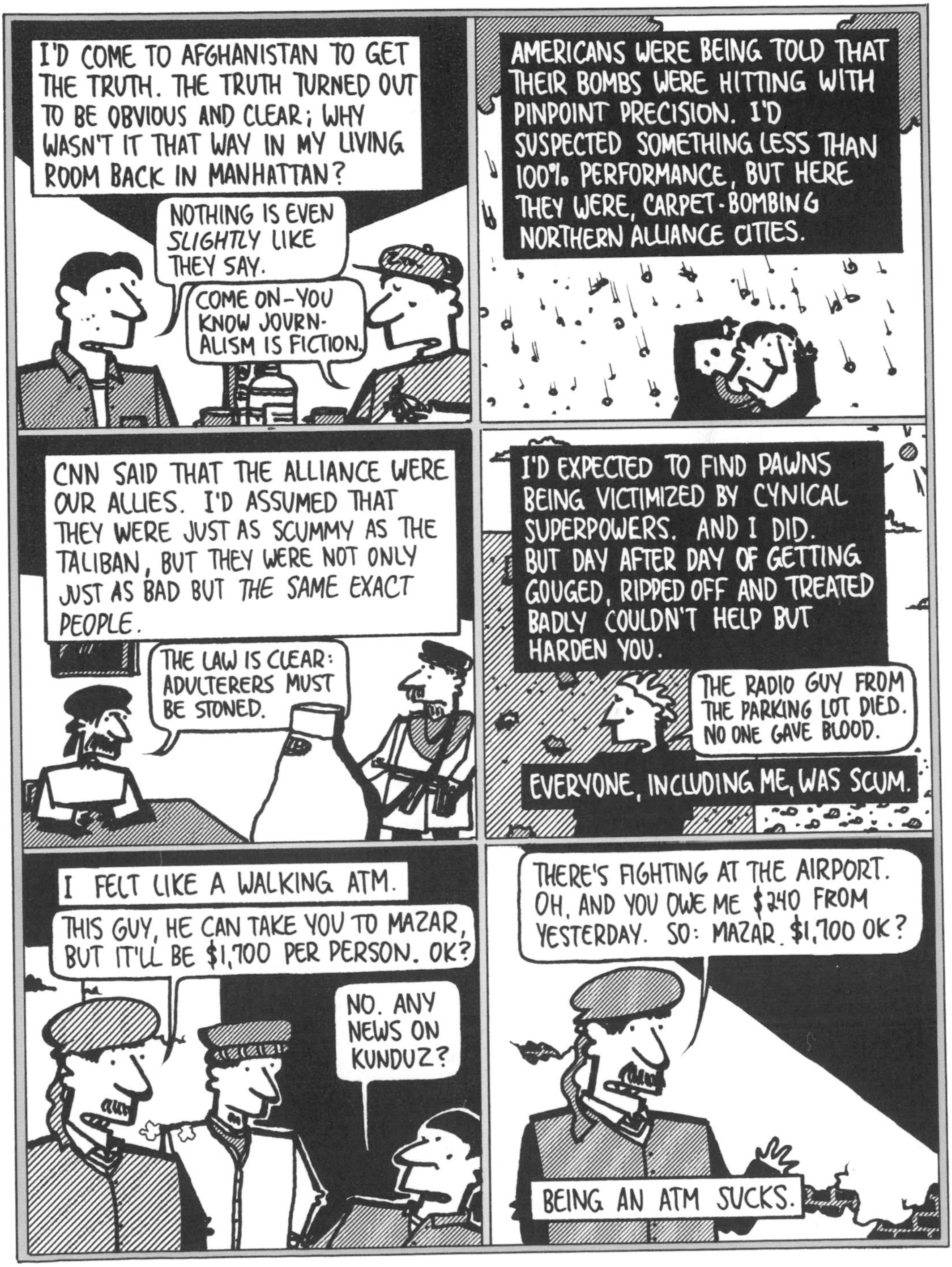
I'D COME TO AFGHANISTAN TO GET THE TRUTH. THE TRUTH TURNED OUT TO BE OBVIOUS AND CLEAR; WHY WASN'T IT THAT WAY IN MY LIVING ROOM BACK IN MANHATTAN?
NOTHING IS EVEN SLIGHTLY LIKE THEY SAY.
COME ON—YOU KNOW JOURNALISM IS FICTION.
AMERICANS WERE BEING TOLD THAT THEIR BOMBS WERE HITTING WITH PINPOINT PRECISION. I'D SUSPECTED SOMETHING LESS THAN 100% PERFORMANCE, BUT HERE THEY WERE, CARPET-BOMBING NORTHERN ALLIANCE CITIES.
CNN SAID THAT THE ALLIANCE WERE OUR ALLIES. I'D ASSUMED THAT THEY WERE JUST AS SCUMMY AS THE TALIBAN, BUT THEY WERE NOT ONLY JUST AS BAD BUT THE SAME EXACT PEOPLE.
THE LAW IS CLEAR: ADULTERERS MUST BE STONED.
I'D EXPECTED TO FIND PAWNS BEING VICTIMIZED BY CYNICAL SUPERPOWERS. AND I DID. BUT DAY AFTER DAY OF GETTING GOUGED, RIPPED OFF AND TREATED BADLY COULDN'T HELP BUT HARDEN YOU.
THE RADIO GUY FROM THE PARKING LOT DIED. NO ONE GAVE BLOOD.
EVERYONE, INCLUDING ME, WAS SCUM.
I FELT LIKE A WALKING ATM.
THIS GUY, HE CAN TAKE YOU TO MAZAR, BUT IT'LL BE $1,700 PER PERSON. OK?
NO. ANY NEWS ON KUNDUZ?
THERE'S FIGHTING AT THE AIRPORT. OH, AND YOU OWE ME $240 FROM YESTERDAY. SO: MAZAR. $1,700 OK?
BEING AN ATM SUCKS.

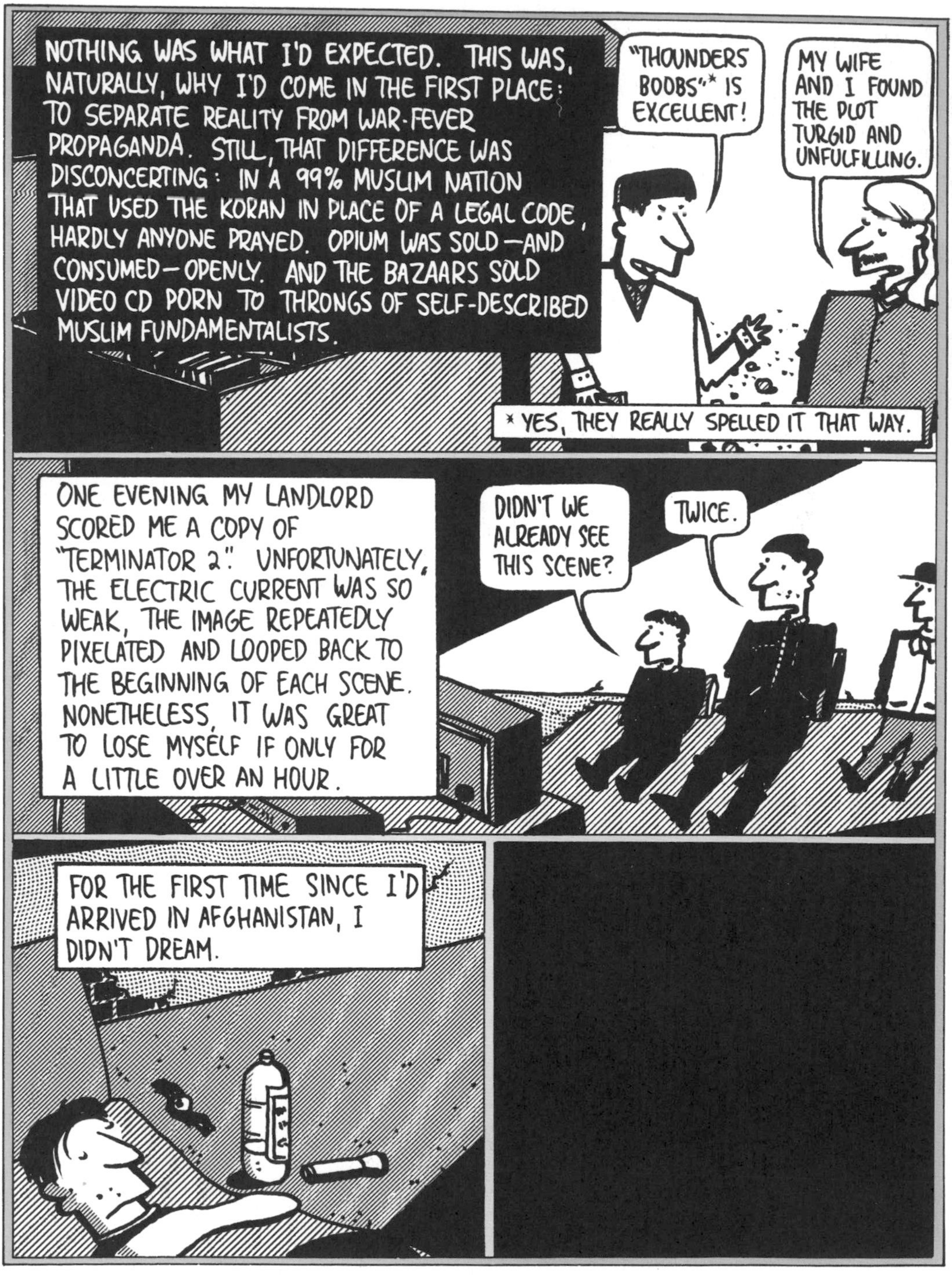
NOTHING WAS WHAT I'D EXPECTED. THIS WAS, NATURALLY, WHY I'D COME IN THE FIRST PLACE: TO SEPARATE REALITY FROM WAR-FEVER PROPAGANDA. STILL, THAT DIFFERENCE WAS DISCONCERTING: IN A 99% MUSLIM NATION THAT USED THE KORAN IN PLACE OF A LEGAL CODE, HARDLY ANYONE PRAYED. OPIUM WAS SOLD—AND CONSUMED—OPENLY. AND THE BAZAARS SOLD VIDEO CD PORN TO THRONGS OF SELF-DESCRIBED MUSLIM FUNDAMENTALISTS.
"THOUNDERS BOOBS"* IS EXCELLENT!
MY WIFE AND I FOUND THE PLOT TURGID AND UNFULFILLING.
* YES, THEY REALLY SPELLED IT THAT WAY.
ONE EVENING MY LANDLORD SCORED ME A COPY OF "TERMINATOR 2". UNFORTUNATELY, THE ELECTRIC CURRENT WAS SO WEAK, THE IMAGE REPEATEDLY PIXELATED AND LOOPED BACK TO THE BEGINNING OF EACH SCENE. NONETHELESS, IT WAS GREAT TO LOSE MYSELF IF ONLY FOR A LITTLE OVER AN HOUR.
DIDN'T WE ALREADY SEE THIS SCENE?
TWICE.
FOR THE FIRST TIME SINCE I'D ARRIVED IN AFGHANISTAN, I DIDN'T DREAM.

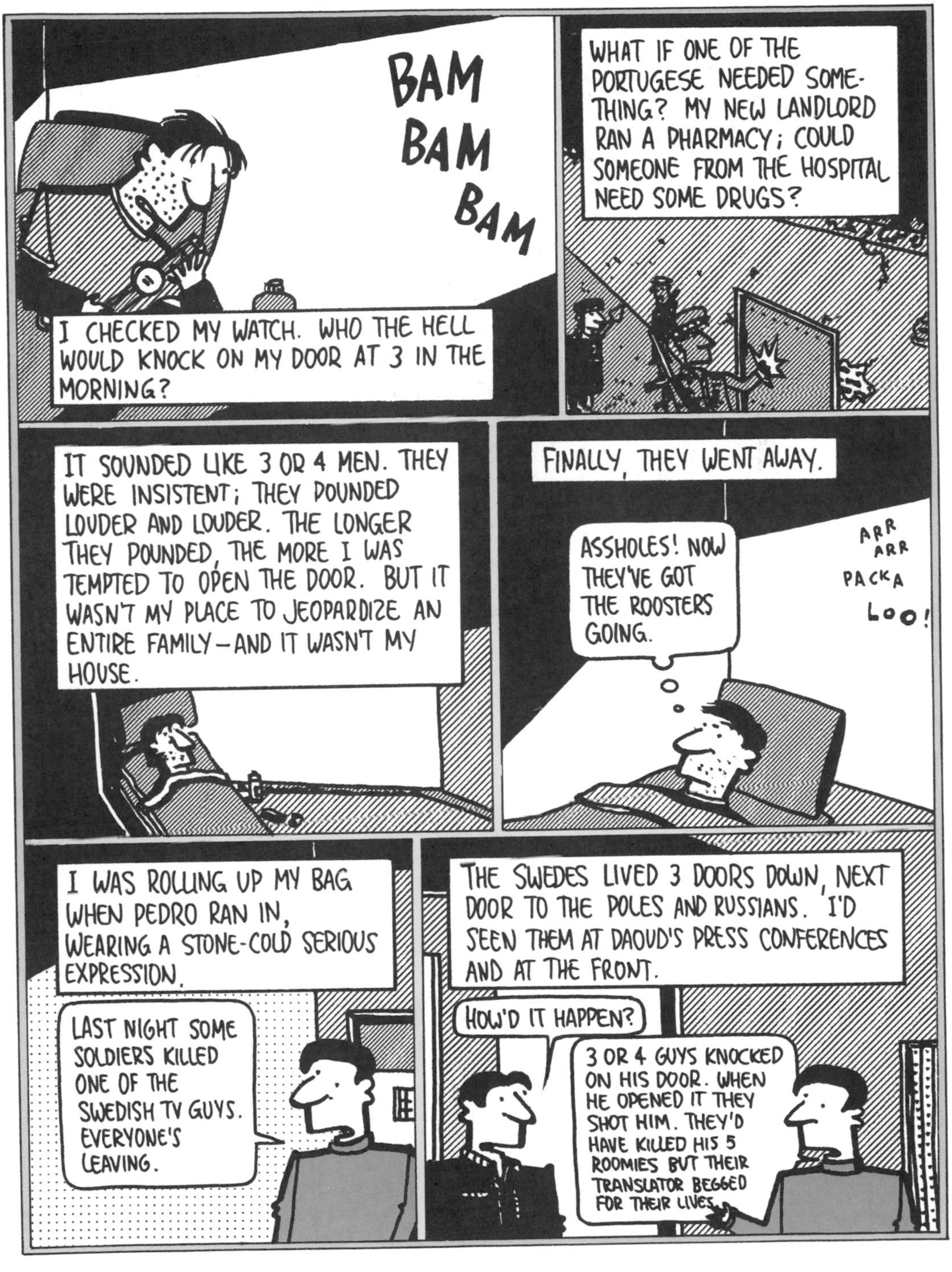
BAM
BAM
BAM
I CHECKED MY WATCH. WHO THE HELL WOULD KNOCK ON MY DOOR AT 3 IN THE MORNING?
WHAT IF ONE OF THE PORTUGESE NEEDED SOMETHING? MY NEW LANDLORD RAN A PHARMACY; COULD SOMEONE FROM THE HOSPITAL NEED SOME DRUGS?
IT SOUNDED LIKE 3 OR 4 MEN. THEY WERE INSISTENT; THEY POUNDED LOUDER AND LOUDER. THE LONGER THEY POUNDED, THE MORE I WAS TEMPTED TO OPEN THE DOOR. BUT IT WASN'T MY PLACE TO JEOPARDIZE AN ENTIRE FAMILY—AND IT WASN'T MY HOUSE.
FINALLY, THEY WENT AWAY.
ASSHOLES! NOW THEY'VE GOT THE ROOSTERS GOING.
ARR ARR PACKA LOO!
I WAS ROLLING UP MY BAG WHEN PEDRO RAN IN, WEARING A STONE-COLD SERIOUS EXPRESSION.
LAST NIGHT SOME SOLDIERS KILLED ONE OF THE SWEDISH TV GUYS. EVERYONE'S LEAVING.
THE SWEDES LIVED 3 DOORS DOWN, NEXT DOOR TO THE POLES AND RUSSIANS. I'D SEEN THEM AT DAOUD'S PRESS CONFERENCES AND AT THE FRONT.
HOW'D IT HAPPEN?
3 OR 4 GUYS KNOCKED ON HIS DOOR. WHEN HE OPENED IT THEY SHOT HIM. THEY'D HAVE KILLED HIS 5 ROOMIES BUT THEIR TRANSLATOR BEGGED FOR THEIR LIVES.

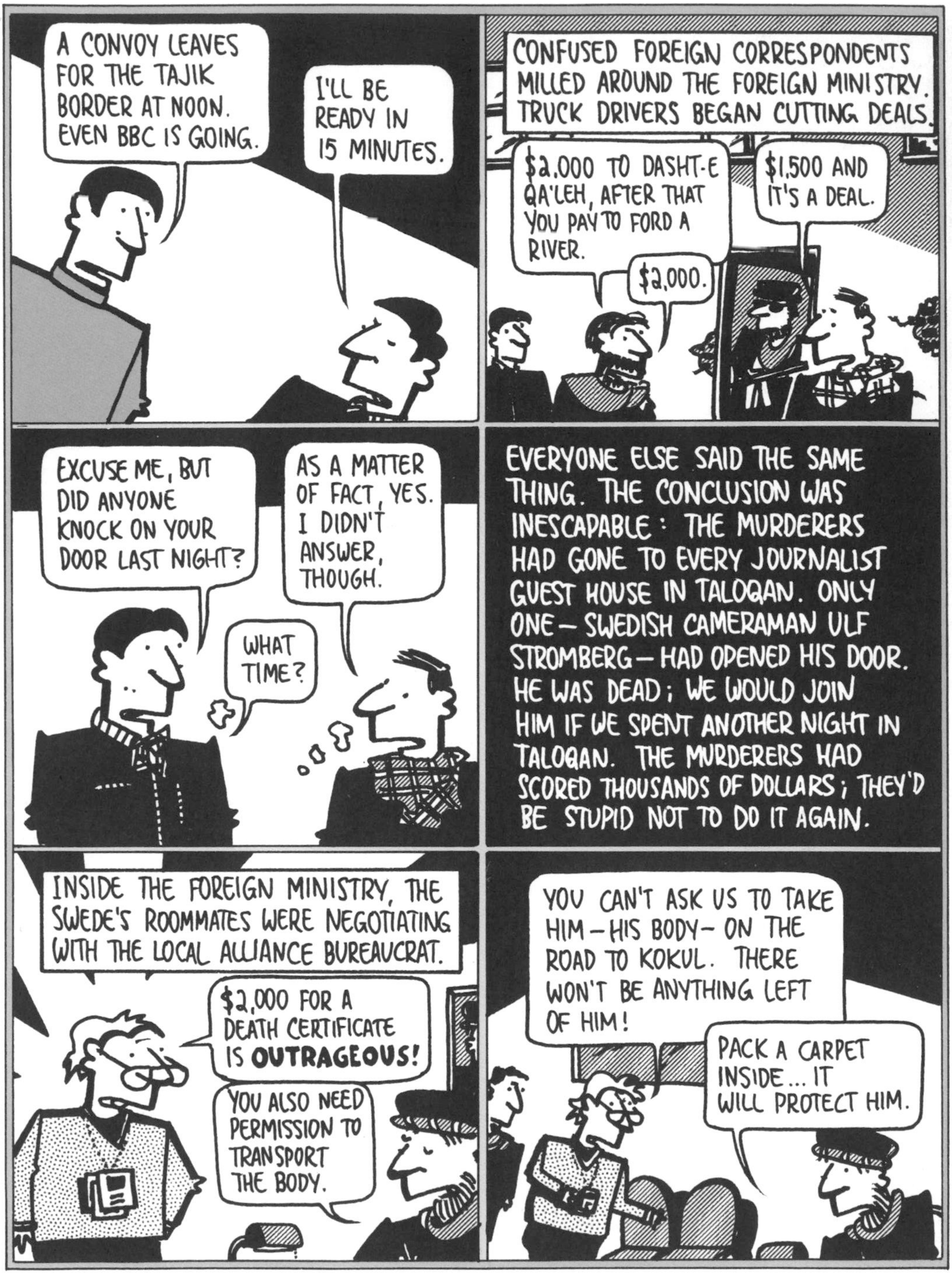
A CONVOY LEAVES FOR THE TAJIK BORDER AT NOON. EVEN BBC IS GOING.
I'LL BE READY IN 15 MINUTES.
CONFUSED FOREIGN CORRESPONDENTS MILLED AROUND THE FOREIGN MINISTRY. TRUCK DRIVERS BEGAN CUTTING DEALS.
$2,000 TO DASHT-E QA'LEH, AFTER THAT YOU PAY TO FORD A RIVER.
$2,000.
$1,500 AND IT'S A DEAL.
EXCUSE ME, BUT DID ANYONE KNOCK ON YOUR DOOR LAST NIGHT?
AS A MATTER OF FACT, YES. I DIDN'T ANSWER, THOUGH.
WHAT TIME?
EVERYONE ELSE SAID THE SAME THING. THE CONCLUSION WAS INESCAPABLE: THE MURDERERS HAD GONE TO EVERY JOURNALIST GUEST HOUSE IN TALOQAN. ONLY ONE—SWEDISH CAMERAMAN ULF STROMBERG—HAD OPENED HIS DOOR. HE WAS DEAD; WE WOULD JOIN HIM IF WE SPENT ANOTHER NIGHT IN TALOQAN. THE MURDERERS HAD SCORED THOUSANDS OF DOLLARS; THEY'D BE STUPID NOT TO DO IT AGAIN.
INSIDE THE FOREIGN MINISTRY, THE SWEDE'S ROOMMATES WERE NEGOTIATING WITH THE LOCAL ALLIANCE BUREAUCRAT.
$2,000 FOR A DEATH CERTIFICATE IS OUTRAGEOUS!
YOU ALSO NEED PERMISSION TO TRANSPORT THE BODY.
YOU CAN'T ASK US TO TAKE HIM—HIS BODY—ON THE ROAD TO KOKUL. THERE WON'T BE ANYTHING LEFT OF HIM!
PACK A CARPET INSIDE... IT WILL PROTECT HIM.

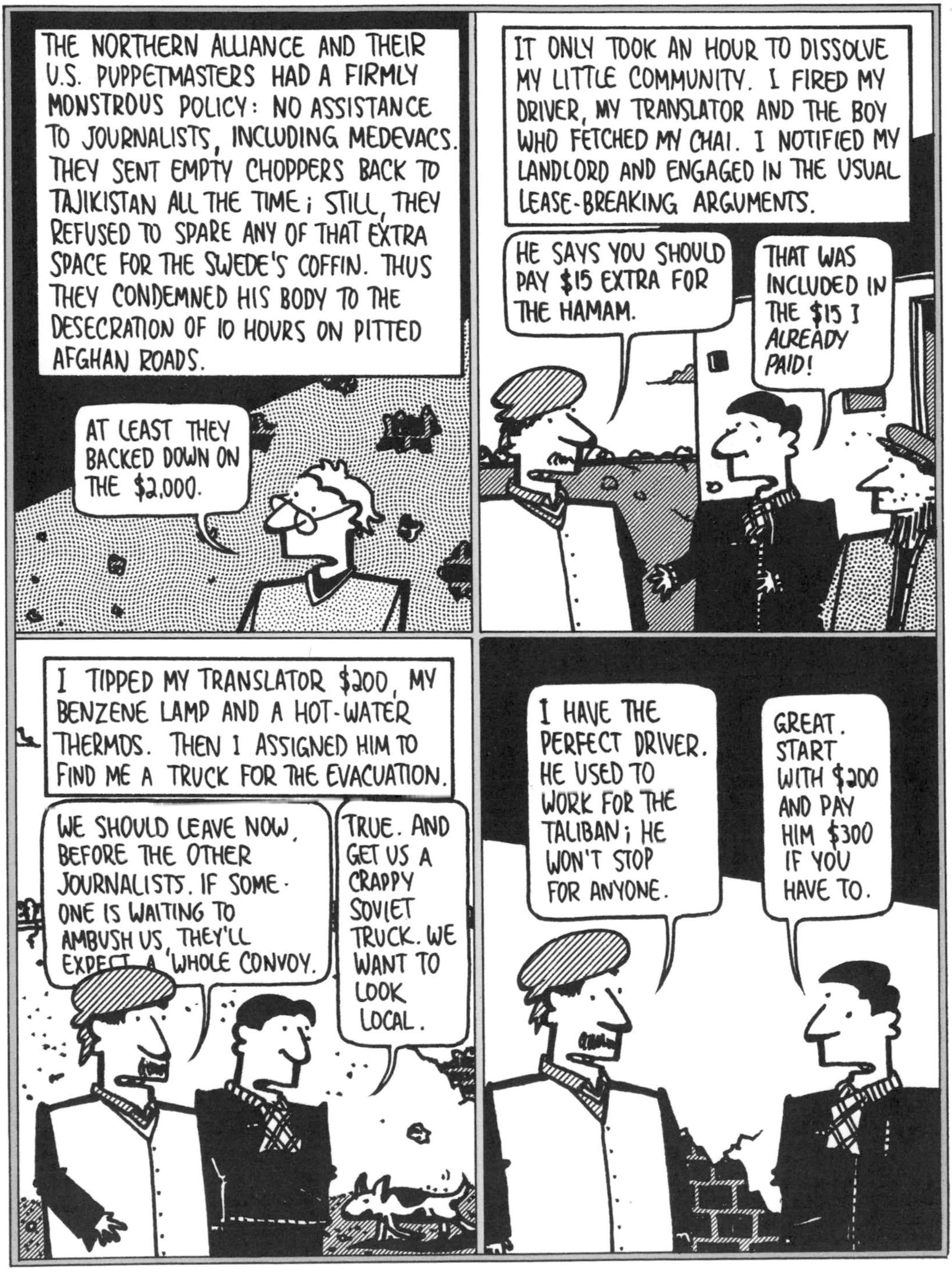
THE NORTHERN ALLIANCE AND THEIR U.S. PUPPETMASTERS HAD A FIRMLY MONSTROUS POLICY: NO ASSISTANCE TO JOURNALISTS, INCLUDING MEDEVACS. THEY SENT EMPTY CHOPPERS BACK TO TAJIKISTAN ALL THE TIME; STILL, THEY REFUSED TO SPARE ANY OF THAT EXTRA SPACE FOR THE SWEDE'S COFFIN. THUS THEY CONDEMNED HIS BODY TO THE DESECRATION OF 10 HOURS ON PITTED AFGHAN ROADS.
AT LEAST THEY BACKED DOWN ON THE $2,000.
IT ONLY TOOK AN HOUR TO DISSOLVE MY LITTLE COMMUNITY. I FIRED MY DRIVER, MY TRANSLATOR AND THE BOY WHO FETCHED MY CHAI. I NOTIFIED MY LANDLORD AND ENGAGED IN THE USUAL LEASE-BREAKING ARGUMENTS.
HE SAYS YOU SHOULD PAY $15 EXTRA FOR THE HAMAM.
THAT WAS INCLUDED IN THE $15 I ALREADY PAID!
I TIPPED MY TRANSLATOR $200, MY BENZENE LAMP AND A HOT-WATER THERMOS. THEN I ASSIGNED HIM TO FIND ME A TRUCK FOR THE EVACUATION.
WE SHOULD LEAVE NOW, BEFORE THE OTHER JOURNALISTS. IF SOMEONE IS WAITING TO AMBUSH US, THEY'LL EXPECT A WHOLE CONVOY.
TRUE. AND GET US A CRAPPY SOVIET TRUCK. WE WANT TO LOOK LOCAL.
I HAVE THE PERFECT DRIVER. HE USED TO WORK FOR THE TALIBAN; HE WON'T STOP FOR ANYONE.
GREAT. START WITH $200 AND PAY HIM $300 IF YOU HAVE TO.

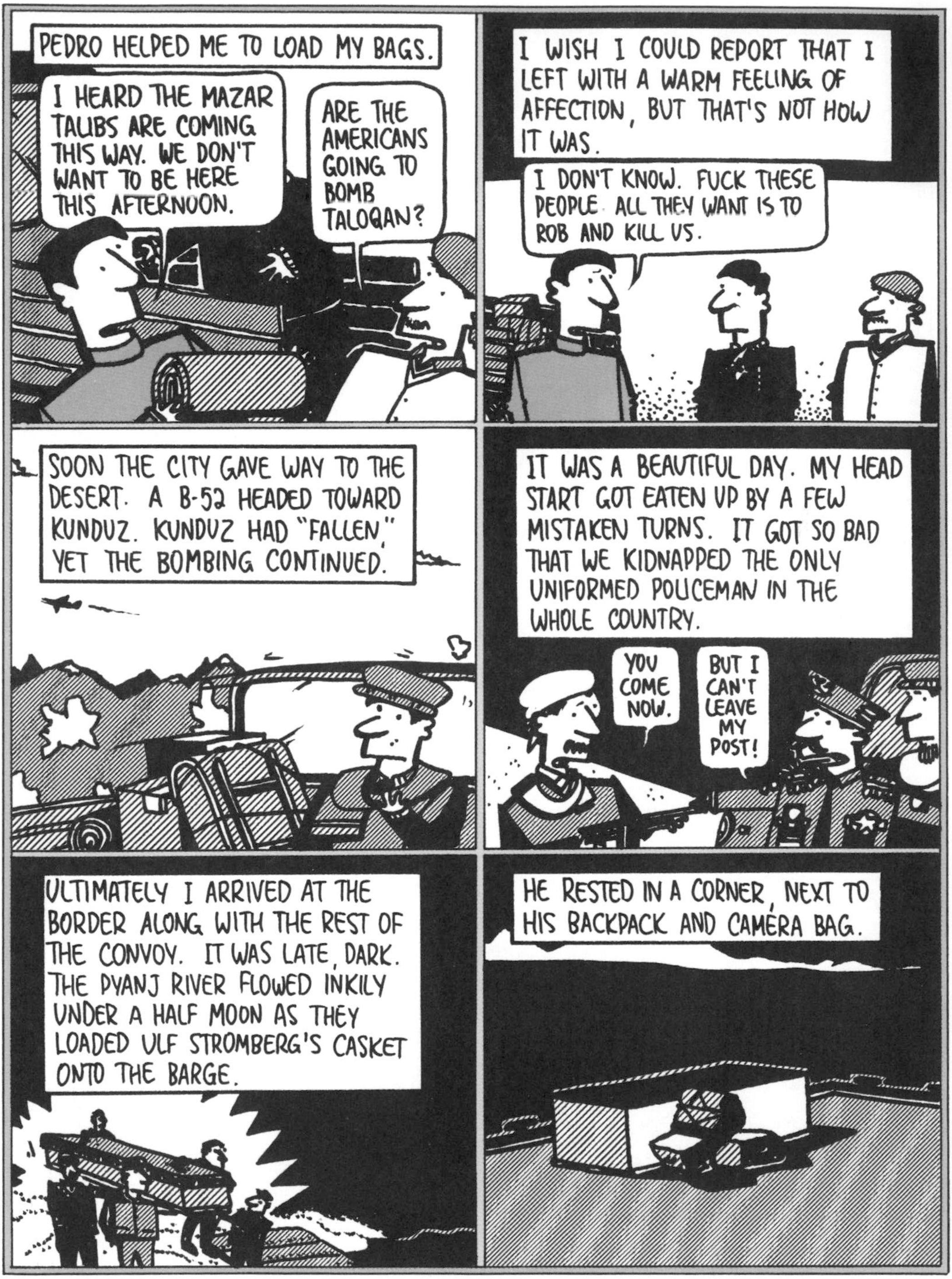
PEDRO HELPED ME TO LOAD MY BAGS.
I HEARD THE MAZAR TALIBS ARE COMING THIS WAY. WE DON'T WANT TO BE HERE THIS AFTERNOON.
ARE THE AMERICANS GOING TO BOMB TALOQAN?
I WISH I COULD REPORT THAT I LEFT WITH A WARM FEELING OF AFFECTION, BUT THAT'S NOT HOW IT WAS.
I DON'T KNOW. FUCK THESE PEOPLE. ALL THEY WANT IS TO ROB AND KILL US.
SOON THE CITY GAVE WAY TO THE DESERT. A B-52 HEADED TOWARD KUNDUZ. KUNDUZ HAD "FALLEN," YET THE BOMBING CONTINUED.
IT WAS A BEAUTIFUL DAY. MY HEAD START GOT EATEN UP BY A FEW MISTAKEN TURNS. IT GOT SO BAD THAT WE KIDNAPPED THE ONLY UNIFORMED POLICEMAN IN THE WHOLE COUNTRY.
YOU COME NOW.
BUT I CAN'T LEAVE MY POST!
ULTIMATELY I ARRIVED AT THE BORDER ALONG WITH THE REST OF THE CONVOY. IT WAS LATE, DARK. THE PYANJ RIVER FLOWED INKILY UNDER A HALF MOON AS THEY LOADED ULF STROMBERG'S CASKET ONTO THE BARGE.
HE RESTED IN A CORNER, NEXT TO HIS BACKPACK AND CAMERA BAG.

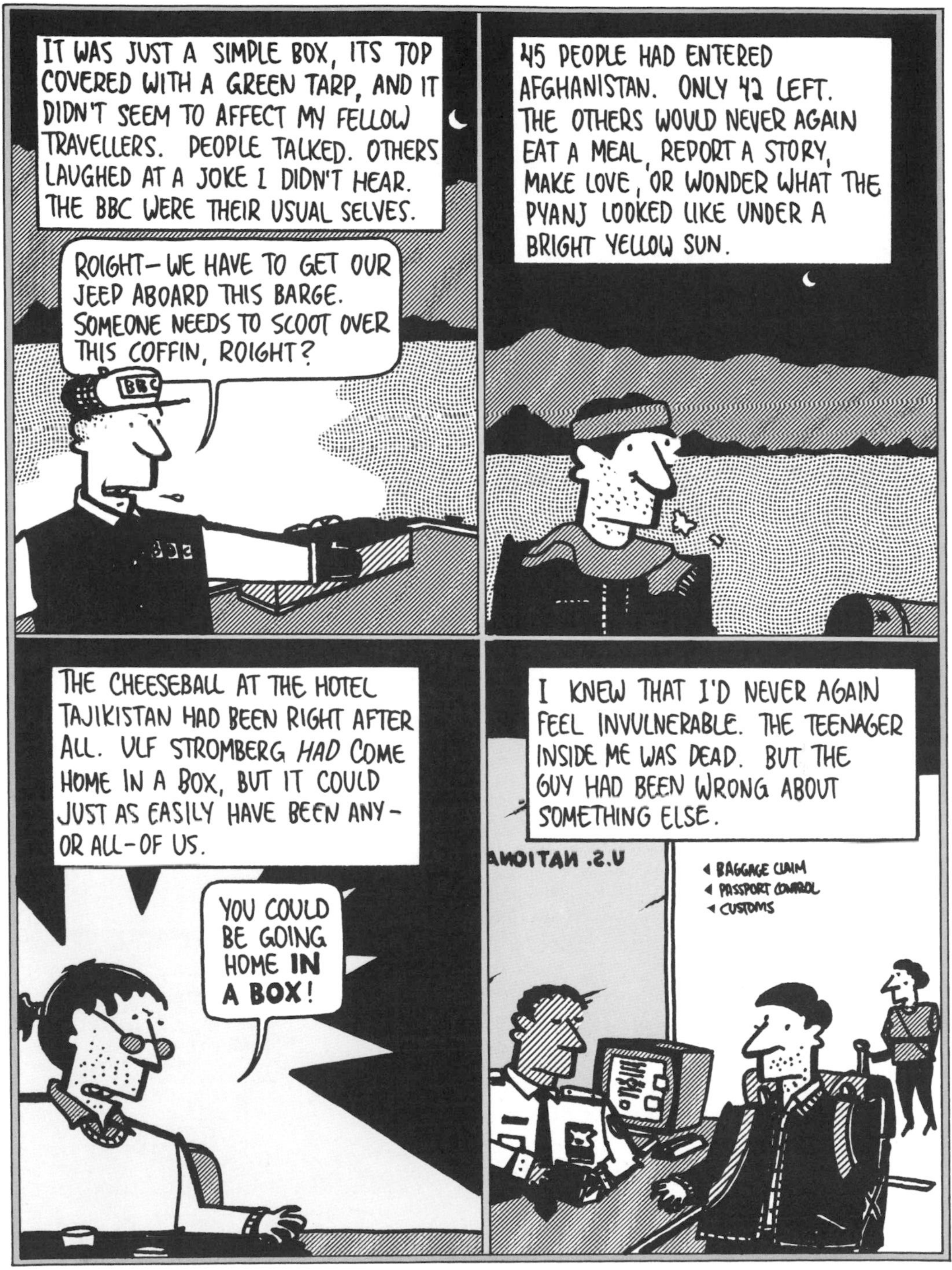
IT WAS JUST A SIMPLE BOX, ITS TOP COVERED WITH A GREEN TARP, AND IT DIDN'T SEEM TO AFFECT MY FELLOW TRAVELLERS. PEOPLE TALKED. OTHERS LAUGHED AT A JOKE I DIDN'T HEAR. THE BBC WERE THEIR USUAL SELVES.
ROIGHT– WE HAVE TO GET OUR JEEP ABOARD THIS BARGE. SOMEONE NEEDS TO SCOOT OVER THIS COFFIN, ROIGHT?
BBC
45 PEOPLE HAD ENTERED AFGHANISTAN. ONLY 42 LEFT. THE OTHERS WOULD NEVER AGAIN EAT A MEAL, REPORT A STORY, MAKE LOVE, OR WONDER WHAT THE PYANJ LOOKED LIKE UNDER A BRIGHT YELLOW SUN.
THE CHEESEBALL AT THE HOTEL TAJIKISTAN HAD BEEN RIGHT AFTER ALL. ULF STROMBERG *HAD* COME HOME IN A BOX, BUT IT COULD JUST AS EASILY HAVE BEEN ANY– OR ALL– OF US.
YOU COULD BE GOING HOME **IN A BOX**!
I KNEW THAT I'D NEVER AGAIN FEEL INVULNERABLE. THE TEENAGER INSIDE ME WAS DEAD. BUT THE GUY HAD BEEN WRONG ABOUT SOMETHING ELSE.
U.S. NATIONA
◂ BAGGAGE CLAIM
◂ PASSPORT CONTROL
◂ CUSTOMS

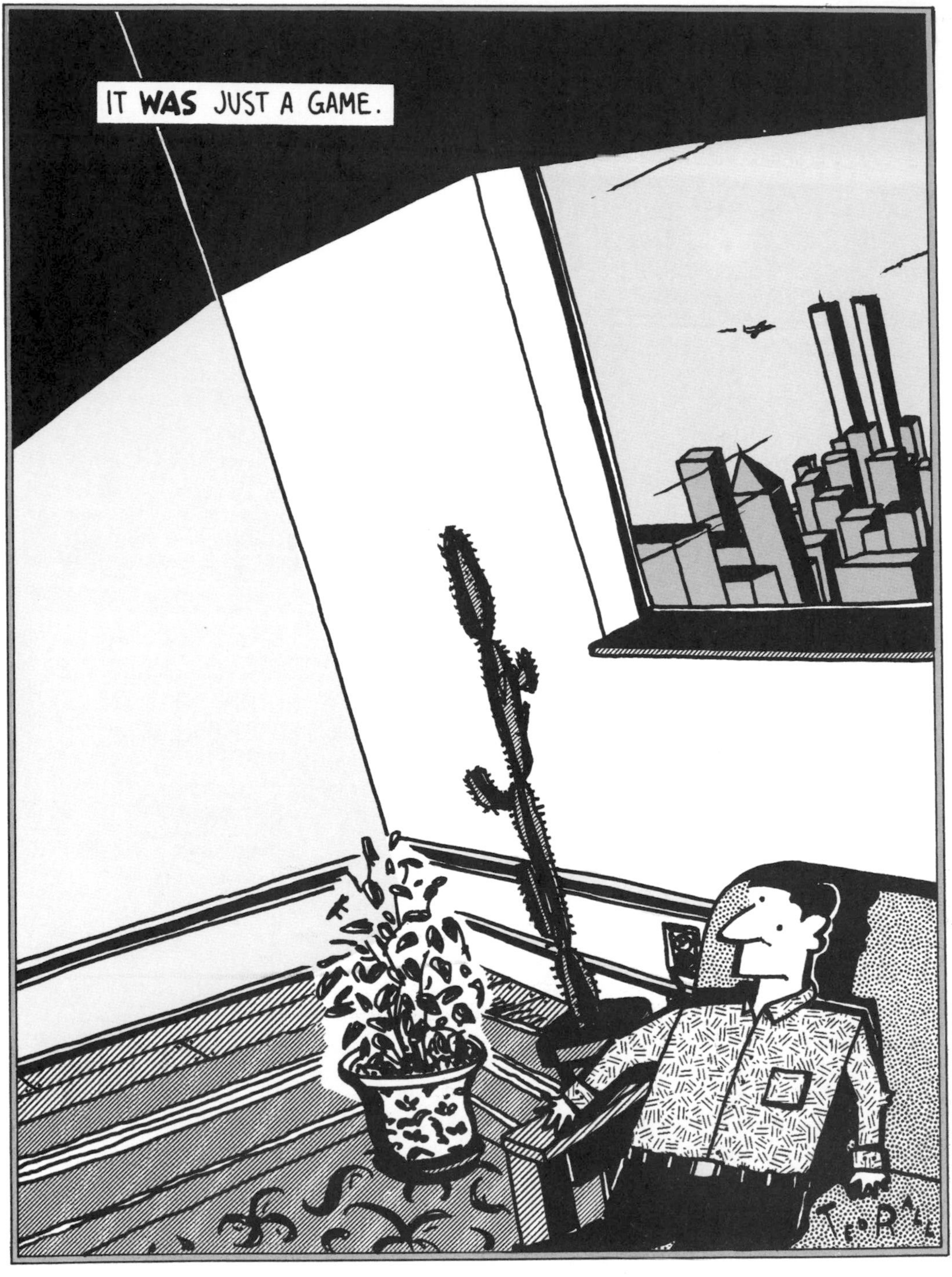
IT WAS JUST A GAME.
TED RALL

7. Taliban Family Values

KHANABAD, AFGHANISTAN, December 5

For several weeks the little boy soldiers and journalist war tourists lurked at a curve in the highway a few kilometers east of Kunduz, waiting for things to open up. American bombs had driven the Taliban and their law-and-order-at-any-price mores to their southern redoubt in Kandahar. All that stood in the way of the Northern Alliance becoming the government of North Afghanistan was an estimated 30,000 diehard Talibs holed up in the otherwise uninteresting provincial capital down the dusty road.

Modern warfare, even in preindustrial Afghanistan, requires asphalt. The road that goes west from the Northern Alliance stronghold of Taloqan to Kunduz continues on to Mazar-e-Sharif, the largest city north of the Hindu Kush. The Alliance needs Mazar in order to get U.S. weapons and troops across the Uzbek border at Termiz, and to run supplies down to Kabul and west to Herat on the Iranian border along the nation's main highway, the A76—one of the five paved roads in the whole joint. You need Kunduz to keep Mazar to keep Kabul to keep from becoming the main event at someone else's mass-execution fiesta.

Traditional Afghan treachery kept the siege entertaining. One Taliban surrender offer after another was followed by torrents of gunfire aimed at their would-be conquerors. "This unacceptable behavior is the influence of the Pakistanis, Chechens, and other foreign elements among the Taliban," Alliance general Daoud announced sternly. "These Arabs will be sent before a judge and executed."

This being Afghanistan, where the only truth is that everything is a lie, nothing of the sort occurred. The Pakistanis flew back home, possibly to rejoin Osama bin Laden's beleaguered but well-funded posse (most Afghans believe that he fled to Kashmir months ago, more likely than not with the help of the C.I.A.), causing many Western media types to wonder aloud whether the Alliance was maturing into the kind of realistic entity that could govern and unify this quintessentially unruly place. Afghans, on the other hand, recognized their new government slipping back into its old ways. Once again, lawlessness, even murder, was going utterly unpunished.

Before George W. Bush decided to avenge September 11th by reordering the Afghan

Women in Burqas, Khanabad. Despite Western news reports, Afghan women continued to wear their veils under Northern Alliance rule.

political landscape with daisy-cutter bombs, the Northern Alliance was an internationally recognized government with hardly any territory to its name. President Burhanuddin Rabbani's Islamic State of Afghanistan had presided in Kabul from 1992 until the 1996 rise of the Taliban, but constant civil war between Rabbani and two warlords, Abdul Rashid Dostum and Gulbuddin Hekmatyar, caused even more devastation than the Soviet war and plunged the country into anarchy.

Though at the price of personal freedom, most famously for the women who were transformed into null social factors, the Taliban's fierce brand of discipline was welcomed by most Afghans when they pushed Rabbani's gang into internal exile in Badakhshan province in the mountainous northeast near the Chinese border. Most people expected the Taliban to finish off the Alliance and its five percent share of real estate by 2002 at the latest. World Trade, saturation bombing, and the traditional preternatural ability of Afghans to react to changing times with instantaneous personal reinvention turned that 95 to 5 equation upside-down in just a month. The Northern Alliance didn't so much conquer Afghanistan as buy it with your tax dollars.

Despite the usual human rights concerns, a few hundred P.O.W.s executed here and there, Alliance troops mainly behaved themselves fairly decently by the admittedly lenient national standards. Even the renewal of factional infighting between Rabbani and Dostum over which army would rule Kunduz after the Taliban departed involved more words over tea than impressive explosions. The question was: Would that decorum devolve into the "Mad Max"-esque mayhem of the early '90s? And given how the Alliance came to capture so much of the country by simply having Talibs hit their local barber shops and trade in their turbans for Ahmad Shah Massoud trademark Nuristani hats, would the Alliance become Talibanized or vice versa, and what would any of it mean?

Even as shells were still flitting about Kunduz's main drag and dawdling Talibs were holding out at the airport three miles away, the answer became clear: In the New Afghanistan, anything goes. Kunduz's newly liberated bazaar, always a festival of free-wheeling capitalism in Central Asia, instantaneously assumed an even more manic tone. Until November 26, the notoriously violent officers of the Ministry for the Promotion of Virtue and the Prevention of Vice (or, informally, the Religious Police) thrashed and jailed men whose beards were too short and women whose burqas showed a little ankle. On the 27th, for 300,000 afghanis (about $5) you could rent a TV, DVD player, and a grab bag of discs of dubious parentage overnight. Television, banned by the eminently uptight Taliban as decadent and foreign, had survived its rule in secret stashes. But now the titles have expanded from such third-world staples as Schwarzenegger's "Commando" and Van Damme's "Universal Soldier" to "Thounders Boobs" (sic), "Climaxic Dyldoos" (sic), and for mujaheddin whose sexual preferences extend beyond or in lieu of their permitted four wives, "Manroot, Twice as Long."

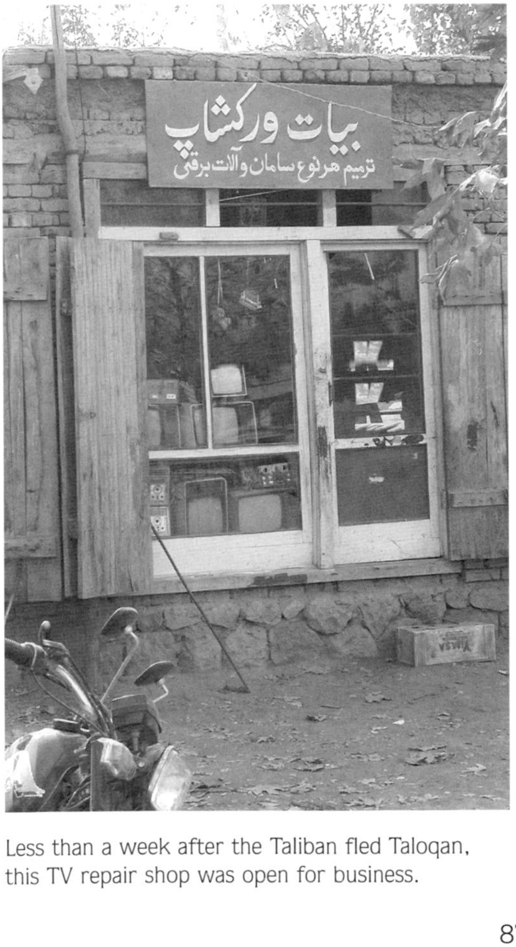
بیات ورکشاپ
ترمیم هرنوع سامان وآلات برقی
Less than a week after the Taliban fled Taloqan, this TV repair shop was open for business.

"You should see 'Thounders Boobs,' my 20-year-old translator, Jovid, told me. "It really is quite excellent." No "Manroot" for him.

Certainly any society that fetishizes women by cloistering them even when they're walking down the street—that much certainly hasn't changed, even in the cities—offers a natural market for dirty-movie entrepreneurs. But the post-Taliban sex life of Afghans is transforming more than just their wet dreams.

Many Afghans are doing the unthinkable: They're dating, or to be more specific, fucking without permission. A week and a half ago, the only way you could

Taliban logo being painted over at a school. They waited a week to be sure the Taliban weren't coming back.

get laid here was to get hitched to your parents' friends' child—and you never got to see what was behind door number one until it was too late. People dodged this convention occasionally, but if they got caught by the Religious Police they were offered an uncomfortable choice—being stoned to death or buried alive. "If I want her to come to me, she does," Jovid confided about his girlfriend. Neither of their parents know about this "secret love."

"Do you two have sex?" I asked.

"Of course!" he brightened.

"And if she gets pregnant?"

"In Afghanistan this kind of relationship is just like marriage."

What a difference a few thousand cluster bombs make: Afghanistan has evolved from the Hephthalites and the Sassanids to "Home Fries" in 10 days. And it's not just the kids: Married women are getting busy on the side while their husbands kill their countrymen at the airport. "The important thing," one thirtyish woman said, "is for him not to know about your secret love."

This brought up an intriguing issue. What about prostitution? Not to worry, half a dozen unrelated sources assured me. Men were pimping their daughters to the highest bidder all over town. The going rate: $100 per night, and an impressive variety of ages and ethnicities—Uzbek, Hazara, you name it—were available.

Striking, about a culture condemned by Iran for taking Islam too far, is the fact that few Afghans deign to heed the call to prayer. In neighboring Pakistan, taxi drivers stop their cars in the middle of the street, whip out a prayer mat, and get busy chatting up Allah whenever a nearby loudspeaker belches out a mullah's beseeching cry; here no one even bothers to blink or roll their eyes as they line up at the bustling opium market to score some Friday night rhapsody to go along with a screening of "Thounders Boobs." No one is frying up a meal of pigs' feet wrapped in bacon, at least not yet, but that's more of a concession to regional culinary preferences than strict adherence to Islam.

Even the daytime Ramadan fast, the only aspect of the Muslim religion still universally observed after Taliban logos started getting painted over, fell by the wayside just days later. Countless vendors fired up their grills and began serving up beef and lamb kebabs to eager customers in mid afternoon. "Isn't that illegal?" I asked one such entrepreneur. "People are hungry," he shrugged. "They've been fasting all day."

Even that simplest of Muslim prohibitions, the stricture against drinking alcohol, is yesterday's news. "Please bring wine" is the second line you'll hear after being invited to dinner. The third is: "How about whiskey?" Supplies are sparse, but the way things are going, expect a fully stocked Cork-N-Bottle to open in Kunduz within minutes.

Petty thievery, punishable by amputation until late, has made an impressive comeback in this brave new world of no payback. Throngs of boys blowing off their *madrassa* studies to hang around the Afghan version of the mall bum-rush the slow, the dimwitted, and the foreign, dozens of little hands eagerly snatching watches from wrists and bundles of afghanis from pockets. Gap-toothed graybeards of 40—half the age you'd guess in America —chortle as these children of the corn grab burqaed butts and scamper off to shoplift Iranian sweaters and Chinese lighters.

The ample supply of opium here comes as a real mystery. About a year ago, the Taliban government had announced that Afghanistan, formerly exporter of half the world's heroin, had virtually eradicated its opium crop by the edict of Supreme Leader Mullah Mohammad Omar. The world didn't trust but did verify, and it turned out to be true. No one at the bazaar could explain where the bricks of brown paste had come from so quickly, but they didn't much care: "It is so much cheaper than food," a toothless codger reasoned.

While I talked to him, a fellow journalist arrived with breaking news: Taliban prisoners had tried to escape in Mazar-e-Sharif and were engaging U.S. and British commandos in a ferocious firefight. Secret Talib cells had ambushed Alliance forces in Taloqan and Dasht-e Qal'eh. Northern Afghanistan, it seemed, was once again in play.

"I'd better go home and smoke this while I still can," the old man told me. "I'm glad I didn't shave my beard."

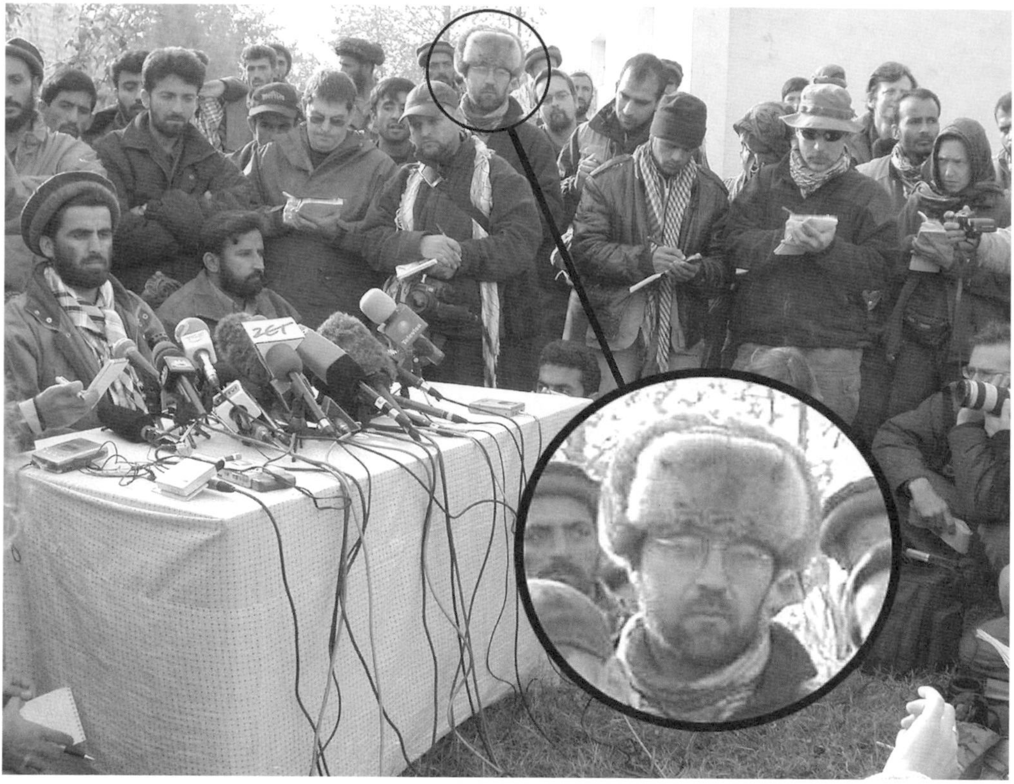
ZET

Press conference given by Northern Alliance General Mohammad Daoud in Taloqan. Insert shows Ulf Stromberg, a cameraman for Swedish TV4. Stromberg was murdered in his Taloqan guest house a few days later.

8. Running the Odds When Nobody Cares

TALOQAN-KOLKUL HWY., AFGHANISTAN, December 3

They came to kill me. I heard them pounding on my metal door. Everyone in this country who can afford metal doors has them: the sky turns pitch-black and the streets turn ugly at 5 p.m.

The murderers were polite at first. Naturally, I didn't answer the door. It was 3 in the morning and it was Afghanistan. Anyone with a hot lead on an exclusive interview with General Dostum or photos of child mine victims could wait until morning.

Then they pounded angrily. I was glad I hadn't gotten out of my sleeping bag.

They came back at 5, I think it was. They had young voices and they spoke Dari, the _lingua franca_ of northeastern Afghanistan and by extension the Northern Alliance. They went away sooner this time.

There were 45 Western journalists living in private homes scattered around Taloqan, a backwater equivalent to a small town in Georgia, which serves as the provincial capital of Takhar Province. Taloqan was just 20 minutes from the front line at Kunduz on a fairly decent road. We were there to cover the siege of Kunduz, the fall of which would also open major roads to Kabul and Mazar-e-Sharif and access to the Uzbek border.

Conditions in the journalists' guest houses were squalid. The better rooms featured a few filthy mats on top of a flea-infested carpet. Heat was furnished by benzene lamps that caused nausea and burning eyes. There was no electricity.

You couldn't eat during the day because it was Ramadan, and you couldn't go out at night. We paid $25 per person per night for these digs. Boiled hot water for bathing was $5 more.

They really got you on food brought in from the bazaar. My favorite price-gouging moment—and there were so many—was my landlord's assertion that eggs were going for a buck each in a country with an average monthly salary of $1.40.

The journalists said that it was all CNN's fault, that the network paid so much for helicopter rides and cool shots of tanks that the Afghans began to believe that all Westerners were made of money. On the other hand, CNN was probably just another victim in a place where taxi drivers think nothing of asking $1,400 for a 10-minute ride.

No one gave a damn about our security. The Northern Alliance never assigned

Khanabad, Afghanistan, east of Kunduz. This area was struck by Taliban shells an hour later. At least one journalist was seriously injured.

guards for our houses or for journalist convoys, which were constantly getting ambushed. And neither the U.S. nor the Alliance would send a chopper for you if you got shot.

The next morning, Nov. 27, I ran into Pedro, a Portugese radio correspondent who lived a few houses away. I asked him if anyone had pounded on his door the night before. "As a matter of fact, yes," he replied.

A few hours later, the news spread that Ulf Stromberg, a 42-year-old Swedish cameraman who'd been living three doors away from me, had answered the door that night to find three or four young men pointing Kalishnikovs at him. When he shouted to alert his roommates, they shot him. The killers robbed the others and fled into the night.

Forty-five journalists had come to Taloqan in my convoy. Stromberg was the third one killed for his money.

I conducted an informal poll of the writers and TV people gathering at the tiny Northern Alliance Foreign Ministry. All had been awakened the night before by knocks at their doors. Only Stromberg had answered. The killers had known where all of us lived. If we had all answered our doors, we all would have been killed for our carefully concealed $100 bills and whatever possessions intrigued them.

"I don't mind dying in battle to get a story," a writer for the French daily *Le Monde* told me. "Getting killed in a stupid street crime is something else altogether."

The Afghans are wrong, of course. We're not loaded. If and when I make it back home, I've got bills piled a foot high to contend with. But they're also right: compared to them, we're zillionaires. One could try a long-term/short-term argument on them—journalists tell the Afghans' story, people back home decide to help out, aid pours in, Afghanistan prospers someday and so do you—but why bother? When the next meal is uncertain, a percentage of the population will act by any means necessary to secure that food and maybe a little extra. The fact that we're taking enormous risks to help them just doesn't matter.

They ripped off Ulf Stromberg again, even after he was dead. Northern Alliance officials initially refused to issue a death certificate or permission to let his body leave the country unless they were paid a $2,000 fee. (This indecent behavior isn't without precedent; another murdered TV man's body was held on the grounds that, like himself, his visa had expired.)

Later that day, Stromberg's colleagues loaded his coffin onto a pickup for the brutal six-hour trip on a bombed-out road to the Tajik border. Both the U.S. and the Alliance refused to send a chopper to spare his corpse this final humiliation.

Finally, at 9 that night, a box containing Stromberg's remains was placed on a tractor-powered barge that crossed the Pyanj River. Next to the coffin rested his backpack and equipment. Covering it was a green tarp covered with the thick, powdery dust of Afghanistan.

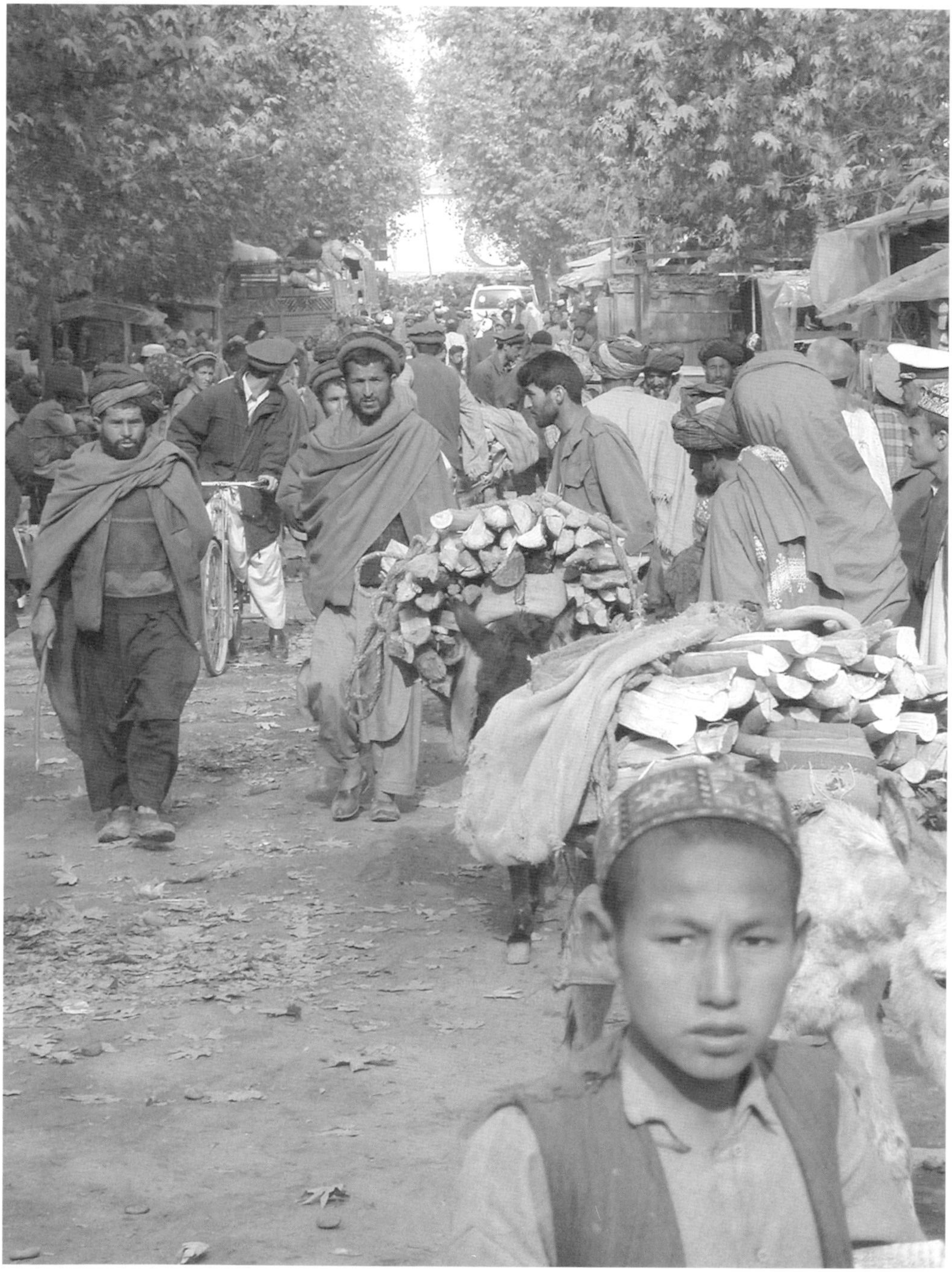

Street scene, Taloqan.

9. Here's to the Middle Ages

TALOQAN, AFGHANISTAN, December 5

You only have to be in this country for a few minutes to understand what an entire presidential administration seated behind faux cherry desks in D.C. hasn't figured out yet: The last thing this country needs is more bombs. Bombing is redundant; death by air strike too pointless to be cruel.

God must have been in a serious funk when He created this geographic leftover between Central and South Asia. Not only did He stick the Afghans with the world's hottest deserts and its coldest mountains, He gave them just two natural resources: rocks and dust. And then, just because He's both ornery and omnipotent, He also gave them neighbors who hate each other so much they won't even touch each other with guns and knives; they let the Afghans do it for them.

"We should nuke this whole country and start from scratch," a New Yorker named David told me over fatty kebabs at the bazaar. And he's a libbie, toiling for a couple of N.G.O. charities here.

Nonetheless, we Americans could learn a lot from the Afghans and their medieval society. Even the most well-traveled visitors here are instantly struck by the way Afghans help one another. To some extent it's self-motivated: helping to push someone's truck out of a ditch gets you moving sooner if it's blocking your way. But the truth is, everyone jumps to the assistance of anyone who needs it without being asked. No one walks by. If you drop a heavy load, a dozen men will rush up and offer not only to assist, but also to carry the item themselves. And no, they're not grabbing your wallet as they do it.

Afghans are rightly famous for their unparalleled skills of subterfuge, dissembling and outright cheating. But things are a lot more complicated than that. Afghans live in a state of perpetual warfare in a land where getting by is tough enough during peacetime. It comes as no surprise that they cut a few corners in the honesty department. What's amazing is how fundamentally decent these people are under such desperate conditions.

As you read this, you're thinking that Americans also help each other in a pinch. But we don't. If we lived like Afghans, you'd stop the instant you saw a broken-down vehicle on the side of the road. So would the car behind you. But you don't stop and neither do I. Afghans don't need an auto club; they have each other.

The tribal system, so detrimental to building an effective multiethnic state, offers tremendous support to people struggling to survive in impossibly difficult times. My translator Jovid's rented adobe-walled box on the outskirts of town here, which would normally house six people, is currently home to 15. Three of them, an old man and his two children, are refugees from nearby Kunduz who walked here after an errant American bomb destroyed their neighborhood. Four more are distant relatives who moved in after four years of drought made farming impossible.

The rest are orphaned children, not even distantly related to Jovid's family. The orphans are from the neighborhood; their mothers starved to death after their fathers died in battle. There are few orphanages in Afghanistan; there's no need for them.

"Someone just takes them in," Jovid replied when I asked him what happens to most orphans. Just to be clear, Jovid's family is desperately poor. Still, it would never occur to them not to feed a hungry person.

After years of reading about a country rigidly divided between a Tajik north and a Pashtun south, in which the Hindu minority was ordered by the Taliban to wear identifying badges—for their own protection, supposedly—I was astonished to discover an altogether different reality. Uzbeks, Daris and Pashtuns not only tolerate one another, they almost all speak each other's languages and partake of various elements of each other's cultures. Tajiks wear Pashtun clothing, Uzbeks eat Turkmen food and Tajiks marry Uzbeks.

While different kinds of Americans live in strictly segregated, monochromatic cities and neighborhoods and can't even stand to hear each other's music, Afghans of all ethnic stripes live side by side in a truly blended nation. This partly explains why yesterday's Taliban can shave, trade his turban for a Nuristani cap, and become Northern Alliance—to jump from a Pashtun- to a Tajik-dominant culture isn't that hard. Afghans make war all the time—it's what they do best—but they fight out of loyalty to a commander or a warlord. They don't shoot each other merely because of the color of their skin. We Americans, who most assuredly know better, do.

And while we've all been treated to vague references to the Afghan tradition of "hospitality to strangers"—mainly to explain the Taliban willingness to eat American lead on behalf of their guest Osama bin Laden—it's something you have to experience personally in order to fully appreciate. To be offered a meal in a home here means that you'll be treated to the equivalent of a Thanksgiving dinner by people who can scarcely afford the minimum caloric intake to get them through the day.

When an emergency arose that required me to go out into the night (Afghans never go out after dark, due to armed rapists and brigands roaming the streets), my hosts insisted that a car and driver be found to take me. Armed to the teeth and willing to risk their lives had I been attacked, they accompanied me to my destination. It was only days later that I inadvertently discovered that they had paid $50—more than a year's salary—for that car.

Crisis, as New Yorkers rediscovered after September 11th, brings people together. If Afghanistan is someday blessed with peace, one hopes that it won't lose the powerful bonds that have kept its people going through the worst that life has to offer.

10. When Life is a
Short-term Lease

"How old are you?" the soldier wanted to know. Resplendent in his spiffy new Northern Alliance hat and shiny Pancho Villa ammo belt and matching AK-47, he tiptoed through what some said was a minefield (though he said they were from Badakhshan Province and didn't know Takhar or the mysteries of its mines) to take a leak.

DUSHANBE, TAJIKISTAN, December 7

"Thirty-eight. How about you?"

"How old do you think I am?"

Salt-and-pepper hair, definitely receding. Not just eye bags, but wrinkles. Subtly hard facial angles; not a gram of baby fat. I thought 42. I said 36 to be polite.

He enjoyed a hearty laugh. "I'm 18!"

Middle-aged teen-agers shouldn't come as much of a surprise in a country with an average life expectancy of 43 (considerably less for front-line troops). But when you spend just a few weeks living the same toxic lifestyle as these poor and unlucky souls, it's amazing that they live as long as they do.

All things considered, I lived considerably better than the average resident of Taloqan, Afghanistan, where I just spent a couple of weeks. For one thing, I was willing and able to pay the extortionate rate of five bucks for the sticks you burn to boil bath water in an ancient tin stove. A hot-water *hamam* goes a long way toward improving your outlook after a night spent watching bombs fall far too close to your home address. And call me a spendthrift if you want, but I always sprang for the 60-cent horse-drawn cart ride across town. Most Afghans didn't.

Otherwise, there were few indignities or inconveniences that my Amex, Visa or carefully concealed wad of crisp hundreds could ease, much less eradicate. Like most Afghans, I slept on a filthy mat along one wall of a freezing-cold room containing said stinky mat on top of one astonishingly dirty red carpet. The foul stench made sleep nearly impossible; strange rashes spread among the press corps. Afghans, when asked about this, shrugged and pointed to their own scary blotches.

Though as an infidel I was technically exempt from the 5 a.m.-to-6 p.m. Ramadan fast, the only way to sneak a snack without causing the highly armed locals to take

Taliban POWs at the Taloqan jail. Saw blades serve as window bars. (Photo: Maryanne Patey.)

offense was to stay home and pay a kid to run to the bazaar. Since I was always out and about, like other journalists I observed a de facto Ramadan fast. Think it's easy? Try it yourself: Move to Arizona and go all day without a sip of water. The principal difference is that Afghanistan is drier and dustier.

Don't get the idea, though, that breaking out that dinnertime flatware after an all-day fast is a big treat. Most people survive on a vegan-unfriendly diet of fatty kebabs and water drawn from the natural goodness of the gutter on the side of the road. When I hungrily inquired about a few plump ducks splashing around in Taloqan's communal bath/drinking fountain/toilet/garbage can, you would have thought I'd said only wimps like AK-47s. "EAT them? Why?" my translator spat in disgust.

"In France," I offered, "ducks are a delicacy."

"Not here," he shuddered. "We need them alive."

"If you don't eat ducks, what good are they?"

"They keep the gutter water clean."

What an atrociously unbalanced and unhygienic diet and American bombs don't finish off, the triple B's—bugs, benzene and breathing—surely will.

For one thing, the nation's bedding supports a thriving ecosystem of fleas, ticks, bed-bugs, lice and other assorted nasties—including everyone's favorite bedtime companion, Mr. Scorpion. Neither warrior nor babe nor Osama himself is safe from the contagion, not to mention painful welts, issued by the local critters. After just one week, I counted 106 bites from Afghan bed fauna, many of them on body parts best left unblemished.

Furthermore, nights are almost always shockingly cold, and so are the days from November through May. Afghans heat their uninsulated mud-adobe homes with Chinese-made camping lanterns fueled by eye-burning, lung-searing benzene. Every teeth-chattering minute offers a terrible dilemma: Which is worse, freezing to death or poisoning yourself on low-grade Central Asian benzene?

Finally, there's the dust. With the consistency of flour, it's kicked up by anything and anyone moving across a 99 percent unpaved landscape. Consequently, everyone in Afghanistan suffers from smoker's cough. I left Afghanistan days ago, yet I'm still ejecting prodigious balls of sandy phlegm.

Perhaps the world will, against all odds, witness the coming of a peaceful, prosperous society in Afghanistan. Maybe Afghans will routinely live well into their 50s. American civilization may bring running water, nay, even clean, fresh Evian, into every home. But who's going to nuke the ferocious fleas I'm bringing home in my luggage?

Rall shopping at the Taloqan bazaar. Huge crowds, unaccustomed to foreigners, followed him everywhere. (Photo: Maryanne Patey.)

THESE SANCTIONS SEND A STRONG MESSAGE TO IRAQ AND AFGHANISTAN FOR SUPPORTING TERRORISM.
THIS TERRORISM SENDS A STRONG MESSAGE TO THE U.S. FOR IMPOSING SANCTIONS.
THESE BOMBS SEND A STRONG MESSAGE TO AFGHANISTAN FOR THE TERRORISM OF SEPTEMBER 11TH.
THEY'RE NOT GETTING THE MESSAGE.
REPEAT AS NECESSARY, BUT LOUDER.
NEVER EVER EVER THE END.

11. A Snake Swallowing A Snake Swallowing Its Tail

T *NEW YORK, October 23*

he terrorists won, and I collaborated with them. And if you've done anything other than deck out your SUV in plastic flags while chanting "YOO-ESS-AY" every time Donald Rumsfeld's smug mug flashes across your screen, you were in on it too.

No one, if the tightlipped Bush Administration is to be believed, has claimed responsibility for the quadruple hijackings and ensuing mayhem of September 11th. But just about everyone agrees that the perps were out to send America some kind of message. Whether that memo reads "quit propping up Israel" or "drop the sanctions against Iraq" or "Muslim fundamentalism is taking over the world so please die and go away" has been debated by every talking head imaginable, but one thing is certain: people fly planes into buildings for a reason.

Suddenly louts who couldn't tell Serbia from Slovenia are fully versed on the Pashtun-Tajik rivalry in Afghanistan, the differences between Sunnis and Shiites and the strategic importance of Mazar-e-Sharif to the Northern Alliance. Recovering ignoramuses who wouldn't have shot a passing glance to a column-inch about the deaths of millions in China are questioning whether State Department policy towards the Arab world may have been so hypocritical and insensitive that it led extremists to get our attention in an incredibly dramatic way.

For the first time in memory, Americans are reconsidering the wisdom of supporting an Israel whose reactions to Palestinian terrorism is itself increasingly indistinguishable from terrorism. We're questioning—not just on the op-ed pages, but in real life—our dependence on foreign oil. We're reevaluating a set of assumptions that has governed American foreign policy since World War II: Isn't it hypocritical for a freedom-loving republic to support repressive dictatorships in Pakistan and Saudi Arabia? Why continue ineffective sanctions that make ordinary Iraqis suffer while Saddam Hussein maintains his luxurious lifestyle?

This new American thoughtfulness, of course, is exactly what the 19 hijackers hoped for during the last few seconds of their lives. Aside from a shot at those newly-famous black-eyed virgins in the post-martyrdom hereafter, they wanted the world's single remaining superpower to stop business as usual in Central Asia and the Middle East. We may be bombing Afghanistan—a tactic that's nothing more than a flashier rehash of Bill Clinton's own Osama fetish—but the days of blindly backing Israel while blindsiding Muslims to get at the oil beneath their sand are *finito*. Terrorism isn't pretty, but it works.

No one wants to cave in to those who massacred thousands of our fellow citizens. But the alternative is even less attractive. If we continue to back every despot willing to run a pipeline through his back yard, his oppressed subjects will invariably strike at the power behind the throne: us. If we refuse to even consider the possibility that our actions abroad are sometimes less than decent and honorable, we can look forward to more such attacks in the future.

On the other hand, even considering—much less meeting—the demands of terrorists invariably leads to more demands. And so the hawks say: Bomb now, think later. Or better yet: just bomb. They have a point, but they're the ones who got us into this mess in the first place.

There is no correct answer to this Escheresque conundrum. Thoughtful reevaluation of American actions throughout the globe, and not just in the Muslim world, is as welcome as it's overdue. Unfortunately, it's also a concession to mass murder. And yet: we obviously can't blunder along as we always have.

Ideally, we Americans and our government would see such events as the bombings

BACK AT JIHAD H.Q.
PRETTY COOL, HUH?
VISIT MECC
TENS OF THOUSANDS OF DEAD... BILLIONS OF DOLLARS IN DAMAGE... OUR MARTYRS KICKED BUTT!
IDIOT! U.S. SANCTIONS HAVE KILLED MILLIONS IN IRAQ AND AFGHANISTAN. THIS DIDN'T BRING THE WAR THERE—IT'S A DROP IN THE BUCKET!
WHAT DO YOU SUGGEST? AIRBORNE BIOTOXINS? DRINKING WATER CONTAMINATION? HACKING INTO NORAD? OUR ECONOMY'S IN RUINS! WE DON'T HAVE THE MONEY!
DON'T WORRY, WE'LL GET THE CASH.
FROM THE AMERICANS?
SOONER OR LATER THEY'LL USE US AGAINST THE RUSSIANS AGAIN.

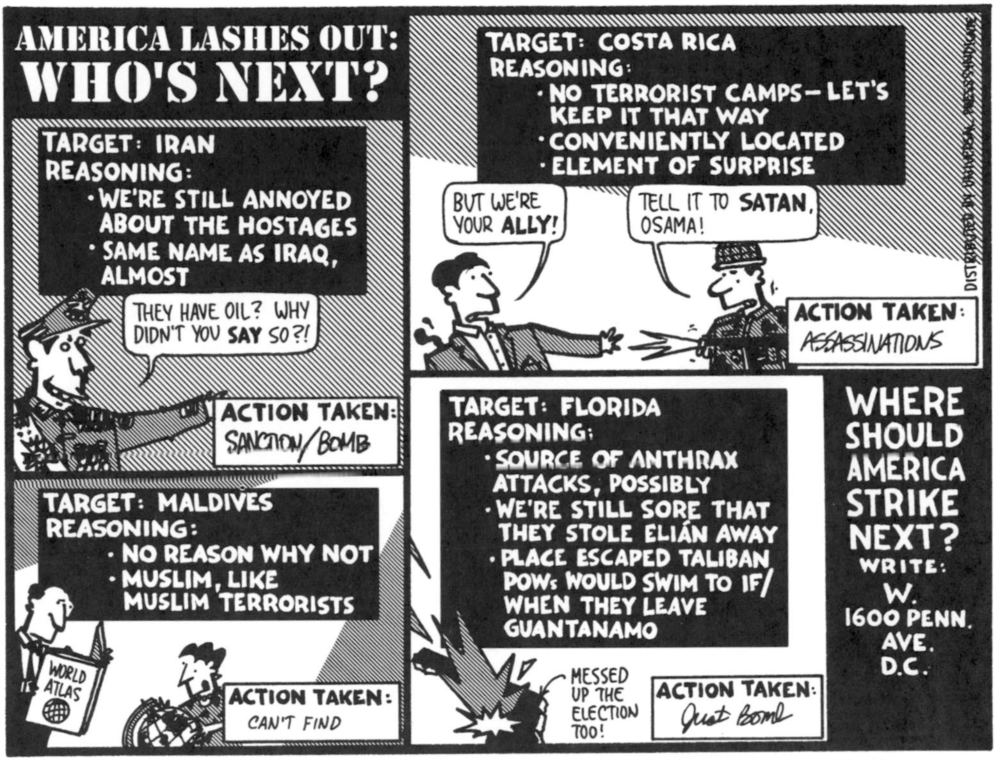
AMERICA LASHES OUT:
WHO'S NEXT?
TARGET: IRAN
REASONING:
• WE'RE STILL ANNOYED ABOUT THE HOSTAGES
• SAME NAME AS IRAQ, ALMOST
THEY HAVE OIL? WHY DIDN'T YOU SAY SO?!
ACTION TAKEN:
SANCTION/BOMB
TARGET: COSTA RICA
REASONING:
• NO TERRORIST CAMPS—LET'S KEEP IT THAT WAY
• CONVENIENTLY LOCATED
• ELEMENT OF SURPRISE
BUT WE'RE YOUR ALLY!
TELL IT TO SATAN, OSAMA!
ACTION TAKEN:
ASSASSINATIONS
TARGET: MALDIVES
REASONING:
• NO REASON WHY NOT
• MUSLIM, LIKE MUSLIM TERRORISTS
WORLD ATLAS
ACTION TAKEN:
CAN'T FIND
TARGET: FLORIDA
REASONING:
• SOURCE OF ANTHRAX ATTACKS, POSSIBLY
• WE'RE STILL SORE THAT THEY STOLE ELIÁN AWAY
• PLACE ESCAPED TALIBAN POWs WOULD SWIM TO IF/WHEN THEY LEAVE GUANTANAMO
MESSED UP THE ELECTION TOO!
ACTION TAKEN:
Just Bomb
WHERE SHOULD AMERICA STRIKE NEXT?
WRITE:
W.
1600 PENN. AVE. D.C.

of the World Trade Center in 1993, our embassies in Kenya and Tanzania and the *U.S.S. Cole* as signals that we were as clueless as we were unprepared. But there's no rolling back the clock, even under a presidency identical in name, personnel and policy to one from 12 years past. The United States is engaged in a negative-sum game; with victory unachievable, cutting losses will have to suffice. Bringing the guilty to justice while considering the possibility that we may not be perfect doesn't exactly set the American heart pounding, but it'll probably have to do.

From now on, we all have to take sides. So let's conduct a brutal self-examination: which are you, a naive sell-out or an ignorant moron?

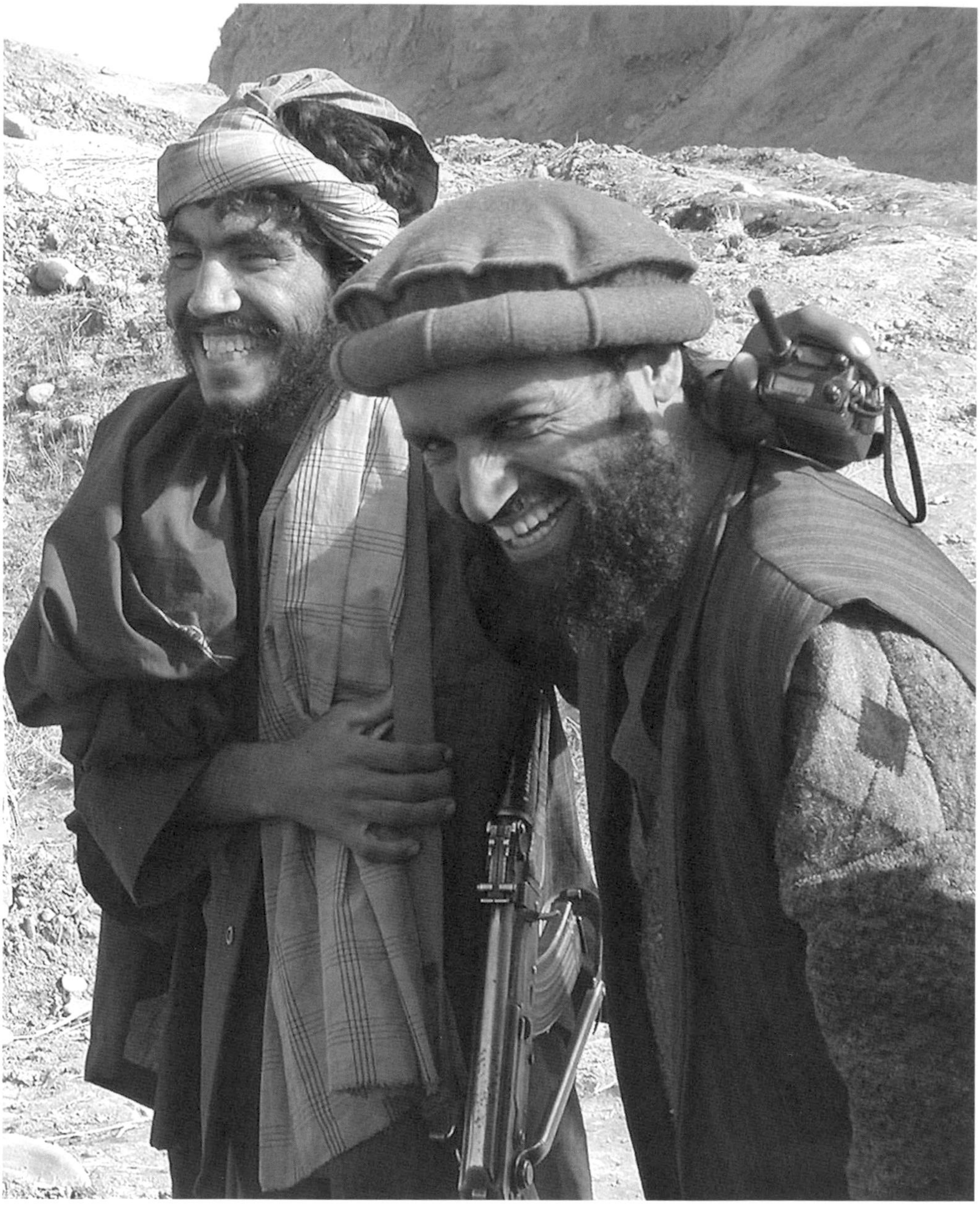

Alliance soldiers, Bangi.

12. How We Lost The Afghan War

DASHT-E QAL'EH, AFGHANISTAN, December 6

We've lost this war. So how much will it cost?

In 1842, the First Afghan War ended with an infamous retreat across the Hindu Kush that cost between 10,000 and 15,000 Brits and their camp followers their lives. One man, a Dr. William Brydon, survived the Afghans to tell the tale upon his return to a remote outpost of the Raj's Northwest Frontier Province. Eventually a retaliatory expedition returned to slaughter the instigators of their humiliation, but this later victory accomplished nothing. Losing this desolate international leftover inspired testy Sepoys to rise up against their supposed betters, sparking a chain of events that ultimately led to Indian independence, decimated the Empire, and reduced England to a European backwater offering neither steady employment nor edible food to its pasty citizenry.

Ditto for the Russians. After the Great Communist Hope took on the U.S. in a decade-long proxy war between slightly different shades of fanatics, the Soviet Union left half its military equipment, economy, and prestige on the ash heap of history. Blame Gorby and Chernobyl if you want, but the USSR's disintegration into mafia banditry owes more to Stinger-shootin' moojes than Berliners dying to shop on the West Side.

Now a Third Afghan War is wrapping up its final act around Kandahar, and a laughable band of charlatans has lobbied in Bonn, Germany, for the right to rule the unruly. Somehow, if the Bushalopes and the Annanites are to be believed, a New Democratic Afghanistan will be cobbled together from the Hekmatyars and Dostums and Rabbanis, all united under the banner of an 87-year-old king who owes more to Fellini than to Shah Mohammed. And get this: After the Afghan parliament gets together, the burqas will come off, the Wendy's will open up next to the main gate of the Kabul bazaar, and that Internet-famous Unocal pipeline project, dormant for far too long, will begin sucking Kazakh crude out from under the Caspian and into the Pakistani port of Karachi. Next mission: bombing Iraq into capitalism.

The networks aired maps turning from Taliban red to Northern Alliance blue, but here on the ground, as people who prefer to remain anywhere-but like to say, no such thing occurred. Dasht-e Qal'eh and Taloqan and Kunduz all "fell," but 99 percent of the conquerors were Taliban troops who shed their beards and turbans and picked up Shah

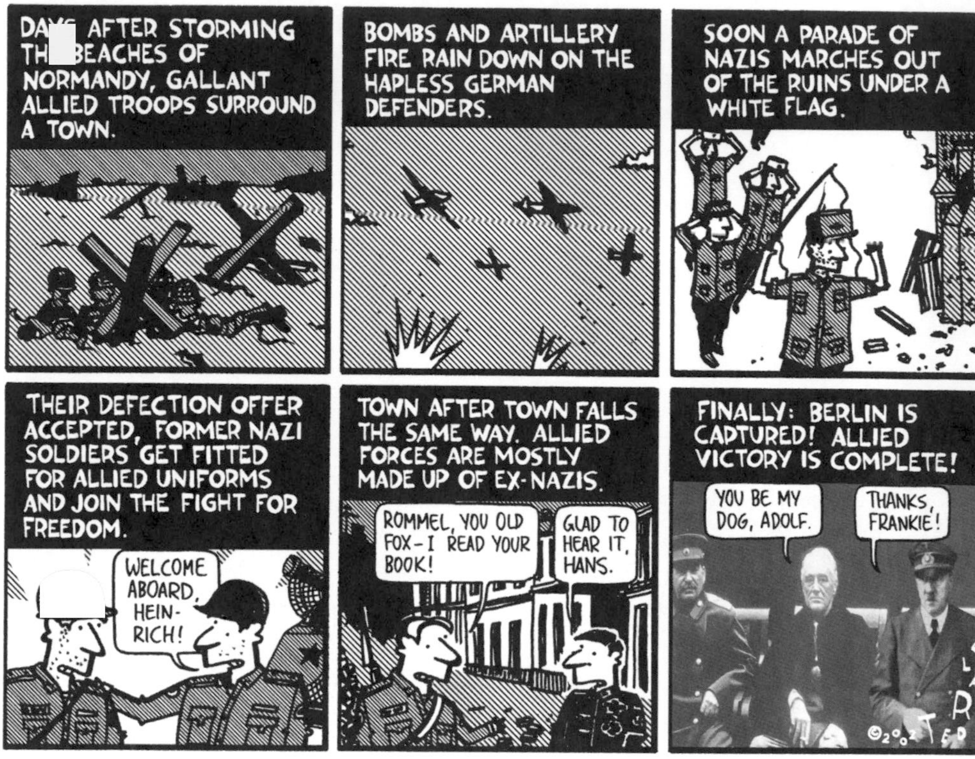
DA AFTER STORMING TH BEACHES OF NORMANDY, GALLANT ALLIED TROOPS SURROUND A TOWN.
BOMBS AND ARTILLERY FIRE RAIN DOWN ON THE HAPLESS GERMAN DEFENDERS.
SOON A PARADE OF NAZIS MARCHES OUT OF THE RUINS UNDER A WHITE FLAG.
THEIR DEFECTION OFFER ACCEPTED, FORMER NAZI SOLDIERS GET FITTED FOR ALLIED UNIFORMS AND JOIN THE FIGHT FOR FREEDOM.
WELCOME ABOARD, HEIN-RICH!
TOWN AFTER TOWN FALLS THE SAME WAY. ALLIED FORCES ARE MOSTLY MADE UP OF EX-NAZIS.
ROMMEL, YOU OLD FOX–I READ YOUR BOOK!
GLAD TO HEAR IT, HANS.
FINALLY: BERLIN IS CAPTURED! ALLIED VICTORY IS COMPLETE!
YOU BE MY DOG, ADOLF.
THANKS, FRANKIE!

Massoud's hip hat for a buck. There were, before September 11, a mere 6,000 to 20,000 Northern Alliance soldiers holding the eastern portion of Takhar province and the extremely mountainous Badakhshan and Wakhan Corridor, an inland peninsula created as a buffer zone between imperial Russia and British India during the 19th century.

When your taxpayer-funded $75,000 bombs began pounding front-line Taliban positions and the not-so-occasional farming village, the age-old Afghan tradition of ideological flexibility and self-preservation led thousands of Taliban to cross the lines to "defect."

"I am so sorry," a Taliban commander cried in the welcoming arms of his Northern Alliance counterpart a day before Kunduz "fell." "We are brothers and should not have fought."

Finally, a rare truth in a land of lies—both men had fought together in the Taliban and before that against the Soviets. The vast majority of "Northern Alliance" fighters now were Taliban a few weeks ago; welcome to the first fashion war of the new millennium.

There are two ways to consider the success of War on Terror, Part One. The first is as an act of retribution against the Taliban for tolerating and supporting Osama bin Laden's Al Qaeda network (never mind that Al Qaeda is bigger and more influential in Pakistan than in Afghanistan or that it is merely one of hundreds of extremist Islamist organizations that trained in Afghanistan). In this view Afghanistan is a source of instability throughout Central Asia and, by extension, for Western oil interests and the West itself. September 11 was merely the latest manifestation of the dangerous extremist phenomenon. Angry Afghans aren't angry at anything America has done, say Rumsfeld and Powell; they're perpetually ornery motherfuckers who have to be kept under lock and key so that the civilized world can get down to the business of the 21st century, which will be one hell of a business if we can ever convince people to stop selling off their mutual funds.

Then there's the liberal, free-market, interventionist approach, which sees the geopolitical collision zone between Central and South Asia as intrinsically doomed by a variety of factors: a strategic location, an absence of natural resources, and far too many guns and mines left over from the '80s. Marshall-Plan the joint, these N.G.O. types say. Build roads, schools, and Virgin Megastores and damn if all of those Uzbeks, Pashtuns, and Tajiks don't simply drop their AKs in favor of Burger King uniforms. And just like that, Americans will be able to shed their fears of 767s cruising through their office towers.

Cooler heads, those who own books by both Rudyard Kipling and Ahmed Rashid, know that Lonely Planet offers the best advice on the best time to visit Afghanistan: "Don't go." But nothing is more certain than this: You can no more control the Afghans than you can help them.

It's a good thing that those snapshots of starving Afghans were taken in refugee camps in Quetta; you have to work hard to find hunger here. That's good too, since Afghans aren't getting any of that much vaunted food aid, unless they pay top afghani

WAR ON TERROR, PHASE 1
THE PLAN IS SIMPLE: BOMB THE TALIBAN, WEAKEN AL QAEDA, PUT OSAMA ON TRIAL AND DECLARE VICTORY!
WANTED
DEAD OR ALIVE
AMERICA'S NEW WAR, PART 2
UM... THE BOMBS SPOOKED OSAMA. SINCE HE'S GONE, WE'RE GONNA NAIL EVIL ONE NUMBER TWO - MULLAH OMAR! WE'VE GOT HIM SURROUNDED!
TARGET: OMAR
OFFICE OF PERPETUAL WARFARE
AMERICA FIGHTS BACK, PORTION 3
MULLAH OMAR OBVIOUSLY HAS SOME INSIDE TRACK WITH ALLAH - HOW ELSE COULD HE HAVE EVADED OUR BRILLIANT TROOPS? BUT DON'T WORRY: WE'VE BAGGED THE FORMER ENVOY TO PAKISTAN WHO GAVE TALIBAN THOSE ANNOYING BRIEFINGS.
EVEN MORE WAR, NO. 4
LIKE, WE'RE ZEROING IN ON A DUDE WHO COOKED KEBABS FOR THE TALIBAN.
IS THAT "KEBAB" OR "KEBOB"?
SEQUELS ARE A CASE STUDY IN ENTROPY.
GETCHER WAR INFO HERE
TED RALL

Coffin of slain cameraman Ulf Stromberg leaves Afghanistan via Pyanj River barge to Tajikistan. (Photo: Maryanne Patey.)

for it at the market.

Feed starving people out of bags covered with your flag and they'll love you, the theory goes. But based on this precept, no one in Afghanistan has any cause to even *like* you.

Even our military contribution isn't earning the U.S. any I.O.U.s. "We appreciate the bombs you dropped on the Taliban," a veteran Alliance commander named Amin (many Afghans use only one name) told me. "But you bombed airports and roads that we need to run the country. And my men are dying because they have old Russian weapons and you Americans won't fully support us."

What do you want from America?

"Go home and leave us alone."

The principal goal of this adventure in imperialistic vengeance, it seems obvious, should be to install a friendly government in Kabul. But we're winning neither hearts nor minds among either the commoners or the leadership of the current regime apparent.

"How can you talk of imposing that old king on us?" Amin snaps. "Even my father doesn't remember who he is."

A bolder nation-building objective, to reshape medieval Afghanistan from a land of donkeys lugging bundles of sticks into something resembling modernity—i.e., us—has actually moved further away since the beginning of the bombing. Along with the demise of Talibanism's more unusual strictures against kites, pigeons, and women, has come a reversion to the pre-nation-state feudalism that prevailed the last time this regime ran things, from 1992 to 1996.

When a Swedish cameraman was murdered in a Taloqan push-in robbery, journalists asked their liaison at Foreign Ministry to advise them as to which authorities would handle the investigation. "There will be no investigation," came the perfunctory reply.

"But a crime has been committed," a Portuguese television editor insisted. "Where do Afghans go to report crimes?"

"They go home. Nowhere."

The system of governance espoused by anarchokids on St. Marks Place is in full effect here beyond Thunderdome. "You can kill anyone you want, provided they don't have any friends," my translator Jovid assured me. "Nothing will happen."

Thus it's no surprise that Afghanistan has become a gangland paradise. Sign up for service with a local warlord and see the world. You'll die young whether or not you join, but at least your friends will kill your killer if you do.

Americans, mostly of the right and the post-9-11 squishy left, want Afghanistan and its jihad boys out of their hair. For the most part, the barn door has long remained open—tens of thousands of jihad grads are everywhere from Alabama to Alberta, and camps remain operational in Pakistan, Tajikistan, Kyrgyzstan, and elsewhere. But even assuming that the locals are mistaken about Osama having packed up for a new cave on the Pakistani side of the Kashmiri Line of Control, closing the Taliban Club isn't likely to put an end to Islamic extremism here. For one thing, the Northern Alliance itself remains a hotbed of Muslim fundamentalism—with few exceptions, women remain out of sight and out of work. Sharia law still enforces stoning as punishment ("but we will use only small stones," Judge Ahamat Ullha Zarif notes), and America is still viewed as a blank-check endorser of Israeli war crimes and Saudi corruption. And for all of America's talk of dropping as many yellow food packs—I haven't seen a single one, by the way—as bombs, Bush Deux is already losing interest in this accursed buffer state just as his father did after the Soviet withdrawal in 1989.

"Next target: Saddam," reads a handwritten sign on a derelict Soviet tank outside a "secret" American base south of the Uzbek border. "It would take billions of dollars to even begin rebuilding this country," an American officer who refused to give his name noted while his driver worked on a flat tire. "Billions of dollars and many, many years. We don't have that kind of attention span. Bombing Iraq will be a lot sexier than teaching Afghans how to read."

And so we've lost this war, not because they're good or we're not, but because of who we are. The American Empire can't spend the bodies or the time or the cash to fix this crazyass place, because in the final analysis, election-year W. was right—we're not nation builders. Guys who once called themselves Talibs switch to something called the Northern Alliance, and we call this a victory. We know it isn't so, but like Nixon's peace with honor, it'll have to do.

Both the Russians and the English lost everything to Afghanistan, but it doesn't have to end that way for us. After all, the same thing happened to us in Vietnam, our first Afghanistan, but we survived it. True, our economy was never the same. Undeniably, it replaced an American Century with postmodern alienation and ironic detachment. But if those estimates are correct and this war is costing a mere billion bucks a month, we ought to tally our dead, write up our losses, and count ourselves lucky to still be called a superpower.

Recommended Reading

Ahmed Rashid's **Taliban: Militant Islam, Oil and Fundamentalism** (Yale University Press, 2000) is the definitive work about Afghanistan and the relationship between the Taliban, the U.S. and Pakistan during the late '90s. For further insight about the region, check out his **The Resurgence of Central Asia: Islam or Nationalism?** (Oxford University Press, 1994). Rashid's Jihad: **The Rise of Militant Islam in Cental Asia** (Yale University Press, 2002) focuses on the former Soviet Central Asian republics but is nonetheless essential for those interested in Afghanistan's regional influence.

Peter Hopkirk's **The Great Game: The Struggle for Empire in Central Asia** (Kodansha America, 1994) is an entertaining look at 19th century superpower politics between Great Britain and Russia. "The Great Game," as Kipling called it, now focuses on a rivalry between the U.S. and Russia.

Though difficult to find, the Swiss-published **Essential Field Guide to Afghanistan** (Crosslines Communications, 1998) is the only serious English-language travel book currently in print about the country.

The **Central Asia Phrasebook** (Lonely Planet, 1998) covers the major languages of the region. The book's Pashto section is useful in Afghanistan; although it omits Dari, the *lingua franca* of the Northern Alliance, Tajik is included.

About
Ted Rall

Pulitzer Prize finalist and twice-winner of the Robert F. Kennedy Journalism Award, cartoonist and writer Ted Rall is one of America's most widely syndicated journalists. **To Afghanistan and Back** is Rall's eighth book, coming on the heels of the widely-acclaimed graphic novel **2024** and the influential political manifesto **Revenge of the Latchkey Kids**. Born in Cambridge, Massachusetts and raised in Kettering, Ohio, Rall graduated from Columbia University with honors in history in 1991. His trips overland from Beijing to Istanbul and along the Karakoram Highway in Kashmir were chronicled in pieces for *P.O.V.* magazine; Rall's journey to Afghanistan was his fifth adventure in Central Asia. His "Stan Watch," a summary and analysis of Central Asian news, has been broadcast frequently on NPR and the BBC. He lives in New York.

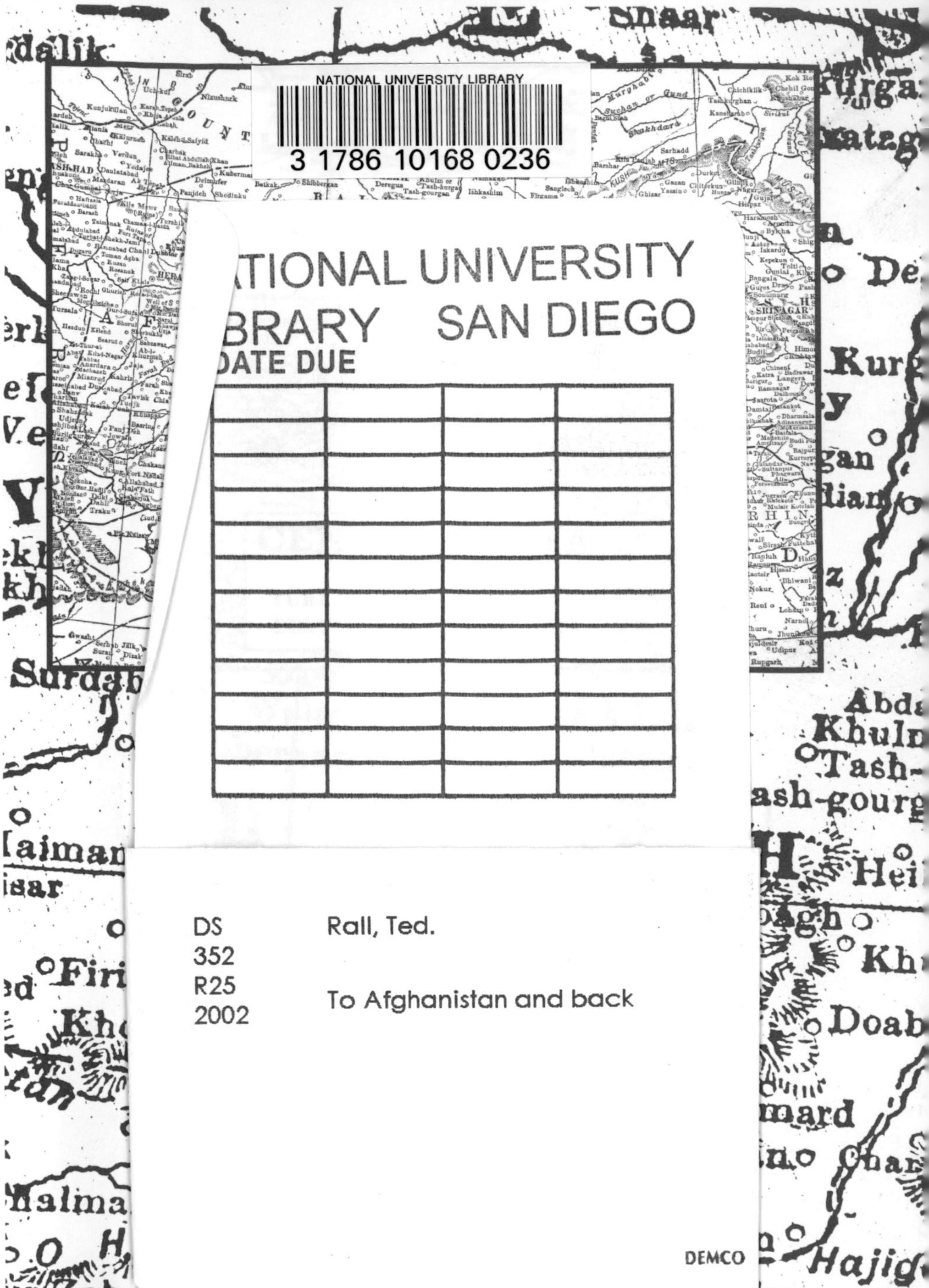
Surdab
Abda
Khulm
Tash-
ash-gourg
Doab
Hajig

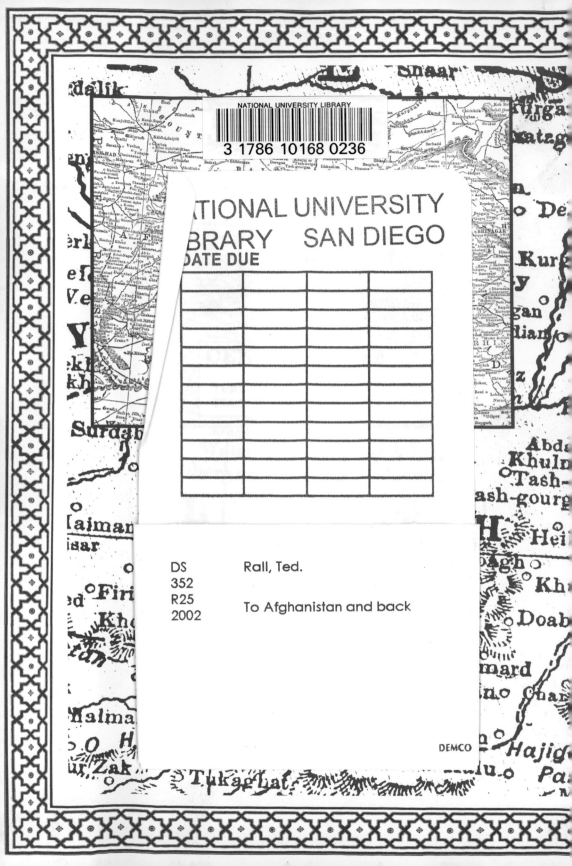